The Poor Bugger's Tool

The Poor Bugger's Tool

*Irish Modernism, Queer Labor,
and Postcolonial History*

Patrick R. Mullen

OXFORD
UNIVERSITY PRESS

OXFORD
UNIVERSITY PRESS

Oxford University Press, Inc., publishes works that further
Oxford University's objective of excellence
in research, scholarship, and education.

Oxford   New York
Auckland   Cape Town   Dar es Salaam   Hong Kong   Karachi
Kuala Lumpur   Madrid   Melbourne   Mexico City   Nairobi
New Delhi   Shanghai   Taipei   Toronto

With offices in
Argentina   Austria   Brazil   Chile   Czech Republic   France   Greece
Guatemala   Hungary   Italy   Japan   Poland   Portugal   Singapore
South Korea   Switzerland   Thailand   Turkey   Ukraine   Vietnam

Published by Oxford University Press, Inc.
198 Madison Avenue, New York, New York 10016

www.oup.com

Oxford is a registered trademark of Oxford University Press

Library of Congress Cataloging-in-Publication Data
Mullen, Patrick R.
The poor bugger's tool : Irish modernism, queer labor, and postcolonial history / Patrick R. Mullen.
p.   cm.
Includes bibliographical references and index.
ISBN 978-0-19-974669-9 (cloth : alk. paper)
1. English literature—Irish authors—History and criticism.
2. English literature—20th century—History and criticism.
3. Homosexuality in literature. 4. Queer theory. 5. Value in literature.
6. Values in literature. 7. Postcolonialism in literature.
8. Nationalism and literature—Ireland—History. 9. Homosexuality and
literature—Ireland—History. 10. Modernism (Literature)—Ireland.
I. Title. II. Title: Irish modernism, queer labor, and postcolonial history.
PR8755.M85   2012
820.9'353—dc23

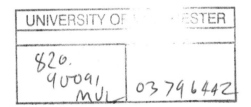
1 3 5 7 9 8 6 4 2

Printed in the United States of America
on acid-free paper

CONTENTS

ACKNOWLEDGMENTS

I would like to thank the remarkable people who have made this work possible. The book is dedicated to my parents, Sandy and Jim. Their humor and adventurous engagement with life have been an inspiration. Seán, Michael, and our newest addition, Anuka, have been a source of unfailing support. Mary Lou and Jim offered their home and warm meals on the coldest winter nights of graduate school.

A wealth of friends have supported me and challenged me to think beyond the walls of the academy, to name but a few: Thomas Bary, Frédéric Biousse, Ann and Jack Brockette, Ed Bucholtz, José and Noreen Cabrera, Tony De Louise, Mike Dyer, Eric Ennis, Frank Fox, Carlos French, Dee Grant, Andy Kearney, Michael Ledford, Dustin Lewis, Mike McQuesten, Brian Mozeleski, Peter Nava, Alex Sosa, and Tommy Wiles.

Two of the teachers who most powerfully touched my life have died. Their loss is a tragedy. Siobhán Kilfeather inspired me to pursue an academic career in a first-year course at Columbia University. She helped me get into graduate school and eventually invited me to speak at Queen's University Belfast in my early days as an assistant professor. Eric O. Clarke was the sweetest of friends and the most daring and glamorous of intellectual mentors. He persists for me in the power of living memory.

Key parts of the book began as a dissertation at the University of Pittsburgh, where I had the privilege to study with Marcia Landy, Jonathan Arac, Colin MacCabe, and Eric O. Clarke. These extraordinary mentors shared with me the passion and style of engaged intellectual work. A wealth of people from my days at Pitt continue to nourish my life and thinking: Anustup Basu, John Beverley, Paul Bové, Petra Dierkes-Thrun, Ronald Judy, Kara Keeling, Todd Marciani, Seán O'Toole, Rich Purcell, Brian Samonek, and Judy Suh.

My colleagues at Northeastern University have offered both encouragement and support, and I'd like to thank Nicole Aljoe, Kimberly Juanita Brown, Elizabeth Maddock Dillon, Carla Kaplan, Kathleen Kelly, Marina Leslie, Mary Loeffelholz, Guy Rotella, Beryl Schlossman, Patricia Sullivan, and Georges Van Den Abbeele. Special thanks to Laura Green, whose friendship and intellectual conversations have helped to sustain me over the past years.

My gratitude to all the people who have helped to shape my thinking, some old friends who have helped me to wrestle with ideas over the years, and some new friends whose conversations have sparked a future of exchanges yet to unfold: Henry Abelove, Nancy Armstrong, Will Bishop, Claire Bracken, Mike Cronin, Sergio Delgado, Marjorie Howes, Seán Kennedy, Nadia Louar, Vicki Mahaffey, Joe Nugent, Joe Rezek, Mike Rubenstein, William Spurlin, Moynagh Sullivan, and Joe Valente.

This book would have been impossible without Pearson McGee and Book Club, and Book Club would have been impossible without a sabbatical from Northeastern University. The University of Pittsburgh generously gave me time to work, through a Cultural Studies Fellowship, a Mellon Dissertation Fellowship, and a postdoctoral position.

I am grateful to audiences at Boston College, Columbia University, Queen's University Belfast, and Northeastern University as well as at the ACLA, the Queering Ireland conference, the MSA, and the NCSA. Thanks to Lucy McDiarmid, who early on invited me to speak on her Roger Casement panel at the MLA. Thanks to *Critical Quarterly* and *Public Culture* for permission to reprint material. Special thanks to the reviewers and editors of the manuscript and to Brendan O'Neill of OUP.

The Poor Bugger's Tool

Introduction

G iven the general misery of life in Ireland at the turn of the twentieth century, James Joyce famously remarks in *Ulysses* that history is a nightmare from which Stephen Dedalus is trying to awake. Less than a hundred years later, at the Lincoln Memorial inaugural concert for Barack Obama, Bono, lead singer of U2, performing the band's tribute song to Martin Luther King Jr., *Pride (In the Name of Love)*, proclaimed to an ecstatic audience that King's dream was "not just an American dream, also an Irish dream, a European dream, African dream, Israeli dream, and also a Palestinian dream." Summing up their support for the new president, Bono exclaimed, "What a thrill for four Irish boys from the north side of Dublin to honor you, sir! . . ."[1] From the claustrophobia of colonial torpor to the glamour of global pop stardom, from being trapped in a nightmare to living the dream, Ireland seemed finally to have stepped from a history of political and economic trauma onto the world stage. Even the ensuing global economic crisis and Obama's political trials were not enough to completely extinguish the emotional power of these images, and the American president rekindled their force during his 2011 trip to Ireland with three simple words: "Is féidir linn. Yes, we can." How are we to understand this political trajectory and the power of these images and affects? How might we account for the movement from the projects of anticolonial nationalism that opened the twentieth century to the productivity of contemporary postmodern culture? How are we to square the history of an isolated and impoverished colony with this international presence and cosmopolitan style? And finally, to invoke the title of U2's song through the trials of another famous Irishman, what is this love that apparently dares to speak its name? *The Poor Bugger's Tool* argues that love, particularly queer love and the discourses of queer sexuality, offer a privileged critical lens on the relations among colonial and postcolonial history, changing forms of capital, and modes of cultural expression, glimpsed briefly in these images. By examining aesthetic articulations of queer sexuality in Ireland, the study argues that novel forms of affective value production are key elements of the historical dynamics of modernist and postmodernist culture.

The title, *The Poor Bugger's Tool*, taken from a bawdy allusion in Joyce's *Ulysses*, styles in a single inscription the work's three recurrent concerns: the queer sexual discourses of Irish modernism, emergent forms of labor and value, and the structures and textures of imperial history. Leaving aside for the moment the specific dynamics of Joyce's joke, I make three central arguments in the book. First, I argue that key male Irish modernists—Oscar Wilde, J. M. Synge, Roger Casement, and James Joyce—deployed queer aesthetic sensibilities to organize anticolonial discourses that read against the grain of British imperial hegemony. Siobhán Kilfeather has claimed that "historically, the primacy of a particular form of masculinist nationalism in Irish writing led, inevitably, to the suppression of a number of counterdiscourses such as feminism, radical socialism, lesbianism and the homoerotic, and therefore in reclaiming liminal and marginalized homoerotic narratives within Irish writing, a common ground for re-appropriation is being realized."[2] Following on this insight, I claim that Wilde, Synge, Casement, and Joyce in diverse ways embraced the inclusive potentials of queer aesthetics in order to articulate open and fluid models of Irish national belonging.

The second line of argument follows the circulation of queer sensibilities in the collaborations of Neil Jordan and Patrick McCabe, and in Jamie O'Neill's seminal novel *At Swim, Two Boys* (2001). I propose that, taken over the course of the last century, Irish queer discourses represent telling reflections on the passage from capitalist modernization, epitomized by mass industrialization, to a postmodern capitalism, reliant on increasingly abstract and immaterial labor. If Irish queer sensibilities in Wilde, Synge, Casement, and Joyce organized political counterdiscourses, in McCabe, Jordan, and O'Neill they come to operate as active expressions of new kinds of affective labor. The cultural products through which queer sensibilities circulate stage what can be thought of as the epistemological crises of modern colonial and postcolonial subjects; they also circulate new kinds of social and cultural values specifically linked to new economic realities. I argue that queer aesthetics are a key site for thinking through national and individual subject formation and modes of capitalist development, and I offer a historical reading of aesthetic forms as simultaneously affective and economic.

Most important, the third line of argument threads through the entire study as a persistent consideration of how the multiple connections among the languages of queer desire and emergent forms of value production and circulation shape and reshape Irish and world history. I consider received versions of Irish history to bring to light occluded narratives and connections.

Through this exploration, I explore the contemporary construction of history in postmodernity and suggest progressive ways of relating to a national past and an increasingly global present.

While Irish literary contributions to international modernism are unmistakable, as this impressive roster of names already suggests, I propose connections among sexual discourses, cultural production, economic developments, and national history that are not fully addressed by current conceptual frameworks. *The Poor Bugger's Tool* calls on an eclectic mix of disciplines and critical conversations, and some preliminary definitions are in order. In particular, I would like to introduce key theoretical discussions that have served as a resource for my own thinking, while suggesting the new connections that my study articulates. These discussions cluster around two concepts: the *queer* and *value and labor*.

To begin, what exactly are the *queer* discourses of Irish culture? And to follow up Kilfeather's formulations, how might these discourses help to realize a common ground for reappropriation within an Irish context or within other contexts? Colm Tóibín, in the introduction to *Love in a Dark Time*, speculates that certain tendencies in what he refers to as "gay writing" have echoes in Irish writing, and in keeping with this suggestion, a range of important scholarship has elaborated the relationships between Irish national and sexual formation.[3] The Queering Ireland conferences (2009, 2011), organized by Sean Kennedy and Éibhear Walshe, have been, to my mind, the most exciting recent development in queer Irish scholarship. These conferences have both showcased important work in the field and provided for an ongoing critical discussion. Particular critics who have examined Irish national and sexual discourses include Joseph Valente; in his writing on Jamie O'Neill, Valente has examined how ". . . Irishness came to be a privileged site for articulating racial and sexual forms of abjection during this period [1916] and to propose how such overdetermined abjection could be transvalued and its revolutionary possibilities mined."[4] Sally Munt, in her examination of Irish culture and politics in *Queer Attachments*, reads "class, sexuality and ethnicity as co-implicated paradigms" and finds the affect of shame to be a particularly apt tool for negotiating among these paradigms.[5] Kathryn Conrad has elaborated the concept of the family cell from the work of Michel Foucault as a lever for the analysis of national and sexual identity in the Irish context, claiming that "the centrality of the family cell to social, economic, and political organization defines and limits not only acceptable sexuality but also the contours of the private sphere, the public sphere, and the nation itself."[6] Margot Backus has examined the authorization of the "heterosexual man as the 'paradigmatic citizen-subject'" (4) and the ramifications of this authorization for Irish culture.[7] Declan Kiberd might also be read as suggesting that Ireland has been strange, if not literally queer, for a long time, particularly in relation to its complicated colonial history. In *The Irish Writer and the World*, Kiberd discusses the Irish rejection of imperialist tropes of "the old stable self of the heroic male" in a way that easily opens the discussion of Irish culture to queer theory: "This explains the androgyny which lasts as a theme from the bardic poets through Wilde and Shaw down to Yeats and Joyce: the constant attraction in texts between manly women and womanly men. It also accounts for a linked phenomenon: if the self can multiply, becoming the opposite of what it seemed by nature and gender, then it may also become multicultural as well."[8] This scholarship has addressed both specific questions of queer sexuality and how the broader dynamics of sexual definition and the politics of gender have played a role in shaping Irish national life.

In this book, I deploy the term "queer" both as a capacious index for a series of non-normative desires, sexualities, people, politics, and cultural expressions and as a term that maintains specific relations, at times contradictory and elusive, with the homosexual and the homoerotic. This definitional slippage will undoubtedly delight some readers and vex others. Exploiting the term's shape-shifting dynamism, my study follows the trajectories opened by queer theory in the 1990s. This vehicular mobility was a salient attribute for many scholars, as it enabled them to bring questions of non-normative sex and sexuality to contexts that previously seemed unmarked by the violent struggle over the borders of homosexual versus heterosexual definition. The pioneering work of Eve Kosofsky Sedgwick, for example, uncovered the deep resonances of sexual politics in previously unimagined venues of Western culture. Along with the work of Judith Butler and Gayle Rubin, Sedgwick opened a vibrant new domain of intellectual inquiry. "Queer" became both a marker of certain texts, attitudes, styles, and cultural practices and its own mode of critical engagement. "Queer" functioned as a potent and frequently polemical adjective to describe a widening array of cultural objects and was transformed into a verb, into a way of looking at images, reading texts, and listening to sounds, as scholars sought "to queer" their fields of inquiry and disciplinary methodologies. The mobility and pliability of the term is what made it, and still makes it, sexy.

This "traveling" queer theory, to invoke the work of Edward Said, also inscribed and circulated particular vernacular resonances attached to gay male culture. Fabio Cleto captures both facets of the term "queer" in his introduction to the reader *Camp: Queer Aesthetics and the Performing Subject.*[9] For *The Poor Bugger's Tool*, Cleto's formulation is doubly emblematic first because he captures the paradoxical openness and specificity of the term "queer" and second because he inscribes the figure of Oscar Wilde as the historical foundation of this paradox. Cleto situates an Irish figure at the origin of queer practice and theory even though queer theory as an academic discipline, in what might be thought of as its first wave, did not largely insist on Wilde's Irish connections.

On the pliability of the term, Cleto explains that "until the end of the nineteenth century, *queer* meant its own *undecidability*, unsettling in itself for the fact that one couldn't settle the sign's meaning, or its *queer(ing) direction* or *sense*" (13). He also traces how the term came to be part of a specific gay male vernacular:

> It was only after the turn of the century that *queer* began signaling, along with its "strangeness," the violence of stigma for "homosexuality," and its first referent in this sense was the effeminate male upper middle-class model, the mode of existence based on Oscar Wilde's "social body"—the effect through his 1895 trials, of an exemplary punishment which turned Oscar Wilde into a public property, a common system of intelligibility, and his effeminate, aristocratic, "aesthetic" *posing* into a sure sign of inner "degeneracy." (13)

This formulation invests the figure of Wilde, in life and in death, with a queer cultural capital that circulates both "public property" and a "common system of intelligibility."

Furthermore, Wilde comes to embody key tenets of queer theory itself, historical lessons gleaned from the reading of Michel Foucault's *History of Sexuality: Volume 1*.[10] These lessons, which circulate in many of the foundational texts of the discipline, are worth citing at length, as my study departs from them in a number of ways. Here, for example, Cleto sketches two notions that have been axiomatic for queer theory:

> The stabilization of the sign [queer] thus seems to move in concert with the birth of the homosexual as a type, that creature brought forth by the nineteenth-century convergence of legal and medical discourses in order to bring queer sexualities within the realm of the knowable, by inscribing the mischievous crime of sodomy on the queer body, by turning an unidentifying practice into an identity (the word "homosexual" itself being a mid-nineteenth-century creature). In Foucault's words, "the homosexual became a personage, a past, a case history, and a childhood, in addition to being a type of life, a life form, and a morphology, with an indiscreet anatomy and possibly a mysterious physiology [...]. The sodomite had been a temporary aberration, the homosexual was now a species" (*History of Sexuality*, 43). Such discursive formation was in fact definitely processed in the English-speaking world through, appropriately we might say, the "processing" of Oscar Wilde, as the readings of popular representations of the 1895 trials in Ed Cohen's *Talk on the Wilde Side*, and the analysis of the semiotics of "effeminacy" in *The Wilde Century* (Sinfield 1994) have shown. What before the trials was *queer*— "strange," slippery and undecidable, "troubling" because failing ontological and

hermeneutical categories, and condemnable for being so—was made into a *queer* stabilized sign denoting the "love that dare not speak its name," and an inverted subjectivity, *anima muliebris in corpore virili inclusa.* Queer became, in short, a sign *decidable* as meaning *homosexual,* within the Wildean model of subjectivity as its imposed referent. (13–14)

The first notion related here is a reading of Foucault that claims that at some point in the late nineteenth century a discursive shift occurred, a sort of historical condensation through which a series of more or less prohibited acts were newly conceived as essential expressions of particular sexual identities. The second suggests that Wilde spectacularly embodies the birth of this new species, the homosexual, for the English-speaking world. I build on and depart from both of these axioms. "Depart" is the precise term: while setting out from the conceptual models and histories that these lessons made possible, I want to focus on different connections and dynamics. In the case of Irish culture in particular, a subterranean vein of queer sexual discourses has provided a dynamic framework for thinking critically about colonial and capitalist exploitation and for undertaking potentially reparative forms of cultural production beyond an American model of identity politics.

The first departure to note is my reading of Wilde. By restoring a queer Wilde to an Irish context, and tracing the resonance of his work through an Irish genealogy, I argue for the queer as a compelling tool for the analysis of colonial and postcolonial life and as a key site for understanding the biopolitics of modern and postmodern capitalism. My reading of Wilde and his oeuvre insists not on the formation of a modern homosexual identity but on the articulation of anti-imperial cultural strategies and the emergence of a queer politics of value. The first chapter of this study elaborates this reading and situates Wilde as a resource for subsequent writers, artists, and thinkers.

The second departure is my reading of Foucault's *History of Sexuality: Volume 1.* I do not focus on the shift from an eroticism organized around "acts" to a sexuality expressive of an "identity"; instead I explore how Foucault helps us to understand the relations among modern discourses of sexuality and the economic and cultural politics of value. My study is not alone in recent attempts to resituate Foucault's work for queer theory. Lynne Huffer, in *Mad for Foucault: Rethinking the Foundations of Queer Theory,* has challenged the formulation that casts Foucault as tracing the movement from erotic acts to sexual identity as a dogmatic and pervasive misreading. Huffer argues that this misreading is partially based on misleading features of the English translation and is partially attributable to the lack of engagement by monolingual English-speaking intellectuals with

Foucault's earlier work in *History and Madness*, a complete English translation of which did not appear until 2006. She describes the famous passage
cited above by Cleto not as the consolidation of a historical identity but
more subtly as a kind of ethical shift: ". . . rather than opposing acts and
identities along the linear time line of Sartrean history, as so many identity-
obsessed readers are wont to do, Foucault describes here an ethical shift
with regard to erotic subjectivity that is perfectly clear if we read the passage through the lens of *Madness*."[11] Huffer tracks the complexity of this
ethical shift through a creative engagement with Foucault and his archive. I
do not enter the debate that Huffer has begun. Nonetheless, my study
departs from the currently dominant reading of Foucault's work to consider
how queer sexual discourses operate beyond the anchor of identity, and in
particular how they come to be a key site of investment for postmodern
capitalism.

I argue that the formulations of value that we can elaborate from queer
aesthetic discourses in the Irish context stand at the crossroads of two powerful yet bifurcated theoretical discussions that trace themselves back to
Foucault's seminal volume: on the one hand, Sedgwick's work on sexual
epistemology, and on the other, Antonio Negri and Michael Hardt's critique
of postmodern capitalism and empire.[12] The scholarship of Sedgwick, Negri,
and Hardt marks key points on the contemporary intellectual map, as these
thinkers have all produced magnetically compelling works that have shaped
their respective fields. Both of these lines of thinking claim Foucault, and in
particular *The History of Sexuality*, as decisively influential, and each takes up
key aspects of his project. However, both also leave aside crucial elements.
Their selective embrace has created a vibrant and productive engagement
with Foucault's thought yet has left their potentially related theoretical un-
dertakings largely estranged. My elaboration of articulations of value in Irish
queer aesthetics enables a return to neglected aspects of Foucault's work
and, furthermore, opens a space for critical dialogue between two important intellectual discourses that are currently largely disengaged from one
another. I do not offer my project as a correction of either of these lines of
inquiry—my own reading and thinking, as this book attests, would have
been impossible without them. I do maintain that the expressions of value
that emerge first in my reading of Wilde both expand on connections
between sexual discourse and economic value that Foucault suggests are
closely linked and offer a perspective from which we might imagine a more
engaged dialogue between queer theory and critiques of global capitalism
and neo-imperialism.

A brief sketch of Foucault's project brings these trajectories into focus.
At the outset of *The History of Sexuality*, he famously rehearses and then
raises serious doubts about the "repressive hypothesis" (10). According to

this hypothesis, the seventeenth century in Europe saw the rise of a re-pressive approach to human sexuality. What had once been relatively unhindered and open increasingly fell under prohibition and censor-ship, culminating in the hypocritical prudery of the nineteenth-century bourgeoisie. Raising serious doubts concerning this hypothesis and the prospects of sexual liberation promised by its supporters, Foucault places it aside in order to focus on his object: "to define the regime of power-knowledge-pleasure that sustains the discourse on human sexu-ality" (11). The subsequent sections of the book track the productive entanglements of power, knowledge, and pleasure through an array of European institutions, perhaps most remarkably in the specific practices and broader disseminations of Catholic confession.

When Foucault sets aside the repressive hypothesis, part of what he brackets are certain ways of conceiving sexuality's relationship to capi-talism. A common sense about capitalism's command over sex and sexu-ality is a key element to the content of the repressive hypothesis and to the success of its historical narrative:

> This discourse on modern sexual repression holds up well, owing no doubt to how easy it is to uphold. A solemn historical and political guarantee protects it. By placing the advent of the age of repression in the seventeenth century, after hundreds of years of open spaces and free expression, one adjusts it to coincide with the development of capitalism: it becomes an integral part of the bourgeois order. The minor chronicle of sex and its trials is transposed into the ceremonious history of the modes of production; its trifling aspect fades from view. (5)

As Foucault explores the discursive productivity of sexuality, he is not thinking about production in primarily economic terms. However, in the book's final section, where he turns to the "right of death and power of life" and theorizes biopower and biopolitics, he explicitly takes up sexuality's relationship to capitalism. Recall first that the deployment of sexuality was "one of the most important" (140) technologies of power from the nine-teenth century, a technology that was invested through and through with emergent forms of biopower. The importance of sexuality is closely tied to developments of capitalism:

> This bio-power was without question an indispensible element in the development of capitalism; the latter would not have been possible without the controlled insertion of bodies into the machinery of production and the adjustment of the phenomena of population to economic processes. But this was not all it required; it also needed the growth of both these factors, their reinforcement as well as their availability and docility; it had to have methods of power capable of optimizing forces, aptitudes, and life in

general without at the same time making them more difficult to govern. . . . The adjustment of the accumulation of men to that of capital, the joining of the growth of human groups to the expansion of productive forces and the differential allocation of profit, were made possible in part by the exercise of bio-power in its many forms and modes of application. The investment of the body, its valorization, and the distributive management of its forces were at the same time indispensible. (140–41)

At the outset of the project, Foucault dismisses a theoretical model that figures sexuality as *directly* responsive to economic demands, a model that would argue that capitalism required a thoroughly rationalized sexuality and therefore repressed freedom-loving libidinal energies except in specific formulations. However, it is important to underline that he does not dismiss the imbrications of sexuality and capitalism outright. After suspending the question of sexuality's relationship to the economic in order to elaborate the productive effects of sexual discourse, he resituates sexuality in a complex relation with the economic, no longer understood as the orthodox last instance:

This is the background that enables us to understand the importance assumed by sex as a political issue. It was at the pivot of two axes along which developed the entire political technology of life. On the one hand it was tied to the disciplines of the body: the harnessing, intensification, and distribution of forces, the adjustment and economy of energies. On the other hand, it was applied to the regulation of populations, through all the far-reaching effects of its activity. It fitted in both categories at once, giving rise to infinitesimal surveillances, permanent controls, extremely meticulous orderings of space, indeterminate medical or psychological examinations, to an entire micro-power concerned with the body. But it gave rise as well to comprehensive measures, statistical assessments, and interventions aimed at the entire social body or at groups taken as a whole. Sex was a means of access to the life of the body and the life of the species. (145–46)

Modern Western sexuality in Foucault's analysis is no longer a direct expression of an economic last instance but is complexly involved in the capillary networks of micropower as well as the broad projections of power at the level of social biology. Mapping sexuality along both of these axes, Foucault allows for a richer consideration of its complex relationship to the economic.

A relatively simple outline comes into view from this sketch of Foucault's project: he brackets the repressive hypothesis, which includes a particular understanding of sexuality's relationship to capitalism; he then explores the performative effects of sexual discourse without recourse to the economic as the last instance; he finally restores conceptual connections between sexuality and capitalist economics in a model of biopower and biopolitics. In light of this outline, the difference between Sedgwick's use of the *History of Sexuality* and Negri and Hardt's deployment of the same text comes into sharp relief. To put it simply: Sedgwick leaves aside sexuality's relationship to capitalism; Negri and Hardt evacuate questions of sexual discourse from the analysis of power in postmodern capitalism and empire.

Sedgwick's deployment of Foucault in *Epistemology of the Closet* is axiomatic, and the particular line of Foucauldian analysis that interests her is clear:

> Furthermore, in accord with Foucault's demonstration, whose results I will take to be axiomatic, that modern Western culture has placed what it calls sexuality in a more and more distinctly privileged relation to our most prized constructs of individual identity, truth, and knowledge, it becomes truer and truer that the language of sexuality not only intersects with but transforms the other languages and relations by which we know.
>
> Accordingly, one characteristic of the readings in this book is to attend to performative aspects of texts, and to what are often blandly called their "reader relations," as sites of definitional creation, violence, and rupture in relation to particular readers, particular institutional circumstances. An assumption underlying the book is that the relations of the closet—the relations of the known and the unknown, the explicit and the inexplicit around homo/heterosexual definition—have the potential for being particularly revealing, in fact, about speech acts more generally. It has felt throughout this work as though the density of their social meaning lends any speech act concerning these issues . . . the exaggerated propulsiveness of wearing flippers in a swimming pool: the force of various rhetorical effects has seemed uniquely difficult to calibrate.[13]

The vitality of Sedgwick's project comes in large part from her acute readerly sensitivity to the social densities contained in speech acts. Her writing so energetically pursues the amplification of these densities that it at first may seem counterintuitive to insist on the selective nature of her project. Nonetheless, as I have already suggested, Sedgwick here takes up the thread of Foucault's analysis that attends to the discourse of sexual definition, but she does not follow this thread through to its knotted entanglement with capitalism. Sedgwick's success attests to the wisdom of this selection. She certainly obtains considerable critical traction by limiting the arena of her concerns to questions of speech and language. The clarity of her decision to not take up the relations between sexual discourse and capitalism stands in contradistinction to Foucault's suggestive, if brief, exploration of these relations.

Negri and Hardt make similarly clear selections in their engagement with Foucault. In the opening of *Empire*, they claim that "the work of Michel

Foucault has prepared the terrain for such an investigation of the material functioning of imperial rule."[14] Their first point is that Foucault's work brings into view the passage from *disciplinary society* to the *society of control*. The second point speaks directly to their engagement with *The History of Sexuality*, which they name as their primary source:

> ... Foucault's work allows us to recognize the *biopolitical* nature of the new paradigm of power. Biopower is a form of power that regulates social life from its interior, following it, interpreting it, absorbing it, and rearticulating it. Power can achieve an effective command over the entire life of the population only when it becomes an integral, vital function that every individual embraces and reactivates of his or her own accord. As Foucault says, "Life has now become ... an object of power." The highest function of this power is to invest life through and through, and its primary task is to administer life. Biopower thus refers to a situation in which what is directly at stake in power is the production and reproduction of life itself. (23–24)

Even as they argue for an analysis of new forms of power that are "open, qualitative, and affective" (24), and even though for Foucault sexuality is one of the most important terrains on which new forms of biopower operate, sexuality does not appear to be a concern for Negri and Hardt. A telling symmetry obtains between these two engagements with Foucault that can be glossed by the fact that just as "Karl Marx" does not appear in the index of *Epistemology of the Closet*, neither "sex" nor "sexuality" appears in the index of *Empire*. *The Poor Bugger's Tool*'s elaboration of formulations of value can be situated at this pivotal moment in Foucault's thought and at this fraught blind spot of contemporary theory.

If this blind spot suggests unexplored relations between sexuality and economic value in the engagement with Foucault's *History of Sexuality*, theorists working in other venues have productively pursued these relations. In *Virtuous Vice: Homoeroticism and the Public Sphere*, Eric Clarke argues that the politics of value can have a transformative effect on the politics of sexuality. Writing in the context of the inclusion debates of the 1990s in the United States, debates that involved both the advancement of civil rights and the visibility of lesbians and gays in commercial culture, he explains:

> ... the issue of value also brings into view the entanglements between representations of homoeroticism and aspects of the public sphere whose concerns are not reducible to sexuality per se (at least as this term has acquired the fiction of a stable referent). Figuring homoeroticism within economies of value whose subject predications extend beyond the erotic—such as norms of citizenship—involves more than the removal of a prior exclusion. As the example of current marketing interests in lesbians and gay men reveals,

inclusion can have far-reaching effects not exhausted by the political goal of fighting homophobia, effects that can change the shape of what "lesbian," "gay," or "queer" could come to mean.[15]

In the Irish context, questions of the public sphere are compounded by the history of colonialism and the new historical possibilities of postcolonial independence. Working within these different historical dynamics, the chapters that follow track the connections among formulations of value and aesthetic representations of queer sexuality. The Irish context confirms Clarke's insight, as my study argues that forms of value have a transformative effect on terms of sexual definition and that queer aesthetic practices come to shape new forms of economic value.

Debates about *camp* are another important resource for this project, particularly as they explore relations among sexuality, aesthetics, and material economy. In his introduction to the work of Andrew Ross, Sascha Torres, and Matthew Tinkcom, Cleto underscores these connections, noting that

> the camp logic of surplus value may in fact be framed as a logic of surplus *counter*-value, for the re-creation of surplus value from forgotten forms of labor was no mere, straight nostalgia: camp enacts a perversion of nostalgia itself, twisting the original circulation and intentions of its objects, reframing them so as to direct them against those very portions of the social body who were "originally" represented by them, thus turning them into powerful signs of oppositional identities (so that Victoriana and the Union Jack, once the signs of British domination, were adopted as signs of fake power—the power of forgery). And yet, the extraordinary significance of camp within the 1960s scene is . . . as an oppositional strategy inherently haunted by its otherness, the specter of complicity. (304)

Chapter 5 of my study, "The Queer Labors of Patrick McCabe and Neil Jordan," investigates the 1960s scene in Ireland, and theoretical considerations of camp offer an important conceptual tool, particularly as camp embodies a queer aesthetic intervention into the realities of life under capitalism.

Camp's status as a strategic aesthetic activity that operates in relation to sexual sensibilities and commodity culture suggests ways to pursue the historical dimensions of queer affects beyond the pursuit of a consolidated identity. In the introduction to *Working Like a Homosexual: Camp, Capital, and Cinema*, Tinkcom explains:

> Despite the apparent distance between the sober, critical assessments of more orthodox Marxist pronouncements and the playful, inconsistent strategies of camp, I would argue,

we can understand camp as a tendency, indeed an insistence on, continually examining the contradictions that capital gives rise to on a daily basis, specifically through the ruptures and fluctuations of monetary and cultural value; and I would heuristically define camp as an alibi for queer men to labor within those contradictions, when paradoxically it would seem that no subject is ever prohibited from exerting him- or herself on capital's behalf.[16]

Here the attitude of camp, its frivolity, is not the essential expression of a gay identity but a philosophical and historical engagement with the material realities of labor. Tinkcom's work suggests one optic through which we can measure the historical and philosophical dimensions of seemingly trivial affects.

These debates about camp are for the most part situated within gay urban venues in postwar Europe and North America and are attached to forms of popular culture, most importantly cinema, music, and drag performance. The larger trajectory of this study suggests that camp might have a broader historical resonance in the cultural strategies that emerge in the Irish colonial context. The homologies between the debates over camp (which bring into concert cultural practices, affects, labor under capitalism, and forms of subjectivity) and critical discussions of Irish culture as it has been produced in the contradictions of imperial history are suggestive. Consider the following passage from Seamus Deane's "Boredom and Apocalypse," the final essay in *Strange Country: Modernity and Nationhood in Irish Writing since 1790*, which introduces prevailing imperialist tropes of the Irish:

Thus the Irish community is consistently portrayed as one that is impossible to recruit into the nineteenth-century normalizing narrative of progress and economic development. Linguistically, it is incoherent; its Irish or English, converted or perverted into one another, its dialects and esoteric vocabularies, indicate as much. Alcoholism, political violence, and economic backwardness are additional marks of the community's improvidence and fecklessness. It is a community that is always *in extremis*, either racked by crisis or constantly manufacturing crisis. Worst of all, even when parts of the Irish community were recruited into existing institutions, like the army or the police, they were often castigated as aliens, traitors in their own country.[17]

Deane here outlines the abject features that ultimately undergird the ethno-erotic analogy that Valente explores between Irishness and the queer in his work on O'Neill. Certainly, we should not flatly equate Irish culture under the contradictory pressures of British imperialism with the urban queer cultural practices of camp, nor should we categorically dissociate them. There are compelling connections to pursue between the Irish colonial situation and the homophobic postwar Euro-American contexts that are analyzed by theorists of camp. In each, abjected subjects face exacerbated and violent economic conditions in which their labor is both required and refused. These subjects have their own cultural heritage and practices that are at once recognized and denigrated by a dominant cultural regime. Both examples, the Irish and the queer, are marked by an affect of excess that is at one and the same time attributed to them by ruling cultural forces and harnessed by individuals as a response to their lived situations. Deane concludes that Ireland, in a certain sense, is a queer country: "The country remains strange in its failure to be normal; the normal remains strange in its failure to be defined as anything other than the negative of strange. Normality is an economic condition; strangeness a cultural one" (197). My reading of this conclusion as "queer" is itself, perhaps, a kind of camp gesture that aims to suggest the contributions to Irish national life made in the name of queer subjects and to sound the Irish valences of queer cultural practices in Ireland as well as those that circulate beyond the island's borders. *The Poor Bugger's Tool*, in this queer sense, takes up the history of Ireland's strange modernity.

While the study engages Irish queer history, it is not in a conventional sense a history of modern Ireland. Instead, it engages aesthetic representations in order to think through the historical dimensions of representational practices. This monograph is neither a history of events, nor a history of ideas, nor an orthodox history of modes of economic development. This work offers what Antonio Gramsci calls an "inventory" of the traces of specific forms of philosophical praxis that emerge in the production, circulation, and consumption of queer aesthetics.[18] As I have already suggested, the book follows an arc, first considering how queer aesthetics helped to organize anti-imperial discourses and then examining how they eventually come to operate as new forms of affective labor. This movement can be seen in broad strokes: The first part of the book will suggest that a key component of the queer sensibilities that emerge in Wilde, Synge, Casement, and Joyce is an affective excess that is framed by their various experimental aesthetic forms. This excess was a critical response to the strictures of a British imperialist imaginary. The second part of the study will suggest that these aesthetic experiments were a success. These Irish modernists were able to transform affective excess into forms of cultural value, and the aesthetic practices of McCabe, Jordan, and O'Neill explicitly engage these earlier writings as repositories of value, particularly affective value. The work of these contemporary writers/artists elaborates relations between value and affect already implicit in the earlier work. The affective labor of these contemporary works produces and circulates values beyond the binary structures that dominated the colonial situation.

The movement from sexuality cast as anticolonial discourse to sexuality as a mode of affective value production comes into critical view at the level of textual analysis. The title of the monograph suggests this shift in a single inscription and also proposes close reading as a specific kind of critical historical methodology for the analysis of this shift. This phrase, "the poor bugger's tool," is the central figure in a sexual joke from the "Cyclops" chapter of Joyce's *Ulysses*. As we will see in chapter 4, the allusion refers specifically to the anti-imperialist activist Roger Casement, and ultimately, through a vulgar amplification, the allusion promotes a queer anality as a trope for collective humanity that challenges the repressive phallic violence of the imperialist imaginary. The phrase inscribes a queer anti-imperialist sensibility in the form of a particular aesthetic—a joke told during a drunken tear at a pub. Beyond this, it also suggests an economic dimension to this aesthetic formulation. It is, after all, the poor bugger's *tool*, a tool of literary production, that produces collective affects in its humor and that predicates subjectivities through a social circulation of value in the text and in relation to the reader. Joyce himself has had both an impressive aesthetic impact and considerable economic resonance. Certainly his work has been one of the most influential aesthetic sensibilities of the last hundred years and has also been a prolific source of value for the multifaceted "Joyce industry." This book's title indexes both of these trajectories: it represents in miniature Joyce's queer aesthetic sensibility, and it inscribes a relation to value, a relation which retrospectively seems entirely apt. This study will argue that the move from questions of discourse to questions of value is already inherent in these modernist texts and that the contemporary engagement with these texts in the work of McCabe, Jordan, and O'Neill is sensitive to this complexity. The monograph activates close reading as a critical historical practice both as it attends to the specificity of the texts and as it attends to the transformations of its objects of study—transformations which, as we have just seen, take place before our very eyes.

Ultimately, the goal of *The Poor Bugger's Tool* is to reveal how the vernacular practices of value of queer Irish aesthetics represent a potentially "world-wide means of expression" (*PN* 325). The study examines how the texts under consideration articulate the contradictions, contingencies, and specificities of their particular contexts. Beyond this, it opens these works to broader contexts, debates, questions, practices, and histories. Writing from the American imperial metropolis, the invocation of the universal ambitions of a scholarly work runs the risk of cultural and political arrogance, epistemic violence, ideological blindness, historical stupidity, complicity, and worse. But perhaps there is a difference between a *dogmatic claim to universality* and the *desire to run the risk of the universal*.[19] The universal as risk: The desire to run the risk of the universal is an open practice; a desire to assemble a commonality; a desire that ultimately traces what must be the failure of the individual intellectual project, even as the trajectories and spaces of collective practice and thinking have opened to new connections, new movements, and new horizons. Edward Said, one of the most forceful twentieth-century critics of European imperialism's claim to a single universal truth, explains the importance of this risk in the introduction to *Representations of the Intellectual*:

> *Universality means taking a risk* in order to go beyond the easy certainties provided us by our background, language, nationality, which so often shield us from the reality of others. It also means looking for and trying to uphold a single standard for human behavior when it comes to such matters as foreign and social policy. Thus if we condemn an unprovoked act of aggression by an enemy we should be able to do the same when our government invades a weaker party. There are no rules by which intellectuals can know what to say or do; nor for the true secular intellectual are there any gods to be worshipped and looked to for unwavering guidance. (My emphasis)[20]

No easy certainties. An eye to the world. No rules. No gods. No guidance. *The Poor Bugger's Tool* follows the pleasures of this risk through the engagement with an eclectic assortment of texts. It explores the political dimensions of affective discourses and the affective dimensions of political and economic discourses and argues for the aesthetic as an important practice in contemporary efforts to create a more just global order.

CHAPTER SUMMARY

Chapter 1, "Oscar Wilde and the Greatest Mystery of Modern Literature," examines two brilliant, yet neglected, works by Wilde, "The Portrait of Mr. W. H." (1889) and "The Soul of Man under Socialism" (1891).[21] In these short pieces, Wilde produces a theory of aesthetic value that undergirds his exposition of the queer epistemological crisis of modernity and offers a politicized model of value redistribution through which we can think contemporary transformations in labor and value. The chapter elaborates a theory of aesthetic and affective value in Wilde and tracks the historical dimensions of that discussion by reading his writings in conjunction with the work of Karl Marx and the post-Marxist theories of Antonio Negri. The chapter resituates the figure of Wilde for queer theory and introduces him into post-Marxist debates over the politics of postmodern capitalism and empire.

Chapter 2, "J. M. Synge and the Aesthetics of Intelligent Sympathy," looks to the work of the playwright and his seminal interpretation by

Daniel Corkery. The chapter makes the connection between Synge's early involvement with experiments in music and literature in Paris and his subsequent involvement with the peasantry of western Ireland. It argues that Synge did not abandon Parisian aestheticism in his engagement with the peasantry and the Irish language; instead Synge highlighted this aestheticism, particularly coded through a queer discourse, in order to reveal the people of the West as active participants in modernity despite the deplorable state of their material conditions. Corkery's work is key for understanding the role of both the homosexual as an identifiable individual and the queer as a form of aesthetic sensibility in Synge. In his foundational *Synge and Anglo Irish Literature,* Corkery argues in effect that while Synge cannot be *identified* with the so-called depravities of an individual like Wilde, his *sensibilities* are too "flamboyant" for the true Irish nature as defined by Catholicism, the land, and sexual chastity. Synge's queer sensibilities come into focus as features of a critical counterdiscourse that connect the national and the international as they develop from his early education in Paris to their condemnation by Corkery. The positive contours of Synge's epistemological project are read through the refractions of Corkery's nationalist anxieties.

Chapter 3, "Roger Casement's Global English: From Human Rights to the Homoerotic," examines Irish nationalist Roger Casement's (1864–1916) humanitarian and sexual writings. The chapter suggests that Casement developed both foundational texts for the emergent human rights movement and a potentially global erotic practice of value in the pages of his famous Black Diaries, which track his homosexual activities and homoerotic fantasies during the course of his career as a British consul. The chapter elaborates the differing spheres of activity in both sets of texts—one as an agent and extension of the state in his human rights interventions and the other as desiring subject constituted in the multilingual, code-switching, punning, eccentric texture of the diaries. The chapter argues that the queer lifestyle that emerges in the pages of the diaries, and in the more recent biographical accounts of Casement, is predicated on emergent forms of queer value that supplement, challenge, reframe, and extend his human rights work. Framing Casement within the trajectory of this study, the chapter represents Casement's queer practice of value as a key supplemental feature of both his international and his Irish national politics. Casement interprets the Irish struggle for freedom through his exposure of imperial brutality in Africa and South America.

Chapter 4, "Ruling Passion: James Joyce, Roger Casement, and the Drama of Universal Love," unpacks James Joyce's engagement with the figure of Roger Casement in the "Cyclops" chapter of *Ulysses.* It argues that the figure of Casement, and the attendant homoerotic affective values circulated by this figure, are key to understanding both a fuller resonance of Bloom's "perversity" and Joyce's attack on the repressive sexual and nationalist politics of the Citizen. In effect, Casement operates as a figure of progressive "vulgarity"—not simply in terms of a (homo)sexual explicitness, but more broadly in terms of a popular or collective language of desire that stands in opposition to the "property" or propriety of chaste and racially exclusive visions of Irishness promoted by the Citizen. Arguing against Enda Duffy's analysis in *Subaltern Ulysses* (1994), which suggests that Joyce deploys a chaste image of a humanitarian and progressive nationalist Casement cleansed of any attachment to the diaries, I argue that the Black Diaries are key to reading Joyce's inscription of Casement and to fully understanding Casement's entanglement with issues of sexuality, language, and politics figured through the representation of Bloom. This reading of Casement's inscription reveals Joyce's deployment of a queer sensibility in the critique of claustrophobic articulations of purified nationalism. Furthermore, it suggests that Casement, as he folds into the figure of Bloom, helps Joyce to direct, harness, and provoke forms of excess in the production of novel forms of cultural value.

Chapter 5 focuses on the collaborations of Patrick McCabe and Neil Jordan, specifically on the novel and film versions of *The Butcher Boy* (1992; 1998) and *Breakfast on Pluto* (1999; 2005). *The Butcher Boy* and *Breakfast on Pluto* offer queer visions of the world, an aesthetic that McCabe has referred to as the "social fantastic." The works explore deeply homoerotic themes and see the queer as a dynamic analogue for an array of outcast social positions, feelings, politics, and people. The queer denotes specific relations to same-sex desires and sexual practices and extends beyond these specificities to bring into focus a complex and vital web of social relations. The chapter argues for a concept of what I term "queer labor." Despite the different contexts and very different stories, the main characters of these works engage the world around them specifically through forms of labor. Examining queer labor through the specific articulations of television and cinema, the chapter responds to the question "What does queer labor do?" The general response suggests four things: (1) queer labor produces and circulates forms of value; (2) queer labor is historical; (3) queer labor reveals the social distribution of contemporary power relations; and (4) queer labor opens the historical lines along which the autopoesis both of the individual and the collective becomes possible in these works.

The sixth, and final, chapter of the study, "'Sinn Feiners, me arse. I'm a socialist, never doubt about it': Jamie O'Neill's *At Swim, Two Boys* and the Queer Project of Socialism," thinks through the queer project of socialism at the heart of Jamie O'Neill's powerful *At Swim, Two Boys*. I argue that the central struggle in the novel, both at the diegetic level of the characters and at the metacritical level of the reader, pits what we might call the institutions of moral abstraction against both politicized materialism (socialism) and forms of organized affect, or forms of queer sentiment. The terms of this political contest are at once sociohistorical and literary-critical. On the one hand there are the forces of the Church, the colonial state, nation, the family, and the sovereign subject, which seek to interpellate the allegiances and desires of the various characters in terms of abstract values and ideals (Christianity, nationalism, or normative sexuality). These forces of moral abstraction are clearly targeted by the novel as it attempts to construct alternative forms of collectivity, historical understanding and memory, and aesthetics. On the other hand there are the forms of organized affect in the emerging queer sentiment and culture which the characters construct and in which the reader participates. The organization of this queer culture appears through the practice of a politicized redistribution of the literary and cultural values of Irish modernism. It is not universal forms of abstraction that organize this counterhegemonic queer culture—those abstractions dismissed as "so much foolosophy" by one of the novel's principal characters, Dermot MacMurrough—but, instead, what we might call a form of affective labor that reorganizes the social relations which emerge from the text and which the text represents. I argue that the reader participates in O'Neill's queer socialist project through the affective redistribution of cultural value.

CHAPTER 1

⌀⌀⌀

Oscar Wilde and the Greatest Mystery of Modern Literature

Aesthetics, Affect, and Value

To introduce the questions of sexual discourse, value, and history that guide this book, I first consider the emergence of these concepts in the work of Oscar Wilde, particularly in two short pieces, "The Portrait of Mr. W. H." (1889) and "The Soul of Man under Socialism" (1891).[1] Between these two brilliant, if neglected, works Wilde produces a theory of aesthetic value that undergirds his exposition of the queer epistemological crisis of modernity and offers a politicized model of value redistribution through which we can think contemporary transformations in labor and value. In keeping with the Wildean notion that the aesthetic must be thought of not just as a form of reflection, but also as a manner of practice, and to cast this segue with proper flair, I offer:

THE GREATEST MYSTERY OF MODERN LITERATURE—SOLVED!

Despite Buck Mulligan's quip in the opening scene of James Joyce's *Ulysses* that "we have grown out of Wilde and paradoxes," Wilde's life and work have continued to be a vital source for Irish and queer culture and critique.[2] Recent scholarship has looked to Wilde's oeuvre—his texts and his performance of lifestyle—as an important intervention into debates over the relation between the aesthetic and the economic. Scholars have also looked to his writing as an expression of an acutely modern sensibility, sensitive to the development of sexuality, the complexities of imperialism, and the contradictions of the capitalist market. In the wake of Michel Foucault's work on disciplinarity and governmentality, scholars have argued for the importance of Wilde's notion of self-fashioning, or autopoesis, both as a precursor to the grand aesthetic gestures of high modernism and as a proleptic and generative camp gesture, fully articulate within the play of the economies of postmodernity.[3] As Colm Tóibín explains, "He invented self-invention."[4] Furthermore, Wilde's critical sense, his understanding and presentation of modern epistemological crisis, has helped to shape subsequent scholarship to a remarkable degree. In discussing Wilde's "genre defying" short story/ critical essay "The Portrait of Mr. W. H.," which claims to have discovered the true identity of the enigmatic Mr. W. H., dedicatee of Shakespeare's sonnets, Rebecca Laroche extends the enthusiasm of Joel Fineman's declaration that Wilde's take represents "the only genuinely literary criticism that Shakespeare's sonnets have ever received."[5] Laroche compellingly maps out how Wilde's subtle piece traces the critical parameters not only of Victorian Shakespeare scholarship but also of modern literary scholarship that was to follow, particularly as his short story moves beyond the limitations of nineteenth-century biographical research to a play with language that would mark much of twentieth-century criticism.

Joyce, as opposed to Mulligan, is more sensitive to the enduring importance of Wilde. Mulligan, after all, dismisses Wilde and paradoxes as an introduction to Stephen Dedalus's famous—and "quite simple"— theorization of Hamlet in which he "proves by algebra that Hamlet's grandson is Shakespeare's grandfather and that he himself is the ghost of his own father" (15). Colin MacCabe has deftly dismantled Stephen's ironic undoing in the "Scylla and Charybdis" section of the novel by pointing out that Stephen is ultimately unable to master language in order to convey the logical patriarchal lineage to which he wishes to sign his own name.[6] The theory's fragile net of weft and warp, slipped together by the uneasy crossings of name and pronoun—even in Mulligan's characterization— unravels. It is unable to establish an identity beyond the play of language. As Haines remarks in response to Mulligan: "What? . . . beginning to point to Stephen. He himself?" (15). Stephen's divestment enables Joyce to pursue the prolific contingencies of the signifier and the productive force of language. Ironically, this lesson, the lesson of Joyce's text, is precisely, as we will see, the lesson of Wilde's "The Portrait of Mr. W. H.": Wilde's story also unravels the certainties of the biographical signature in the play of language and desire. It thus stands in relation to Stephen and his theory not as outmoded precursor, but as a critical prolepsis, or even a failed prophylactic. The emphasis in Joyce's text is not therefore on the dismissal of Wilde but on the rejection of Haines's containment of Stephen as an exemplar of Irish paradox:

> They halted while Haines surveyed the tower and said at last:
>   —Rather bleak in wintertime, I should say. Martello you call it?
>   —Billy Pitt had them built, Buck Mulligan said, when the French were on the sea. But ours is the *omphalos*.
>   —What is your idea of Hamlet? Haines asked Stephen.
>   —No, no, Buck Mulligan shouted in pain. I'm not equal to Thomas Aquinas and the fiftyfive reasons he has made to prop it up. Wait till I have a few pints in me first.
>   He turned to Stephen, saying, as he pulled down neatly the peaks of his primrose waistcoat:
>   —You couldn't manage it under three pints, Kinch, could you?
>   —It has waited so long, Stephen said listlessly, it can wait longer.
>   —You pique my curiosity, Haines said amiably. Is that some paradox?
>   —Pooh! Buck Mulligan said. We have grown out of Wilde and paradoxes. (15)

From the invocation of the Martello towers, a series of defensive forts constructed throughout the British Empire in the nineteenth century, and within the overall context of the opening chapter, which records Haines's *amiable* consumption of all things Irish, the context of this exchange is markedly colonial. While Mulligan maneuvers to provoke an invitation to a round of pints by withholding the explanation of Stephen's theory, Haines attempts to secure Stephen and his theory as an object of colonial knowledge. It is not so much that either the characters, or Joyce, have tired of *Wilde and paradoxes*, but perhaps that they have tired of *Wilde as paradox*, where paradox operates as a figure of the power of containment. Mulligan's exact phrase, truncated from the initial grumbling, reads quite literally as a generative endorsement of Wilde: *We have grown out of Wilde and paradoxes*. It is precisely the complex nature of this growth that we must address. In particular, this introductory chapter will examine the questions of sexual discourse, value, and history that Wilde's work sets in motion for modern Irish culture.

Laroche introduces "The Portrait of Mr. W. H." as "a pre-eminent work of modern criticism as well as a consummate Victorian creation" (392). The story tracks the circulation of a theory that claims to have discovered the identity of Mr. W. H. from the dedication of Shakespeare's *Sonnets*. Focused through the point of view of a nameless narrator, the story opens with a discussion between the narrator and his older friend Erskine. Erskine reveals that a "wonderfully handsome" school friend of his, Cyril Graham, claimed to have solved the mystery of the inscription by following a series of linguistic clues in the sonnets themselves that point to one

Mr. William Hughes, an Elizabethan boy actor. Erskine is at first seduced by his friend's reading of the poems, but ultimately remains skeptical because no independent historical evidence seems to exist to corroborate its conclusion. Then a portrait appears—a portrait that seems by all indication to provide precisely the evidence that the insular theory lacks. Erskine is at this moment convinced by the veracity of his friend's idea. However, while the two make arrangements to publish a new edition of the *Sonnets* (which is to include an elaboration of Graham's theory), the portrait is discovered to be a forgery. Erskine recants his belief. Graham commits suicide in order to insist that even if the portrait is a fake, the theory itself is not and must be brought to the world. As the details of the story and its circulation unfold in the dialogue between the narrator and Erskine, the narrator becomes increasingly infatuated. He declares at one point that Graham had discovered the solution to "the greatest mystery of modern literature" (48): none other than the true identity of the enigmatic Mr. W. H. Despite various moments of enthusiasm for the theory, the story ends on an ambiguous note, as the narrator reflects: "But sometimes when I look at it [the forged portrait which Erskine bequeaths him upon his death], I think that there is really a great deal to be said for the Willie Hughes theory of Shakespeare's Sonnets" (101).

"Perfectly wild with delight" (37) and paradox, the story both promotes and undermines its central theory. The value of Wilde's story therefore ultimately lies not in the content of Graham's proposition—the plausibility of locating a historical Mr. Hughes—but in the staging of its own theoretical reflection. Even as the identity of Willie Hughes emerges as fictive—there is no "demonstrable proof or formal evidence" (41) to support it—the critical sensibility that Wilde reveals in the investigation of the figure, that "spiritual and artistic sense" (41) that circulates in the curious friendships of the story's three main characters, emerges as the expression of a compelling historical and aesthetic sensibility, a sensibility particularly related both to the emergent Western discourses of the homosexual and to the Irish anticolonial struggle.[7] Instead of delineating evidence in the mode of traditional literary-historical scholarship, the story tracks the circulation of homoerotic desire and affect in order to reflect on how that circulation traces the social dimensions of sexual epistemologies.[8] Wilde's text smartly distills the contradictory force of its queer epistemology when describing the attraction commanded by Cyril Graham himself, claiming that he "fascinated everybody who was worth fascinating" (36)—and the same can be said of Graham's theory of Willie Hughes. The power of fascination drives the plot of the story as the characters exchange the theory, alternating between rapt belief and sober dismissal. This power also hails the reader, who is queerly seduced, at least through the development of the narrative intrigue, by the forged image of the beautiful young man, conjured by the suggestiveness of Wilde's reading of Shakespeare despite the absence of traditional scholarly evidence of his existence.

From one critical perspective, Wilde's story brings into focus what Eve Kosofsky Sedgwick has dubbed the epistemology of the closet, whose contradictory significations have indelibly marked Western culture's most "prized constructs of individual identity, truth, and knowledge."[9] The story's queer sensibility, styled as fascination, is both an expression of desire and a form of knowledge. Pathbreaking queer scholarship of the 1990s traced the complicated politics of desire and knowledge, and Wilde's work was a key site for thinking through the social aspects of modern epistemological relations. However, as Wilde's language suggests, fascination in the story is not simply predicated by desire (the theory does not just *fascinate all who are fascinated*)—it is predicated and mediated by a *form of value* (the theory fascinates everybody who is *worth fascinating*). Value is a key concept for Wilde's aesthetic that has not been adequately addressed in his critical reception.[10]

The opening paragraph of "The Portrait of Mr. W. H." introduces the discussion of value in terms of the problem of artistic forgeries. Contravening the view that a forged work of art is false and therefore ethically objectionable, the narrator instead argues that "all Art being to a certain degree a mode of acting, an attempt to realize one's personality on some imaginative plane out of reach of the trammeling accidents and limitations of real life, to censure an artist for a forgery was to confuse an ethical with an aesthetical problem" (33). For Wilde, the aesthetic is not a mode of direct and authentic expression; rather, as he claims in "The Soul of Man under Socialism," the artist "stands outside his subject, and through its medium produces incomparable artistic effects" (14). An ethics of verification, organized by true/false evaluations, is unable to account for the differential shifts among "imaginative plane[s]" (33), the movements and relations among artistic modes that are key to his understanding of the aesthetic. In other words, Wilde sees the ethics of verification as an evaluation "standing on its head," and he sets it right in "The Portrait of Mr. W. H." by inverting its terms: instead of looking for proof that a work of art is authentic, he offers a forgery in order to prove a theory.[11] The "wonderful portrait" (35), with its power of "strange fascination" (35), ultimately does not confirm or authenticate the identity of Willie Hughes. Instead, it brings into relief a series of catachreses. Despite these catachreses, the multiple disjunctions and contradictions that the portrait inscribes, it proceeds to convince, at least at certain moments, the story's characters. Also calling on Shakespeare, Karl Marx offers a formulation of the money form that aptly describes the portrait as that which represents "the equation of the incompatible."[12] Much like

Marx's money form, the portrait represents not simply identity but an array of incompatibilities, yet it nonetheless manages to circulate.

Both Wilde and Marx look to the Shakespearean text to enhance a concept of value. And when read in conjunction with Marx, Wilde's insistence on the question of value finally comes into critical view. As a form of value, the power of fascination in Wilde's story does not express identity—the tautological fascination of the fascinated—but expresses a social mode of equivalence that operates in relation to difference. Marx introduces the concept of value as the functioning representation of a differential relation: "We have seen that when commodities are in the relation of exchange, their exchange-value manifests itself as something totally independent of their use-value. But if we abstract from their use-value, there remains their value, as it has just been defined. The common factor in the exchange relation, or in the exchange-value of the commodity, is therefore its value."[13] Value thus operates, on the one hand, as a form of representation that circulates use-value, and, on the other hand, as something "totally independent," as an indifferent form, as exchange-value that does not, and cannot, represent the contingencies of use-value. The "crystals of this social substance" (C 128) figure the social dimensions of differential relations, as Marx describes it in a famous passage from the *Grundrisse*:

> The reciprocal and all-sided dependence of individuals who are indifferent to one another forms their social connection. This social bond is expressed in *exchange value*, by means of which alone each individual's own activity or his product becomes an activity and a product for him; he must produce a general product—*exchange value*, or, the latter isolated for itself and individualized, *money*. On the other side, the power which each individual exercises over the activity of others or over social wealth exists in him as the owner of *exchange values*, of *money*. The individual carries his social power, as well as his bond with society, in his pocket. (156–57)

As Wilde explores the fascinating theory of Willie Hughes, he does not gradually reveal an authentic historical identity but instead develops a differential concept of aesthetic value, a concept that is at the heart of both "The Portrait of Mr. W. H." and "The Soul of Man under Socialism." This concept of aesthetic value structures Wilde's queer epistemology.

THE PORTRAIT AND THE MONEY FORM

Let us begin with the notion that the portrait brings into relief a series of catachreses. Despite originally having concluded that the theory of Willie Hughes is false, after receiving a detailed and passionate letter from the story's unnamed narrator Erskine changes his mind and proclaims, "You have proved the thing to me. Do you think I cannot estimate the value of evidence?" (96). What precisely is the evidential value of the portrait? On first look, the portrait seems to be perfectly adequate proof of Graham's theory. Indeed, the portrait is in some sense called into existence by the very structure of the theory, which, "working by purely internal evidence, had found out who Mr. W. H. really was" (37). Given the internal mechanics of Graham's theory, the portrait secures its authority by being external. As Erskine reasons, "I began to see that before the theory could be placed before the world in a really perfected form, it was necessary to get some independent evidence about the existence of this young actor, Willie Hughes" (43). Even the gestural arrangement of the image and its frame emphasizes external contiguity: "Here was an authentic portrait of Mr. W. H., with his hand resting on the dedicatory page of the Sonnets, and on the frame itself could be faintly seen the name of the young man himself written in gold uncial letters on the faded *bleu de paon* ground, 'Master Will Hews'" (44).

This independent and external authority, however, also emerges as indifference. When Erskine visits the studio of the young painter, Edward Merton, to commission a piece for the cover of Graham's edition of the sonnets, he discovers that Graham had paid Merton to produce the purportedly authentic portrait. Wilde's text emphasizes the multiple and layered moments of exchange—intellectual, conversational, affective, and economic—that have produced and circulated the portrait:

> "Where on earth did you get that?" I said. He grew rather confused, and said—"Oh, that is nothing. I did not know it was in this portfolio. It is not a thing of any value." "It is what you did for Mr. Cyril Graham," exclaimed his wife, "and if this gentleman wishes to buy it, let him have it." "For Mr. Cyril Graham?" I repeated. "Did you paint the portrait of Mr. W. H.?" "I don't understand what you mean," he answered, growing very red. Well the whole thing was quite dreadful. The wife let it all out. I gave her five pounds when I was going away. (46)

Precisely in these moments of exchange, the independent and external authority of the portrait is simultaneously revealed as its formal indifference: it both acquires and sheds different forms of value; it both secures and loses various expressions of authority.

The portrait's formal indifference points to a more deeply seated structure of contradiction within the theory of Willie Hughes. The portrait indexes a series of metalepses among the multiple artistic modes or imaginative planes that the theory engages as well as affective disjunctions among the theory's interlocutors. The portrait renders visual the metonymic shifts that lie at the heart of Graham's theory: Graham argues that Mr. W. H. was a beautifully seductive actor named Willie Hughes *and* that Hughes was the true inspiration for Shakespeare's more artistically important dramatic works. The narrator points to the importance of the difference in genres: "It was also extremely suggestive to note how here as elsewhere Shakespeare promised Willie Hughes immortality in a form that appeared to men's eyes—that is to say, in a spectacular form, in a play that is to be looked at" (58). The portrait is therefore theoretical in the root sense of this word: it is the expression in a visual discourse of a name that is first coded through a series of puns in the poetic discourse of the sonnets, that stands in for a person whose image appears originally in dramatic discourse.[14] These entangled metonymic substitutions occur within a story that is sharply observant of the differences among various aesthetic media. Within its first pages, Wilde's story invokes a remarkable variety of artistic modes, including the forged works of Macpherson and Chatterton, which involve translation; Irish bardic and medieval poetic traditions; the drama and sonnets of Shakespeare; the short story and the Platonic dialogue (both suggested by Wilde's own work); Elizabethan, French, Flemish, and Italian Renaissance portraiture; and, finally, painted late nineteenth-century imitations of historical styles.[15] Even as a theorized object of Shakespeare's adoration, the figure of Willie Hughes is a passion without requital. As the narrator explains, the figure sets in play elemental contradictions: "He could act love, but could not feel it, could mimic passion without realizing it" (60).

If at first the portrait seems to be the perfectly adequate evidence to prove Graham's theory, ultimately it is as queer as a three-dollar bill. However, as Marx notes, the queer status of the fake bill does not mean that the bill won't circulate:

> But if a fake £ were to circulate in the place of a real one, it would render absolutely the same service in circulation as a whole as if it were genuine. . . . The genuine pound, is therefore, in this process, nothing more than a *symbol*, in so far as the moment in which it realizes prices is left out, and we look only at the totality of the process, in which it serves only as medium of exchange and in which the realization of prices is only a *semblance*, a fleeting mediation. (*G* 210)

Similarly, when taking the entire circulation of the portrait into account—and by extension the circulation of the theory of Willie Hughes—we note that despite its status as a forgery and the numerous disjunctions, contradictions, and misfits that it brings to light, it nonetheless captivates the imaginations of the protagonists, and potentially readers, who find themselves "always on the brink of absolute verification" (70) without ever really being able to attain it. Perhaps strangely, this fascinating power of the theory does not stem from a form of emulation through which characters come to believe what those they admire believe. As the narrator explains: "Emotional forces, like the forces of physical life, have their positive limitations. Perhaps the mere effort to convert any one to a theory involves some form of renunciation of the power of credence" (90). In a similar vein, the theory seems most compelling when the speaker who is expounding it is himself no longer convinced. This disjunction between expression and belief appears numerous times in the story.[16] An important example occurs when the narrator's letter convinces Erskine of the theory—for a second time— to the utter disbelief of the narrator himself:

> "But there is no evidence at all," I groaned, sinking into a chair. "When I wrote to you I was under the influence of a perfectly silly enthusiasm. I had been touched by the story of Cyril Graham's death, fascinated by his romantic theory, enthralled by the wonder and novelty of the whole idea. I see now that the theory is based on a delusion. The only evidence for the existence of Willie Hughes is that picture in front of you, and the picture is a forgery. Don't be carried away by mere sentiment in this matter. Whatever romance may have to say about the Willie Hughes theory, reason is dead against it." (96)

Erskine, considering his friend's response, comments, "I see that you don't understand the theory" (96).

What are we to make of this circulation of belief on the back, or in this case *dans le visage de femme*, of the forged image?[17] Marx explains that "money is the physical medium into which exchange values are dipped, and in which they obtain the form corresponding to their general character" (G 167). Marx's gilded metaphor recalls Wilde's interest in physical beauty, and it is suggestive to think that in this passage from Wilde, the medium into which the theory of Willie Hughes is *dipped*, and the general character through which it becomes valuable, is homoerotic affect. The silly enthusiasm, the emotional touch of the story of Cyril's death, the same-sex romance at the heart of the theory itself, the wonder and novelty of the whole idea that unfolds in the intimacies of male friendship, the fascinating power of the portrait with its "extraordinary personal beauty ... [that is] evidently somewhat effeminate" (34)—these are the expressions of homoerotic affect, the medium which makes the theory valuable, that is, compelling and believable, and, at the same time, merely a notion to be dismissed, a hint, a tone, a fleeting semblance. We have already briefly considered the epistemological structure of homoerotic affect, which operates through connotation and suggestiveness, and thus equally, and strategically, through denial and evasion. These doubly bound epistemological dynamics appear here in the exchange and circulation of the portrait, and the theory of Willie Hughes, as the differentials of a practice of value. To recall Marx, "The reciprocal and all-sided dependence of individuals who are indifferent to one another forms their social connection." Homoerotic affect as a value form produces and circulates just such a modern fascinating social indifference in Wilde.

A QUEER SOCIALISM

The preceding discussion of "The Portrait of Mr. W. H." begins to suggest that thinking about homoerotic affect as a value form is quite different from conceiving a model of communal sentiment.[18] Thus even as the text privileges homoerotic affect as the medium through which the theory of Willie Hughes circulates, it also warns against the sentimental: "Don't be carried away by mere sentiment in this matter." "The Soul of Man under Socialism" will draw a distinction between the sentimental and what I am calling a form of affective value. Wilde casts this as the difference between "sympathy with suffering" and "sympathy with thought" (127). While the homoerotic affective exchanges in "The Portrait" entail both a shared sensibility and moments of difference, the sentimental "sympathy with suffering" that Wilde targets in "The Soul of Man" manifests the coerciveness of the "clamorous claims of others" (127). A key aspect of sentimentality that Wilde attacks in this essay is the notion of the virtuous poor. With full flair, he takes on this notion specifically in terms of sentimentality:

> The virtues of the poor may be readily admitted, and are much to be regretted. We are often told that the poor are grateful for charity. Some of them are, no doubt, but the best amongst the poor are never grateful. They are ungrateful, discontented, disobedient, and rebellious. They are quite right to be so. Charity they feel to be a ridiculously inadequate mode of partial restitution, or *sentimental dole, usually accompanied by some impertinent attempt on the part of the sentimentalist to tyrannize over their private lives.* Why should they be grateful for the crumbs that fall from the rich man's table? They should be seated at the board and they are beginning to know it. (130; my emphasis)

Sentimentality is a tool of what he refers to as the *authoritarian*[19] precisely because it enforces imitation: "All imitation in morals and in life is wrong. Through the streets of Jerusalem at the present day crawls one who is mad and carries a wooden cross on his shoulders. He is a symbol of the lives that are marred by imitation" (137). Wilde's queer practice of value avoids the dangers of sentimental authoritarianism while maintaining the possibilities for imagining shared sensibilities.

Unlike certain strains of high modernism that will denigrate feminine sentimentality in favor of masculine intellectual abstraction—one thinks

particularly of the works of D. H. Lawrence—Wilde does not oppose masculine reason to feminine sentiment.[20] Instead, Wilde opposes the sentimental, figured as *sympathy with suffering*—with all of the authoritarianism
that he reveals in this phrase—to an alternative form of emotion or affect
figured as *sympathy with thought*. This notion of sympathy with thought
points to an expanded and elaborated understanding of the social role of
sympathy:

> When man has realized Individualism, he will also realize sympathy and exercise it freely
> and spontaneously. Up to the present man has hardly cultivated sympathy at all. He has
> merely sympathy with pain, and sympathy with pain is not the highest form of sympathy.
> All sympathy is fine, but sympathy with suffering is the least fine mode. . . . One should
> sympathize with the entirety of life, not with life's sores and maladies merely, but with
> life's joy and beauty and energy and health and freedom. The wider sympathy is, of
> course, the more difficult. It requires more unselfishness. Anybody can sympathize with
> the sufferings of a friend, but it requires a very fine nature—it requires, in fact, the nature
> of a true Individualist—to sympathize with a friend's success. . . . And when Socialism
> has solved the problem of poverty, and Science solved the problem of disease, the area of
> the sentimentalists will be lessened, and the sympathy of man will be large, healthy, and
> spontaneous. Man will have joy in the contemplation of the joyous life of others. (157)

In this description of the expansive power of sympathy, Wilde takes his
place in a long-standing and rebellious philosophical countertradition that
sets itself against a sentimental morality of suffering. The passage echoes
Spinoza's basic premise that an increase in joy involves an increase in agency,
a widening of the sphere of action and influence; it echoes the young Marx
of the *Economic and Philosophical Manuscripts of 1844*, in which he describes
the utopian dimensions of humanity's universal personality; finally, it
recalls the Friedrich Nietzsche of *The Genealogy of Morals*, in which he de-
constructs the foundations of Christian morality, and "The Uses and Disad-
vantages of History for Life," in which he traces the interactions of human
affect and historical culture.[21]

Even as Wilde promotes the expansion of the powers of sympathy in
terms of the "individualist," he nonetheless clearly traces the social dimensions of this transformed and invigorated affect. If the sentimental offers a
model of the social organized around the coercion of imitation, the philosophical expansion of the concept of sympathy offers a socialized model of
affective value. Wilde emphasizes the notion of affect at the core of the
human personality. Paraphrasing the message of Christ, whom Wilde separates from the institutions of Christianity, he writes: "What Jesus meant
was this. He said to man, 'You have a wonderful personality. Develop it. Be
yourself. Don't imagine that your perfection lies in accumulating or

possessing external things. *Your affection is inside of you'"* (my emphasis).[22] This affection, or perfection, is not some essential form of being—Wilde claims that all one can know about human nature is that it changes ("SM" 155)—and the social realization of this affect is not simply a matter of the will to expression. Wilde, one could say, prefigures the concerns of Walter Benjamin, who claims in "The Work of Art in the Age of Its Mechanical Reproducibility" that fascism allows for expression without transforming the organization of social relations, while socialism will work to transform social relations and thereby create new forms and avenues of expression.[23] Wilde sees the transformation of the organization of property relations as crucial to the realization of the human personality, and he links his notion of affect with a model of value production through which the sympathetic structure of the individual is mediated by social relations. He thus predicates the expression of individualism through a socialized notion of labor, not as compulsion, but as freedom:

> For while under the present system a very large number of people can lead lives of a certain amount of freedom and expression and happiness, under an industrial-barrack system, or a system of economic tyranny, nobody would be able to have any such freedom at all. It is to be regretted that a portion of our community should be practically in slavery, but to propose to solve the problem by enslaving the entire community is childish. Every man must be left quite free to choose his own work. No form of compulsion must be exercised over him. If there is, his work will not be good for him, will not be good in itself, and will not be good for others. And by work I simply mean activity of any kind. (131–32)

Wilde's socialist society is one in which the conditions of private property have been transformed and individuals are free to express their personal affection through work—understood as a liberated aesthetic, as *activity of any kind*—that will be immediately social.[24] Here again Wilde follows Marx's vision of the transformed limits of communism in which the vitality of labor is immediately universal.[25] This concept of work is not the authoritarian expression of sentiment but a materialist transformation of the social that will allow for the production or expression of individualist affect as a universal form of value. "The Soul of Man under Socialism" thus offers a theoretical and polemic expansion of the model of affective value that lies at the heart of "The Portrait of Mr. W. H." Michael Rubenstein submits that the relationship between the aesthetic and the utilitarian, or what we are discussing here as "work," has a particular historical resonance for the Irish "born of Ireland's early and traumatic experience of modernity and modernization. It was never that the Irish lacked modernity or development, but rather that they had too much of it, and without the protections of national sovereignty to soften its violent transformations."[26] Wilde's promotion of a liberated aesthetic for activity of any kind bears the trace of this history.

DECONSTRUCTING HISTORY

As Wilde himself notes, the image of an order in which personal affection is expressed as spontaneous social value is decidedly utopian. While Wilde endorses the importance of the utopian, Marx famously has a more vexed relationship with strains of utopian socialism.[27] Nonetheless, the imbrication of questions of epistemology, affect, and value in Wilde has a number of important consequences for thinking about history, both as theory and practice, within the critical trajectories opened by Marx. I would argue that by linking questions of epistemology to questions of the economic through a model of affective value, Wilde allows us to think through some of the historical dimensions of his influential aesthetic sensibility.

The progressive expansion of a socialized concept of affective value in "The Soul of Man" is marked by a subjunctive futurity—"The chief advantage that would result from the establishment of Socialism is . . ." (127).[28] The tracking of the production and circulation of affective value in "The Portrait of Mr. W. H." is, as Marx says, *post festum*, which has consequences both for historical investigation and for philosophical presentation: "Man's reflections on the forms of social life, and consequently, also, his scientific analysis of those forms, take a course directly opposite to that of their actual historical development. He begins, *post festum*, with the results of the process of development ready to hand before him" (C 168). In a similar manner, the theory of Willie Hughes attempts to recover a lost past, and the narrative grammar emphasizes the layers of anteriority, the long history of exchanges, that have brought the theory to the present of the moment of reading: "I had been dining with Erskine in his pretty little house in Birdcage Walk, and we were sitting in the library over our coffee and cigarettes, when the question of literary forgeries happened to turn up in conversation. I cannot at present remember how it was that we struck upon this somewhat curious topic" (33). As Erskine enjoins the narrator in conversation, the focus of the story is pushed even further into the past: "'Yes,' he answered, throwing his cigarette into the fire,—'a great friend of mine, Cyril Graham. He was very fascinating, and very foolish, and very heartless. However, he left me the only legacy I ever received in my life" (33–34). These differences in temporality are not just related to the differences in genre, the essay versus the short story, but are more fully understood as characteristic of the complex historicity of the value form—note the insistence on *legacy*—that Wilde marshals both in looking to the past and in working toward the future. The affective practice of value that Wilde presents circulates shared sensibilities and differential relations, layers of the past in the congealed forms of the present, and fragments of futurity awaiting elaboration. The temporal dynamics of the aesthetic emerge as historical qualities in Wilde.

The temporal dynamics of history emerge at key moments as aesthetic qualities in Marx. Explaining that critical philosophy cannot just track the objective succession of historical modes of production, but instead must think succession through particular conjugations of the relations of production, Marx writes in the introduction to the *Grundrisse*:

> In all forms of society there is one specific kind of production which predominates over the rest, whose relations thus assign rank and influence to the others. It is a general illumination which bathes all the other colors and modifies their particularity. It is a particular ether which determines the specific gravity of every being which has materialized within it. (106)

For modern bourgeois society, this means one must think through the contemporary form of capital that is the "all-dominating economic power" (107):

> It would therefore be unfeasible and wrong to let the economic categories follow one another in the same sequence as that in which they were historically decisive. Their sequence is determined, rather, by their relation to one another in modern bourgeois society, which is precisely the opposite of that which seems to be their natural order or which corresponds to historical development. (107)

In these passages, the dominance of a particular form of social production is predicated as an aesthetic: *the general illumination which bathes all the other colors and modifies their particularity*. The aesthetic maintains a complex relation to history in Marx, and it is a crucial tool for the creation and presentation of critical philosophical concepts. The analogous structures and functions of Wilde's portrait and Marx's analysis of the money form considered earlier are not fortuitous connections. Rather, they point to a shared understanding that forms of aesthetic and economic value influence and shape one another. The argument is not that the relation between Marx and Wilde is genetic but that their works critically enhance each other. The historical temporalities in Wilde's work—the progressive vision of the future and the critical recovery of the past, both of which circulate in the differential value practices of the present—correspond in many ways to Marx's theory of history. Similarly, Marx's understanding of the value of the aesthetic in these passages can be read quite fluently as a description of Wilde's short story. Wilde's story, after all, rejects the historical practices of traditional literary scholarship in favor of an analysis of the production of the theory of Willie Hughes. And the value of this theory, figured by the portrait, bathes all the other values in the story in its general illumination.

The historical dimension of "The Portrait of Mr. W. H." is in some sense its most blatantly dubious feature. It revolves, after all, around both a forged image and a rather ambitious, if charming, decoding of an imagined identity. The piece nonetheless presents a compelling reading of history against the grain, challenging the limits of conventional historical scholarship and producing its own counterhistory as a practice of value.[29] While the story may never conclusively prove the existence of Willie Hughes, it does present a legitimate principle of historical theory that could have been taken from Marx himself: behind the work of art—behind the aesthetic value form—is an occluded social history that entails the history of production. Wilde casts this insight in terms of classical homoerotic relations: "So it had been with others whose beauty had given a new creative impulse to their age. The ivory body of the Bithynian slave rots in the green ooze of the Nile, and on the yellow hills of the Cerameicus is strewn the dust of the young Athenian; but Antinous lives in sculpture, and Charmides in Philosophy" (90). Certainly, one way of reading these examples is to maintain that the aesthetic formulations of these particular human lives are their most enduring legacy. A systematic reading, one (again) in tune with Benjamin and his famous aphorism on culture and violence, is also apparent, which is that, ultimately, behind the beautiful form of the statue is the dissolved body of the slave and the forgotten history of a whole social structure, economic as well as affective. As he claims in "The Soul of Man," "The fact is that civilization requires slaves" (141). This is not a promotion of human slavery; rather, it is (1) a historical insight into the gruesome connections between slavery and culture, that is, the super-adequation that has been the source for the production and command of culture; and (2) a motivation for the materialist transformations of socialism, which will allow everyone to participate in the life of culture. Wilde foresees these transformations through the "slave labor" of machines, which will redistribute wealth for the general welfare.

Wilde plays with the figure of the slave in two directions. The body of the slave does not simply point to forgotten labor but also represents the ruins of a queer romance. He suggests therefore that the production of affective labor is congealed in the aesthetic object as hieroglyph. He sketches, in the imaginative musings of the story's narrator, the queer recovery of that affective history:

> If this was so—and there was certainly no evidence against it—it was not improbable that Willie Hughes was one of those English comedians (mimœ quidam ex Britannia, as the old chronicle calls them), who were slain at Nuremberg in a sudden uprising of the people, and were secretly buried in a little vineyard outside the city by some young men "who had found pleasure in their performances, and of whom some had sought to be instructed in the mysteries of the new art." (89)

The alternative practices of these young men, who have found an unforeseen pleasure in the production of the new art, have left their traces in the social text. If the forms of capital obscure the general social contributions that go into the work of art, they also obscure the affective labor that has congealed in the work of art as a value form. In the traditional discursive parameters of art history, this passage provides no evidence for its claim. However, the theoretical insight of the passage suggests a compelling project for critical historical scholarship: the recovery of the history of the affective labor that has contributed to the social production of the work of art.

Perhaps the most poignant, as well as the most bathetic, trace of affect that circulates in Wilde's story is the act of suicide. In keeping with the dynamics of paradox and reversal that saturate Wilde's work, suicide is not always what it appears to be. For example, consider Erskine's final announcement in a letter to the narrator that he too intends to take his own life in order to prove the theory of Willie Hughes: "The truth was once revealed to you, and you rejected it. It comes to you now stained with the blood of two lives—do not turn away from it" (98). The narrator reacts to this declaration with dread and exclaims: "I felt sick with misery, and yet I could not believe it. To die for one's theological beliefs is the worst use a man can make of his life, but to die for literary theory! It seemed impossible" (98–99). The end of the story of course reveals that Erskine's performance is just that, a mode of dramatic expression, as he does not die by his own hand but instead succumbs to consumption. More puzzling than Erskine's suicidal declaration, though, is the narrator's reaction to it. After all, this expression of disbelief that there actually exists *a literary theory to die for* occurs at the end of a story that has narrated just that theory. Erskine relates at the outset of the story that according to his suicide letter Cyril Graham killed himself "to offer his life as a sacrifice to the secret of the Sonnets" (46). This "impossible" self-sacrifice thus reprises the impossible possibility of the theory of Willie Hughes itself.

What are we to make of the instabilities of this suicidal expression, and how might it represent a critique of the limits of traditional historical discourse? Despite ambiguities of meaning and inscription, suicide does eloquently express the violence of certain historical realities. For example, Cyril's act of self-sacrifice gestures to the tragic historical connections between queers and suicide.[30] These connections are all too contemporary for the scores of youth who absorb and enforce through their own self-destruction a social mandate of violence and hate. The urgent political connections between homophobic violence and suicide may well exceed the parameters of historical verification—even in Wilde's story—but that makes opposition to these pernicious connections all the more urgent and necessary. Wilde's story, by challenging models of historiographic verification while maintaining the legitimacy of alternative historical narratives, invites us to read against the grain and to see in the complex figuration of suicide the horrific traces of a queer counterhistory.

The other counterhistory expressed through Wilde's figuration of suicide is, I would argue, Irish. As Seamus Deane has noted, "It is no news to anyone that Irish writing in the English language is recurrently obsessed with the problems involved in the idea of representation."[31] Wilde's story offers an example of this obsession, as it is precisely in the long history of Irish anticolonial struggle that the death of the political rebel comes to signify the possibilities of an entirely different world order—*truth stained with the blood of lives*.[32] We have already seen that Wilde promotes the rebellion of the poor, and his language in "The Soul of Man" is quite clear: "Disobedience, in the eyes of anyone who has read history, is man's original virtue" (130). Here Wilde both historicizes and reverses the values of Christianity. In keeping with the tendencies of recent scholarship, it is hard not to read in the promotion of the political rebel the trace of Wilde's Irish upbringing and his Irish sympathies.[33] Suicide in light of this scholarship inscribes what Deane calls the "unsayable" aspects of Irish history, the "realm of atrocity, communal immiseration, ethnocide" (119). According to Deane, a history of death haunts Irish representations, leaving its mark even when not explicitly engaged. So, for example: "Although the English-language literature of the Irish Revival rarely mentions, and much less deals with, the Famine that preceded it by a generation, it nevertheless meditates endlessly upon the linguistic condition that was part of that event's cultural inheritance" (119–20). In Wilde, the denotative ambiguities of suicide, in conjunction with the exposure of the theoretical limitations of projects of verification, paradoxically enrich the historical resonance of the story. There persists what David Lloyd describes as that "ineradicable trace" that lingers in Irish representations and memory.[34] Violence against queers and the Irish political struggle, while never directly engaged, both emerge as legitimate and powerful counterhistories in the subtle play of Wilde's elusive prose. The invocation of these counterhistories emerges even as "reason is dead set against it" (190).

MAKING HISTORY

To track the figure of suicide in Wilde's text is to deconstruct history with an affective tool. Affect also functions as part of a constructive historical practice in Wilde, and we must turn to the productive vitality of affective value to conclude our introductory discussion.

In both Marx and Wilde the dynamic interaction of the aesthetic and the historical reproduces a dialectic modernity in which fundamental social contradictions find their resolution in the imaginative plane of art, a resolution as yet unachieved within the processes of historical development. Both Marx and Wilde also offer glimpses of historical theory and practice beyond the formal movements of the dialectic, particularly as formulations of value intersect the power of affect. Gilles Deleuze and Félix Guattari, Gayatri Chakravorty Spivak, Jacques Derrida, and Antonio Negri have all sought in diverse ways to think beyond the dialectic in Marx, to find, in Negri's words, a *Marx beyond Marx*.[35] In Negri's recent work, affect plays a key role both in his analysis of the development of nondialectical forms of postmodern capitalism and in theorizing potentials for the radical transformation of contemporary social relations. A brief introduction to his analysis can help to locate in the intersection between Marx and Wilde a practice of value that supersedes the dialectic traditions of romantic anticapitalism and brings into focus the transformative potentials of the power of affect.

In "Value and Affect," Negri argues that while the contemporary agents of capitalism understand that value production is increasingly reliant on affect, capitalist power structures cannot truly measure the value of this affect; instead they can only seek to control and direct it, to market it, to discipline it at the level of its biopolitical production.[36] Writing within critical trajectories opened in different ways by Spinoza and Nietzsche, Negri thus extends one of Marx's basic arguments—that while capitalism in the nineteenth century was able to subsume labor power into its profit calculations, it has never been able to measure or represent its true power, to unleash its full potential as collective living activity. Negri suggests that, since affective value registers as a contradictory opacity from the perspectives of the power structures "from above," it therefore must be considered "from below" in the fields of collective activity in which it plays a vital role. His extended analysis offers a dense and richly suggestive theorization of the role of affect in global postmodernity.[37] Wilde elaborates a remarkably similar theory of affect, though in a different context than Negri, as we will see. In brief, Negri proposes a central paradox to describe the contemporary role of affect:

The more the measure of value becomes ineffectual, the more the value of labor-power becomes determinant in production; the more political economy masks the value of labor-power, the more labor-power is extended and intervenes in a global terrain, a bio-political terrain. In this paradoxical way, labor becomes affect, or better, labor finds its value in affect, if affect is defined as "the power to act" (Spinoza). The paradox can thus be reformulated in these terms: The more the theory of value loses its reference to the subject (measure was this reference as a basis of mediation and command), the more the value of labor resides in affect, that is, in living labor that is made autonomous in the capital relation, and expresses—through all the pores of singular and collective bodies—its power of self-valorization. (79–80)

In this formula, it is precisely labor-power as affect that fuels the global economy. Or in Marx's terms, affect as labor-power is the form of "production which predominates over the rest, whose relations thus assign rank and influence to the others" (*G* 106). While capitalist power structures in some ways recognize this, they cannot represent this productive power of affect, which becomes increasingly alienated in the exploitative processes of capitalist expropriation. For Negri, two crucial examples of this paradoxical process are the domestic labor of women as wives and/or mothers, and the investments of desire that fuel "the economy of attention," the media of mass communications.[38] In both of these contexts, value is stripped from forms of affect whose productive traces haunt capitalist profit as both a new figure of alienated labor and the potential for radical transformation and intervention.

Elaborating from this paradox, he offers four hypotheses to define value-producing affect. Fundamentally, Negri suggests: "Affect can be considered . . . as *a power to act* that is singular and at the same time universal. It is singular because it poses action beyond every measure that power does not contain in itself, in its own structure, and in the continuous restructurings that it constructs. It is universal because the affects construct a commonality among subjects" (85). This power to act opens into three expressions: the power of transformation, the power of appropriation, and the power of expansion—each of these powers describes the constructive and generative power of affect, its living ability to produce value and sociality.[39] Political economy—the capitalist State—recognizes the contemporary transformations in the value form. However, despite this recognition, it can only attempt to control the expressive vitality of affect:

The latent recognition that political economy gives to the fact that *value* is now an *investment in desire* constitutes a real and proper conceptual revolution. . . . In any case, this revolution in political economy is revealing in that it involves dominating the context of the affects that establish productive reality as the superstructure of social reproduction and as the articulation of the circulation of the signs of communication. Even if the measurement of this new productive reality is impossible, because affect is not measurable, nonetheless in this very productive context, so rich in productive subjectivity, affect *must* be controlled. Political economy has become a deontological science. In other words, the project of the political economy of conventions and communications is the control of an immeasurable productive reality. (87)

Michael Hardt is right to caution that an analysis of the potentially subversive qualities of affective labor must be thought in relation to the fact that "the processes of economic postmodernization that have been in course for the past twenty-five years have positioned affective labor in a role that is not only productive of capital but at the pinnacle of the hierarchy of laboring forms" (90). Nonetheless, I believe that it is both the entanglement of affective labor in the production of value, as well as the simple clarity of this involvement, that presents a radical potential for intervention, transformation, and new forms of social practice.

The intersection of concepts of value in Marx and Wilde can be read through Negri's postmodern formulations. To begin, Wilde also proposes a model of value beyond measure, and not simply in the slipperiness of paradox and irony that marks the circulation of the theory of Willie Hughes. In "The Soul of Man," when describing the dimensions of personal affection, Wilde explains:

He who would lead a Christlike life is he who is perfectly and absolutely himself. He may be a great poet, or a great man of science; or a young student at a University, or one who watches sheep on a moor; or a maker of dramas, like Shakespeare, or a thinker about God like Spinoza; or a child who plays in a garden, or a fisherman who throws his net into the sea. . . . There are as many perfections as there are imperfect men. (137–38)

The immeasurable quality of this affect—immeasurable insofar as it represents an open trajectory of activity and being—is not just the banal reprisal of the liberal humanist commonplace that each individual is unique. The measureless measure of Wilde's individualist—which we should remember is ultimately an expression of socialism—is specifically cast as a rejection of the Enlightenment measurements of liberalism. Arguing that "all authority is equally bad," Wilde writes: "There are three kinds of despots. There is the despot who tyrannizes over the body. There is the despot who tyrannizes over the soul. There is the despot who tyrannizes over the soul and body alike. The first is called the Prince. The second is called the Pope. The third is called the people" (153–54). He makes similar jabs at feudal, religious, and populist forms of authority throughout the essay. What is important, in the context of the philosophical problem of measurement, is that each of these regimes offers figures for the measurement, division, organization, and control of individual and collective humanity—all figures that are rejected by Wilde's insistence on a radical ontology of "the true personality of man":

> It will be a marvelous thing—the true personality of man—when we see it. It will grow naturally and simply, flowerlike, or as a tree grows. It will not be at discord. It will never argue or dispute. It will not prove things. It will know everything. And yet it will not busy itself with knowledge. It will have wisdom. Its value will not be measured by material things. It will have nothing. And yet it will have everything, and whatever one takes from it, it will still have, so rich it will be. It will not always be meddling with others, or asking them to be like itself. It will love them because they will be different. And yet while it will not meddle with others, it will help all, as a beautiful thing helps us, by being what it is. (34)

Coded here through a natural aesthetic, this ontology of human affect operates as a challenge to the classical measurements of the Enlightenment. Utopian, flowery, queer, dreamy, femme, stylish, campy, contemplative, silly, artistic, loving, limitless—this passage offers a radically democratic glimpse of what the rational institutions of the Enlightenment, with its figures of the people, the citizen, the state, the property owner, the White European, and Man, could not embrace: the affects of the multitude.[40]

This list of adjectives is in some sense idiosyncratic and impressionistic, a weak and affective intervention against the institutionally sanctioned categories I have set them against. Nonetheless, a number of recent critics, working in diverse contexts, have made a case for the public role of affect and the aesthetic, cases that attempt to enrich rational models of the social with a publicity of feeling that ultimately contributes to our understanding of political agency and our role as critics. In "The Aesthetic Dimension of Kantian Autonomy," Jane Kneller expands on Hannah Arendt's engagement with Immanuel Kant's *Critique of Judgment*. Kneller explicitly argues for an expanded understanding of the publicity of affect that emerges in aesthetic experience:

> It is important to look more closely at Kant's views on the nature of judgments of taste than Arendt does. An explicit aim of Kant's "Critique of Aesthetic Judgment" (roughly the first half of the *Critique of Judgment*) is to show that we have the capacity, in addition to the capacity for publicity of thought, for publicity of feeling. This latter capacity (i.e. the *sensus communis aestheticus*) makes possible the communicability of certain feelings a priori. . . . Thus a kind of universality, "universal communicability," is possible for feelings of pleasure. This willingness to grant the existence of such pleasures in universal conditions a priori is a landmark new position for Kant.[41]

Kneller argues that the affects of aesthetic experience can play an important role in a broadened social sense of autonomy and in deepening our sense of rational political agency. Through Kneller, we can see that Wilde's apparent aestheticism and frivolity might actually engage deeper issues of universal communication and critical political autonomy.

In *Poetry against Torture: Criticism, History, and the Human,* Paul Bové argues for the importance of a humanist literary criticism based on a love of language and books as a supple model of social engagement that must be pursued in addition to sheer oppositional analytic critique. The point is not that Bové might endorse my particular characterization of Wilde's language but that in his promotion of what he terms "criticism" we can imagine a context in which the value of multiple affective literary glosses of language emerges. Bové points to a historical example to make his claims:

> In fine, we might say that Al-Andalus was a philological culture and polity; it was an enactment of the love of language and of books. . . . Criticism cannot be afraid of contradictions. I cannot hope to expunge them and be responsible to the real that humans are and create. It cannot become rigid in its intolerance of the side-by-side that enriches presences and promises futures that are unknown and uncertain. Standing in front of uncertainty and contradiction without reaching for reason—that is, as Keats told us, a poetic strength. It requires a quality, a virtue, much greater than that of reversibility, which Foucault enshrined as the place of love and as the opposite of torture. Surely, about torture, Foucault was right: where there is no chance of changing places, there is only such domination as to make the existence of the dominated subject impossible or nearly so. Nevertheless, reversibility is not the opposite of such domination. We need another term for a society or culture that commits itself to games of truth enhanced by power as forms of absolute domination, or that self-understands its play as a game of "power/knowledge"; such a society lacks a love of language.[42]

Bové's description here echoes Wilde in key points: the poetic embrace of contradictions, a certain lyricism that performs its own kind of critical work, the invocation of love. Most important, Bové's book provides a historical context through which we can think about the affective intensities of Wilde's utopian description.

Finally, Sedgwick offers a lens through which we might consider what's at stake in Wilde's affective theory of the truths of human personality. In her essay "Paranoid Reading and Reparative Reading," she argues that paranoid readings have the power to expose with "conceptual economy and elegance" the deceptive mechanisms of power and that a paranoid methodology has come to dominate contemporary theory.[43] The tools of paranoid reading have a close connection in particular with the development of queer theory. In its early stages queer theory took as a central task the unmasking of the violent paranoid structures of homophobia and heterosexism. A historical problem developed, one that marked her own early writings: "Paranoia thus became by the mid-1980s a privileged *object* of antihomophobic theory. How did it spread so quickly from that status to being its uniquely sanctioned *methodology*?" (126). As a response, Sedgwick sets out to theorize a mode of reparative reading in the essay, and it is through this mode, which she refers to as a weak yet affectively rich theory, that we can see a place for the multitude of affects that Wilde casts as truths of the human personality:

> It is not only important but *possible* to find ways of attending to such reparative motives and positionalities. The vocabulary for articulating any reader's reparative motive toward a text or a culture has long been so sappy, aestheticizing, defensive, anti-intellectual or reactionary that it is no wonder few critics are willing to describe their relations with such motives. The prohibitive problem, however, has been in the limitations of present theoretical categories rather than in the reparative motive itself. No less acute than a paranoid position, no less realistic, no less attached to a project of survival, and neither less nor more delusional nor fantasmatic, the reparative reading position undertakes a different range of affects, ambitions, and risks. What we can best learn from such practices are, perhaps, the many ways selves and communities succeed in extracting sustenance from the objects of a culture—even of a culture whose avowed desire has been not to sustain them. (150–51)

Kneller, Bové, and Sedgwick all point to the need for a theory of affect and the aesthetic that is both thoroughly historical and attentive to the rich textures and idiosyncrasies through which people confront themselves and the world. I argue that Wilde's concept of affect, particularly as it emerges in a theorization of socialism, makes an important contribution to such a project.

We can grasp the importance of Wilde's theorization of socialism by returning to our discussion of Negri. As in Negri's analysis, the struggle to control affect in "The Soul of Man" occurs in the context of its biopolitical production; it is in this light that we must read Wilde's extended discussion of the artist's relation to the public as intimately connected to his promotion of socialism. While the above passage from Wilde insists on a radical individualist concept of affect, it also suggests that, in the theater of its production, affect produces commonality among subjects, a form of the universal that Wilde analyzes through the problem of aesthetic taste. In exploring the problem of the determination and formation of the public's aesthetic taste, Wilde both chastises the public for tyrannizing over the work of the artist, and imagines the possibility of refining or defining public sensibilities, the possibility of producing what he terms "the temperament of receptivity":

In both of these theaters [the Lyceum and the Haymarket] there have been individual artists, who have succeeded in creating in their audiences . . . the temperament to which Art appeals. And what is that temperament? It is the temperament of receptivity. That is all. If a man approaches a work of art with any desire to exercise authority over it and the artist, he approaches it in such a spirit that he cannot receive any artistic impression from it at all. The work of art is to dominate the spectator: the spectator is not to dominate the work of art. The spectator is to be receptive. He is to be the violin on which the master is to play. And the more completely he can suppress his own silly views, his own foolish prejudices, his own absurd idea of what Art should be, or should not be, the more he is likely to appreciate the work of art in question. . . . A temperament capable of receiving, through an imaginative medium, and under imaginative conditions, new and beautiful impressions, is the only temperament that can appreciate a work of art. ("SM" 150)

If the previous passage argues for a radical ontology of affect—a measure-less expression of being—then this passage presents the construction of what Negri terms the universal in relation to that ontology. Unlike the Enlightenment's propagation of a purportedly "universal" rational sub-ject—whose occluded determinations ultimately belie the prospect of its universality—Wilde here assembles a commonality precisely through the erasure of such determinations. As with his figuration of an elaborated form of sympathy, here Wilde proposes a productive receptivity that would be the social relation necessary for the realization and expression of the bound-less vitality of affect.[44] As in Negri, the struggle is over the productive con-text, in this case the theater and the social production of aesthetic taste, the site at which affect produces value and sociality. In the production of public taste, the singular or individualist expression of affect—that of the work of art—is transformed into a common sensibility among subjects. To call on another of Wilde's seminal essays, "The Critic as Artist," the production of an aesthetic sensibility also represents this transformation in the opposite direction—the individuation of the universe of new impressions in the temperament of receptivity, as the development of a critical sensibility itself becomes a mode of artistic expression. It is in this sense that Gilbert in "The Critic as Artist" can claim a creative power for criticism: "Nay, more, I would say that the highest Criticism, being the purest form of per-sonal impression, is in its way more creative than creation, as it has least reference to any standard external to itself, and is, in fact, its own reason for existing, and, as the Greeks would put it, in itself, and to itself, an end."[45] The temperament of receptivity as it interacts with the work of art repre-sents both an individuation of a universal and the expansion of the indi-vidual into universal dimensions. The seemingly hermetic aesthetic of *art for art's sake* that characterizes much of Wilde's work thus emerges not as an escapist flight from history but as an attempt to think through an autonomous form of self-valorization—the power of affect—that challenges the structures, expressions, forms, and potentials of the historical.

To come full circle to "The Portrait of Mr. W. H." and the theory of Willie Hughes that "fascinated everybody who was worth fascinating," we can now see that far from being an exercise in ahistorical fancy, the productive queer affective value of the story shapes history in precisely the ways Negri argues affect transforms, appropriates, and expands in, through, and beyond the terrain of postmodern global capitalism. *Reading,* figured as the circulation of the theory of Willie Hughes, emerges proleptically in Wilde's text as a biopolitical praxis through which contemporary history can be thought. Just as in "The Critic as Artist," where, as we have seen, reproduction is absorbed by the powers of production, *reading,* as the production and circulation of affect, is not simply a practice marked by the slippages of a modernist irony, but a postmodern practice that inscribes the limits and potentials of contemporary living labor. Unlike political economy's sociological account of affect's relation to the global economy "from above," *reading,* as we have theorized it through Wilde's work, offers the chance to think through the power of affect, as Negri says, "from below." The solution to the greatest mystery of modern literature, the secret to this social relation, thus lies in the reader's hand.[46]

CHAPTER 2

✺

J. M. Synge and the Aesthetics of Intelligent Sympathy

At first glance, it might seem that the Irish Literary Revival, inspired by such things as the bucolic sentiment of William Butler Yeats's *Celtic Twilight*, the translations of Irish folk culture by Douglas Hyde in *The Love Songs of Connaught*, and the religious themes of Edward Martyn's plays, turned away from Oscar Wilde's modern aesthetics and urbane sensibilities. By most accounts, the Revival preferred the apparent authenticity of the Irish peasant to the artifice of Wilde's dandy. Of course, both the Irish peasant and the dandy were characters who embodied worldviews and promoted values that challenged philistine and imperialist strains of British culture. However, the cliché of the peasant was in certain ways cast as the antithesis to the dandy: sexually modest as opposed to sensual and pleasure-seeking, religious and devout as opposed to secular and ironic, Irish-speaking and of Gaelic origin as opposed to cosmopolitan and polyglot, rural and not urban, interested in spiritual reward rather than earthly riches; and certainly, so the story went, this sincere Irish peasant was not queer. This image of the authentic peasant was largely conjured and circulated by the cultural nationalists of the urban (Anglo-Irish and Catholic) bourgeoisie, and ultimately the promotion of this modest figure, and the culture it represented, proved to be more incendiary than the Revivalists at first imagined. Despite early attempts to insist on the political neutrality of the project, the cultural revival of Gaelic Ireland in this period paved the way for the political upheaval and transformations that came about with the 1916 Easter Rising and the subsequent War for Independence (1919–21).

This chapter will argue that in the work of John Millington Synge, the revival of the Irish peasant and Irish national culture was not only politically volatile in unforeseen ways, but was a surprisingly queer project. In particular, I maintain that Synge's peasant is a figure whose discursive dynamics are much closer to those of Wilde's dandy than has been allowed. Furthermore, by expanding our understanding of the queer beyond the confines of sexual identity to include a range of non-normative affects, desires, and cultural strategies, this chapter argues that Synge should not be read as turning from Wildean artifice to embrace a rural authenticity but instead should be seen as extending a queer aesthetic project along new lines.

INTELLIGENT SYMPATHY

Of all the people to address the representation of the Irish-speaking peasant, Synge did the most to disrupt burgeoning orthodoxies, and presented the most complexly modern view of the peasantry and its conception of the world. Synge combined a rigorous engagement with Irish speakers—he took the time to learn the living Irish language, to consult experts within the Irish-speaking populations, and to learn to read notoriously difficult Irish-language manuscripts—with a subtle understanding of the contradictory forces at play in the representations of folk culture. In *Tinkers: Synge and the Cultural History of the Irish Traveller*, Mary Burke reveals the depth and range of Synge's engagement with diverse elements of Irish rural society.[1] She establishes his sophisticated understanding of the rich history of representations that converge in the figure of the "tinker," a nomadic element of Irish rural life distinct from both rural and urban sedentary cultures. She shows that Synge's portrayals of "tinkers" are "more nuanced than those of his Revival peers in subtly unfolding the European literary origins of the motif" (59). Furthermore, she examines how this understanding of the literary origins of the motif enables Synge to bring into focus the diversity of Irish cultural life that is at once national and cosmopolitan. She explains: "The complex figure Synge depicts is indisputably Irish, but possesses an Irishness that encompasses what he recognizes to be that identity's multifarious discursive roots. In short, Synge's tinker is cosmopolitan on two levels: it is a construct understood to be of sundry cultural origins and reality that exemplifies Irish cultural diversity" (59).

This chapter will elaborate a concept of "intelligent sympathy" as a way to describe Synge's aesthetic engagement with Irish folk culture. The phrase recalls Wilde's insistence on *sympathy with thought*, which we encountered in the last chapter, and both concepts represent attempts to track the social and historical dimensions of affect. The phrase "intelligent sympathy" comes from Synge's own work and appears in a favorable review of Stephen Gwynn's travel guide, *The Fair Hills of Ireland*. Synge claims that Gwynn's book is "likely to bring many minds into a more intelligent sympathy with Ireland, where, for good and for bad, the past is living and the present so desirous to live."[2] Gwynn's book interests Synge because it forges an intimate and critical relationship with Ireland by taking the inventory of both the contemporary country and the historical legacy that has left its traces on the landscape:

> *The Fair Hills of Ireland* is a guide-book, in the best sense of the words, addressed to travelers and friends of Ireland rather than to ordinary tourists. At the same time it is a sort of popular history, telling its story topographically instead of chronologically, and yet so effectively that one does not grumble at the confusion of the ages that some are likely to fall into, as the author passes back and forward from the times of Cuchulain to those of O'Connell and from the route of the Danes at Clontarf to the modern affairs of the new Irish creameries. (387)

This chapter argues that Synge fashions his own intelligent form of sympathy in his encounter with Irish folk culture. He does not simply offer a chronological historical account of the peasantry, but through his aesthetic style he takes an inventory of the historical traces that circulate in the representations of rural Irish life and suggests a critical form of sympathy as a mode of national affiliation. Using Daniel Corkery's seminal *Synge and Anglo-Irish Literature*[3] to trace the contours of Synge's project, this chapter shows that the playwright uses a queer aesthetic to shape a model of Irishness that both engages the national specificity of Irish history and situates Ireland within a global modernity. Corkery's critique functions as a sort of photographic negative for the argument of the chapter. On the one hand, I look to his work to validate my own reading of the queerness of Synge's sensibilities. On the other hand, while Corkery rejects the queer excesses of the playwright's aesthetic as un-Irish, I situate Synge's artistic practices in a persistent, if subterranean, queer genealogy of modern Irish culture.

Corkery's work on Synge is impressionistic. Its rambling style is rife with contradictions. Nonetheless, there are fundamental values which anchor his romantic nationalism and through which he measures Synge's work. Nationalism for Corkery is a value of "every normal people" (2) and is set against what he refers to variously as the "freakish" (93), the "queer" (101), and the "international" (236). According to Corkery, the Irish nation is Gaelic, Catholic, and intimately attached to the land and rural work. Following the work of Kathryn Conrad and Margot Backus, we can see Corkery's work as part of the broad discourse of heteronormative nationalism. Conrad and Backus explore this discourse through the figure of the heterosexual "family cell" in Irish culture and politics.[4] Conrad explains the historical rise of the family cell as an organizing unit of Irish culture and political life: "In other words, the dual forces of Christianity, which reinforced a patriarchal system of familial relationships, and British colonialism, which divided the land and penalized social formations that did not further British interests, helped to fix the heterosexual nuclear family as the primary unit group of Irish society" (5). She further explains the political and discursive dynamics that this structure produced: the cell "is a method of concealing any instability within the cell in order to present the image of control. If the cell is stable so are the social institutions built upon it, and one can present to the world one's capacity to rule. Instabilities must therefore be constructed and treated as foreign—not only to the family, not only to one's political position, but also to the nation as a whole" (9–10). This discourse projects heteronormative sexuality onto the national stage and connects the sexual norms that govern individual subjects to national questions of colonialism and the postcolonial state. Mutations of this normative heterosexual discourse run throughout Corkery's analysis, in which he articulates Irish national politics through the micropolitics of sexuality, for example in his invocation of the revival of Irish culture through a sexualized framework: "The national virtue of the country had been led astray, *perdu*, in some wayside cavern: only the temerity of lovers could reach to it and rescue it" (100).

The target of Corkery's most vigorous critical attack are the writers of the Protestant Anglo-Irish Ascendancy, whom he condemns as both unbalanced and foreign. Corkery is at pains to distinguish Anglo-Irish Synge from this cohort. However, he is never able to render the playwright fully "normal," and a queer trace remains. Corkery can praise Synge in nationalist terms: "Here, by one stroke, to show how [Synge] stands apart from his fellow Ascendancy writers, it is but necessary to state, that he, an Ascendancy man, went into the huts of the people and lived with them" (27). Nonetheless, he ultimately claims that Synge's writings reflect an imaginative and emotional decadence that distracts from their historical and political validity. At suggestive flashpoints in his analysis, Corkery formulates this imaginative and affective excess through a euphemistic homophobic discourse made culturally available in the wake of Wilde's trial. The figure of Wilde and the specter of the queer operate in subtle, and perhaps unconscious, ways in the text. Within the broader promotion of a heteronormative nationalism, these flashpoints come to suggest that *while Synge might not be queer himself, at times he writes dangerously as if he were.*

What interests me is the power of Corkery's formulation. What is important in it is not the blunt fact of identity but rather the structure of an analysis that can organize its force through the threatening specter of a particular characteristic—as in the example of Wilde, whose queerness operates as definitively homosexual—and yet still target someone whose particular self-definition does not seem to conform to this identity: Synge is targeted as dangerously close to the definitively homosexual. Eve Kosofsky Sedgwick has analyzed this dynamic as a form of emotional terrorism that circulates as homosexual panic.[5] I would like to turn the phobic flashpoints in Corkery's analysis on their head in a slightly different way and to use them to stage questions about Synge's aesthetic. By engaging Corkery as a kind of litmus test of the queer dynamics in Synge, I want to ask if it is not possible that a writer who did not himself identify as gay or homosexual, such as Synge, might adopt queer aesthetic strategies because he sees in them a creative and critical vitality, a power that can shape more progressive models of social belonging and historical understanding. As a reader trained in the recuperative queer context of the 1990s, it seems to me that Synge's work readily responds to queer readings. My strategic reliance on Corkery's phobic responses to Synge's project is an attempt to transform a symptomatically aggressive reading into a queer affirmative one and to keep in critical view the violence of such hostile evaluations in an attempt to diffuse and redirect their power. Moving beyond Corkery's panic, I argue that the playwright harnesses a queer affective excess both to detach Ireland from clichéd relationships to its own history and to connect the nation with a global modernity.

The compelling critical reasons to analyze Synge's concept of "intelligent sympathy" specifically in terms of queer cultural aesthetics are thus manifold, stemming from Synge's own language and the critical role that affect plays in his writings to the terms and tone of Corkery's critique. The preponderance of the term "queer" as a qualifier of emotional states and relations in Synge's work begs for elaboration. The term appears throughout *The Playboy of the Western World*: Pegeen is referred to as the "queer daughter" and Michael James as the "queer father."[6] Lynching is referred to as the villagers' "queer joy" (100). Shawn Keogh accuses Pegeen's interest in Christy of being a "queer story" (122). The village itself appears as a particularly queer place full of macho women (Pegeen Mike the bartender and the Widow Quin husband-killer) and feminized men (the spineless Shawn Keogh and the cross-dressing Christy). It is not clear that any of the characters in the play are involved in same-sex erotic practices; nonetheless, the preponderance and fluidity of the term invites critical attention. According to the *Oxford English Dictionary* (*OED*), the term in Irish dialect operates as a general intensifier. It has the meaning of both the peculiar and the derogatory. As early as 1894 the term had a homosexual valence, quoted by the *OED* from a letter of the Marquess of Queensberry: "I write to tell you that it is a judgment on the whole lot of you. Montgomerys, The Snob Queers like Roseberry & certainly Christian hypocrite Gladstone." Likewise, an emotional and aesthetic sensibility circulates in the body of Synge's work that at times takes on a specifically homoerotic syntax and at other times sheds this homoerotic specificity yet suggests a relation to it. Even Synge as a writer is a sort of queer figure.[7] He is difficult to categorize in generic terms and does not present a clearly systematized aesthetic practice.[8]

Corkery indicts "the narrowness of Synge's range of mind" as well as "the promiscuity of his mannerisms" (viii). In this formula, we begin to see the phobic tensions that animate the discourse of heteronormative nationalism. In the calculus of this observation, the target both has a narrow obsession with a singular topic, an obsession that marks a degenerate interiority, and is inappropriately expressive, as this interior obsession becomes socially legible in the promiscuity of mannerisms. This dynamic has a sexual valence that Corkery here marks with the word "promiscuity." Looking back to the public assault on Wilde in the trial, we see a similar dynamic invoked against the writer: "His adversary Edward Carson read out one of [Wilde's] clever paradoxes—'Wickedness is a myth invented by good people to account for the curious attractiveness of others'—and asked whether this was 'a safe axiom to put forward for the philosophy of the young.' To which Oscar replied, 'Most stimulating.' Carson read out another seditious maxim and again asked, 'Is it good for the young?' 'Anything is good that stimulates thought at any age.'"[9] In this exchange we can read the contradictions that subtend the public legibility of private vice. From Carson's aggressive point of view, that legibility is necessary for the containment of the purportedly vicious. From Wilde's position that same legibility is highly unstable and offers a potential point of reversal as "wickedness" is detached from the object of scorn and is used to measure those who would project it as an epithet. For Wilde, the term ultimately marks not the degeneracy of its target but the curiosities of those who deploy it. Corkery's characterization of Synge reprises the same dynamics, and in the wake of Wilde's trial the fear of promiscuity in Corkery's logic is marked by a fear of the homosexual. It is important to note that Corkery does not name Synge as homosexual even as he marshals the syntax of assault made available by Wilde's trial. Consider the use of this syntax, for instance, in his dismissal of the macho women of *The Playboy* in a passage that clearly calls to mind Wilde's *Dorian Gray*, without, however, claiming anything about Synge's identity: "Little else do they possess, except their tomboyish spirits. By the fitful light of their unruly hearts they live. The only evil they fear is the quenching of that light. Old age may quench it, bringing not lack of love so much as lack of lovers. Nothing matters only the retaining of their good looks, by virtue of which their lovers may be retained" (102).

As a way of understanding the ambiguous status of the queer in Synge's work, the fleeting presence of the homoerotic, the emphasis on the strangeness of emotions, and the conflicting responses that the playwright provokes in his critics, I would like to call again on a concept of affect derived from Spinoza.[10] We know from Synge's diaries that he was at least familiar with the philosopher, and we will analyze later in the chapter traces of Spinozist thought in his work. For now, Spinoza's concept of affect can serve as a critical tool for elaborating his queer aesthetic practice. Gilles Deleuze defines Spinoza's use of affect in a passage that compellingly evokes the transitory and dynamic nature of affect in Synge:

> Therefore, from one state to another, there are transitions, passages that are experienced, durations through which we pass to greater or a lesser perfection. Furthermore, these states, these affections, images or ideas are not separable from the duration that attaches them to the preceding state and makes them tend towards the next state. These continual durations or variations of perfection are called "affect," or feelings (*affectus*).[11]

The particular composition of affects in Synge might at times invite the reader to assign a stable identity, yet they ultimately resist any such assignment, insofar as they are "variations" in Deleuze's terms. In this sense the affective quality of his work and the preponderance of the queer intersect. Throughout Synge's work, affects are channeled in chains of shifting analogues that at times take on a homoerotic valence and at times shed all but the trace of this valence as they acquire new forms. These affects need to be theorized in the movement of their variations, and the musical connotations of this movement will prove very important. While the uncongealed nature of these affects makes them difficult to measure, four key features do emerge. These affective variations point to (1) an embracing of theatricality, (2) an attachment to the nomadic forces of international circulation, (3) an emphasis on the powers of the feminine, and (4) the accentuation of "perverse" sexuality. Understood in their transformative dynamic, these affects provide a critical version of Irishness that extends the importance of queer sexual discourse, economic forms, and modes of cultural expression seen in Wilde.

A taxonomy of affects can be routed through a characterological interpretation, and in the context of Irish culture the biographical implications of the queer have been especially important in the representations of Oscar Wilde and Roger Casement. However, in Synge affects do not primarily play a role in the identification of the subject; rather, they are indissolubly linked with the historico-political narratives of Irishness in an international frame. Affects in Synge intersect the subject, yet they also exceed this particularity and form part of the fabric of the social. They are examples of what Vicky Mahaffey has theorized as *micronationalism*: "Micronationalism . . . bypasses the predictable opposition of nationalism and internationalism. Micronationalism is a concentration on highly local and sometimes submerged features of a country, a person, or a text that are never taken as 'representative,' but which instead initiate an expansive and energizing process of connection (as opposed to a movement of consolidation)."[12] The expansive dimensions of affect in Synge have implications for the tracking of queer valences in his work: the genetic project of locating the emergence of the homosexual as modern individual seems misguided because queer features do not condense into the figure of a particular subject. Rather, in Synge the queer measures the historico-political and cultural forces that intersect and collide in the Irish situation. This chapter, therefore, will not attempt to recover the identity of a particular psyche— it will not attempt to claim, for instance, that Synge was gay—but will instead measure what Synge refers to as "the psychic state of the locality" (Corkery 185), the intersection of forces that define the Irish situation. The queer will be a particular aesthetic rendering of intelligent sympathy, a particular mode for reading the social dimensions of affect in the Irish situation.

The chapter proceeds in three sections. First I look at the production of Synge's aesthetic sensibility through the staging of affective intensities. The theatrical staging of affects in his writing produces a mode of aesthetic consciousness; the queer is key for understanding the social dimensions of this aesthetic consciousness. Second, I track the deployment of this affective sensibility in his aesthetic encounter with Irish folk culture. Specifically, his engagement with experimental continental literature enables a particularly sophisticated and subtle presentation of the peasantry. The chapter argues that the writer takes an inventory of the social and historical situation of the peasants through the aesthetic presentation of an intense array of affects. I read this critical engagement as an "intelligent sympathy" and suggest that Synge's representation of the peasantry points to an expanded understanding of modernity in which the social dimensions of aesthetic experience are able to recast and redirect the dichotomies and power trajectories of the modern imperial imaginary. The model of intelligent sympathy that emerges in Synge's practice of montage allows for the reversal of one-way colonialist subject/object imaginary that situates the colonized merely as objects of metropolitan speculation and consumption. Finally, in a reading of *The Playboy of the Western World*, I explore the socialization of Synge's affective sensibility in the "queer" little village on the west coast of Mayo. Synge reveals the perimetric figures of the Irish peasantry as engaged participants in world modernity.

QUEER ORCHESTRATIONS

Affect has an irreducible social quality in Synge's thought. This social quality is apparent in his brief early *Autobiography*, in which he marshals a network of queer tropes and connotations to describe the emergence of his aesthetic sensibility. The *Autobiography* should not be read simply as presenting the formation of an individual identity, but as tracing the deployment and circulation of a social and affective mode of being in the world. "Mode" is a richly suggestive term in this context and offers a compelling way for thinking about affect in Synge's work beyond the consolidation of sexual identity. Based on the definitions in the *OED*, "mode" has a number of valences that connect with the articulation of affect in Synge's writing, particularly as its connotations connect to the related term "mood." "Mode" has grammatical connotations, in the *mood* of a verb as either active or passive, and in the character of modal propositions that are either necessary, contingent, possible, or impossible. In relation to these grammatical senses, a *mode of being* points to the affective complexity that circulates in and through language. Mode also has musical denotations, describing the tonal and temporal qualities that produce melody, rhythm, and musical style. As we will see, music is a very important art for Synge and is connected with the Spinozist variations of affect discussed above. The word "mode" points generally to a style or manner of acting, and even of fashion or dress. In its Middle French roots it meant "a collective manner of living or thinking proper to a country or age." These senses will be directly invoked in *The Playboy*. Finally, in its philosophical registers "mode" is an elastic and interstitial term, pointing to "a manner or state of being of a thing; a thing considered as possessing certain non-essential attributes which may be changed without destroying its identity."

Synge links his development as a young artist and the emergence of his aesthetic sensibilities with a queerly acute emotional sensitivity. His heightened affects are predicated through ambiguously queer fantasies—though the result of this predication is not the constitution of a homosexual identity but the staging of an emotional and aesthetic sensibility that will later be used in his engagement with Irish folk culture. To understand Synge's engagement with folk culture properly, we must first examine the emergence of this receptivity. In the following passage, the development of Synge's artistic awareness coincides with a homoerotically inflected friendship:

> Although I had the usual affection for my near relations I began while still very young to
> live in my imagination in enchanted premises that had high walls with glass upon the top
> where I sat and drank ginger-beer in a sort of perpetual summer with one companion,
> usually some school fellow I hardly knew. One day the course of my class put me for a
> moment beside my temporary god, and before I could find a fit term of adulation he
> whispered an obscene banality which shattered my illusions. (6)

The eruption of explicitly sexual content within a same-sex, and therefore a putatively (by a normative estimation) nonsexual companionship, gives this scene its charge. Notice that the content of the obscenity and the motivations behind its circulation are missing. Was it meant to shock, seduce, disgust? The passage, even as it registers the eruption of the sexual, also suggests repetition: it is *usually* some school fellow he hardly knows. The experience is both marked by the unknown obscenity that breaks the frame of the narrator's consciousness and is part of the regular rhythm of experience. Synge is both accustomed to this experience and surprised by it, and readers are similarly both knowing and unknowing participants in the dynamics of the passage. Synge here describes the growing autonomy of his aesthetic powers through a queer syntax. The fantasies of his imagination are charged with a homoerotic value as they coalesce around a sort of romantic attachment to his male schoolmate. The passage, with its emphasis on the young boy's enchantment and delicacy, also delights in the subversion of normative gender roles, a subversion that has a long history in Irish writing.[13] However, neither his aesthetic powers nor the queer syntax point to a particular identity (one could no more say that he is an artist because he daydreams than that he gay because he daydreams of his schoolmate). Instead, both appear as modes of being in the world; they point to the extension of personal affects into the dimensions of the social.

Synge does in fact describe his affections for and relations with girls—indicating that his sexual orientation in this sense might more properly be considered heterosexual. However, he presents heterosexuality in a peculiarly queer mode that rejects, rather than reinforces, normative regulations of desire. Synge here is queer before queer, in a sense, as it is the tropes from an emerging queer culture that are capacious enough for him to articulate his desires. So despite cross-sex affections and attractions, he insists throughout the *Autobiography* on his separation from the normative structures of heterosexual identification and courtship. As he separates himself from these normative structures and the circuits that direct, conduct, and regulate normative desires, his affect and affectations acquire a queer charge. In this way, the queer articulates his broader rejection of a normative conception of the world and his attempt to forge his own critical understanding of his place in society. For example, in the following passage he links his poor health with a rejection of marriage:

> I surmised that unhealthy parents should have unhealthy children—my rabbit breeding may have put the idea into my head. Therefore, I said, I am unhealthy, and if I marry I will have unhealthy children. But I will never create beings to suffer as I am suffering, so I will never marry. I do not know how old I was when I came to this decision, but I was between thirteen and fifteen and it caused me horrible misery. (9)

The theatricality in the passage is high camp: the sickly and effeminate teenage boy who prefers to spend his time daydreaming of palaces and of sipping ginger-beer, faced with the coarse actualities of rabbit breeding, divorces himself from the prospects of marriage (perhaps more accurately described as the physicality of "breeding" in this passage), and resigns himself to misery. The passage is camp insofar as it is the queer inflection of normative culture with an alternative sensibility. Synge literally opts out of the normative arrangement of desire by refusing marriage and ends on a note of affective excess. This excess is not an irony through which the "real" meaning of the passage is conveyed to an elite audience. Instead, it is part of a melodramatic camp imaginary that is ultimately more capacious than irony in that it allows for a richer and more complex network of associations. The passage operates through the reversal of gender and sexual norms and culminates in dramatic excess. It is precisely this excess that later writers will harness as they extend the queer aesthetic practices of modern Irish culture.

In both of these passages it is not exactly a question of Synge's actual sexual inclinations or practices that is at stake. Rather, the theatrical intensity of the affect measures the distance between Synge and a normative conception of the world. The passages are organized not around the facts of sexual inclinations and activities, but around the staging of the affect itself. This staging or theatricality is a question not of authenticity of a particular identity, but of the intensity, tone, and charge of the affect, which in these passages evoke a cultural network of queer allusion and connotation.

Synge also separates himself from the normative structures of religion. He explains that reading Darwin led him early on to adopt atheism. Much as with his rejection of marriage, Synge's atheism isolates him from certain dominant social relations and intensifies a particular affect—in this case the affect of misery: "The story is easily told, but was a terrible experience. By it [his atheism] I laid a chasm between my present and my past and between myself and my kindred and my friends" (11). The misery or suffering that Synge describes in the previous passage has a queer valence in that it makes him recuse himself from the structures of normative hetero-sexuality. Here misery has lost the specifically homosocial content it pos-sessed in the passage with his foul-mouthed schoolmate, but still maintains a queer trace insofar as misery is again the affective intensity used to stage Synge's relation to the social. As Synge separates himself from the physi-cality of sex, from the normative structures of heterosexual courtship, and from a belief in God, an aesthetic sensibility emerges. This aesthetic sensibility is attached to affective forces and brings key figures into a constellation:

> Vulgar sensuality did not attract me but I was haunted by dreams of the verdant liberty
> that seemed to reign in the pagan forests of the south. . . . I think the consciousness of
> beauty is awakened in persons as in peoples by a prolonged unsatisfied desire. . . . The
> feeling of primitive people is still everywhere the feeling of the child; an adoration that
> has never learned of or wished to admire its divinity. (12–13)

The queer, the child, the pagan, and the primitive share in Synge's view a heightened sensitivity and an aesthetic sensibility or "consciousness of beauty." This constellation of figures, each organized around a heightened sense of affect, disrupts a certain Eurocentric narrative of modernity's pro-gress and sets the stage for the disruption of clichéd representations of Irish folk culture and sensibilities. Synge tracks the emergence of an aesthetic consciousness in these four figures not to repeat the familiar trope of infan-tilization of purportedly primitive cultures, but to reveal the modern sensi-bilities of these supposedly peripheral figures. Synge does not cast the pagan and primitive as left behind by progress, or the queer as a perversion of progress. Through Synge's representations of these figures we can high-light the progressive tendencies available to the queer, the child, and the primitive pagan.

The disruption of a dominant imperialist narrative of European progress—one that yokes scientific, cultural, and political advancement with the "mature" civilization of Europe—becomes clearest in the discussion of sexuality. This is particularly important in the Irish context because of the colonial program, which involved the emasculation and infantiliza-tion of the indigenous culture, and because of the intensely contested nature of sexuality in the Irish national and religious imaginary. In the following passage, Synge describes how he and a young girlfriend devel-oped their understanding of the sexual. The primitive in this passage should be read both as a recoding of the value of the indigenous "primi-tive" culture in the colonial context, and as another mode of affective sympathy, as another sort of intelligent feeling that takes an inventory of social relations:

> We were always primitive. We both understood all the facts of life and spoke of them
> without much hesitation but a certain propriety that was decidedly wholesome. We
> talked of sexual matters with an indifferent and sometimes amused frankness that
> was identical with the attitude of folk-tales. We were both superstitious, and if we
> had been allowed . . . we would have evolved a pantheistic scheme like that of all
> barbarians. (7)

It is true that here Synge links barbarians with the creation of superstitions.
However, through the deployment of the primitive—including folktales,
barbarians, and superstitions—the children also share a decidedly modern
relationship to the sexual. The children's discussions and pagan folktales
adopt a relaxed and open attitude toward the sexual. The declaration that
"we were always primitive" does not work to mark the backwardness of the
"primitive"; instead it points to an understanding of modernity from which
the primitive is not excluded. The primitive in this case is not so much a
sociological condition as an analogous affective mode in the circulation of
a modern sensibility.

Synge is at pains to separate himself from prevailing social structures and
to isolate an intensity of affect that links his own aesthetic sensibilities with
the peripheral figures of the queer, the child, the pagan, and the primitive.
The dominant metaphor that situates Synge's understanding of affect is musical. He explains:

> Every life is a symphony, and the translation of this life into music, and from music back
> to literature or sculpture or painting is the real effort of the artist. The emotions which
> pass through us have neither end nor beginning—are a part of the sequence of
> existence—and as the laws of the world are in harmony it is almost the cosmic element
> in the person which gives great art, as that of Michaelangelo or Beethoven, the dignity
> of nature. . . . I do not think biography—even autobiography—can give this revelation.
> But while the thoughts and deeds of a lifetime are impersonal and concrete—might
> have been done by anyone—art is the expression of the essential or abstract beauty of
> the person. . . . If by the study of an adult who is before his time we can preconstruct the
> tendency of life and if—as I believe we find in childhood perfect traces of the savage,
> the expression of a personality will reveal evolution from before history to beyond the
> silence of our own époque. (3)

This passage in particular, and his interest in questions of affect and pan-
theism more generally, bear the mark of Synge's reading of Spinoza. According to this passage, affects do not point to the authenticating inner truth of
the individual; rather, they are variations in the subject's implication in the
"sequence of existence." Synge will take up affect not to measure the truth
of identity but to measure this exteriorized sequence that passes through

the figure of the subject. Consider Spinoza's description of how the affects represent the human's implication in the order of nature:

> Most of those who have written about the affects, and men's way of living, seem to treat, not of natural things, which follow the common laws of Nature, but of things which are outside Nature. Indeed they seem to conceive man in Nature as a dominion within a dominion. For they believe that man disturbs, rather than follows, the order of Nature, that he has absolute power over his actions, and that he is determined only by himself. And they attribute the cause of human impotence and inconstancy, not to the common power of Nature, but to I know not what vice of human nature, which they therefore bewail, or laugh at, or disdain, or (as usually happens) curse. . . . But my reason is this: nothing happens in Nature which can be attributed to any defect in it, for Nature is always the same, and its virtue and power of acting are everywhere one and the same, that is, the laws and rules of Nature according to which all things happen, and change form to another, are always and everywhere the same. So the way of understanding the nature of anything, of whatever kind, must also be the same, namely through the universal laws and rules of Nature.[14]

Affects in Synge and Spinoza index the implication of the subject within the sequence of existence; affects index the human's encounter with the order of nature as opposed to the expression of a human separate from the natural. The sympathies that we have been tracing—the queer, the primitive, and so on—have all pointed not to the truth of the individual but to the implication of the subject within a larger fabric. This use of affect to explore the social is part of the Spinozist inflection of Synge's work.

The queer has been a particularly important mode of being and evaluation in the *Autobiography*, and playing on the musical metaphor, Synge ends the text with a declaration that reinscribes a particularly queer tone. As a way to fashion a subjectivity that is attentive to the movement of these affects—understood both as a question of the kinetic and as a question of musical rhythm and composition—Synge declares himself a musician. This particular modality of aesthetic consciousness reintroduces a queer valence: "For the hypersensitive organization the musical excitement is perhaps too powerful, too nearly a physical intoxication, but it is not surprising that when I found in the orchestra the world of magical beauty I dreamed of, I threw aside all reasonable counsel and declared myself a professional musician" (15). Here Synge's subjectivity is organized around a hypersensitivity to music that borders on physical intoxication. This hypersensitivity is another analogue in the chain of affective intensities and modes we have traced thus far. Interestingly, the passage also marks a seminal—though ironic—avowal. The intensity of his affect and the discovery of others who share this affect lead him to an ambiguous declaration: finally discovering the "world of magic and beauty" that resonates with his "hypersensitive or-ganization," he throws off "all reasonable counsel" and declares himself a "musician." The tone and the metaphor of the passage evoke a sort of com-ing-out narrative, although rather than coming out as a particular identity, Synge "outs" his aesthetic sensibility. (In fact Christopher Isherwood, in *Christopher and His Kind*, points out that the term "musical" was common English-language slang for homosexuals in the first half of the twentieth century.)[15] His declaration is not an act of authentication—Synge *comes out* only as a musician. The passage points to the theatricality of its staging rather than the authenticity of identity.[16] This aesthetic sensibility, which is here again coded as queer, is essential for understanding Synge's aesthetic engagement with Irish folk culture.

Corkery also registers the queer valence of the aesthetic sensibilities pre-sented in the *Autobiography*. Measured against what he refers to as "normal" Irish identity, Corkery describes the young Synge as "delicate," "strangely reserved and even unboyish to a certain extent" (32). This unboyishness and delicacy come to influence his creative work. Corkery explains that Synge's work is "emotional rather than intellectual" (35). This emotional character will direct the type of nationalist that Synge will be. He is an emo-tional nationalist who sees the Irish peasantry through eyes lit by the "flame of love" (38). Consider how the following description by Corkery rein-forces this chapter's reading of the queer affective mode in Synge's descrip-tion of the formation of his aesthetic sensibilities:

> Picture him: the boy, one of a large family, left, one thinks, much to himself, not robust
> enough to join in the usual games—and how much that means in the development of a
> boy's character!—driven in upon himself, finding solace in nature and the wild,—
> companionship that does not betray. He takes to music also, the most social of the arts,
> yet it was for himself, and not for others he was accustomed to play. . . . Always therefore
> desiring affection yet always afraid of it, such a one wanders with his dog and mumbles
> snatches of lyric poetry to himself as he makes across the hills. All softness in a certain
> sense, yet untamable also. . . . No if Synge was such as we imagine it is not the politics,
> naturally part and parcel of Irish nationality, that would coax him to its service; rather it
> is the folk, the Gaelic-speaking peasantry, with their immemorial lore, their aloofness
> from the modern world, their simple life; for going to them would be for him a way of
> extending the passions that warmed his breast in boyhood. (55)

Synge is effeminate, receptive, sensitive, and separated from the normal development of boys—this characterization of his artistic sensibility has a queer tone, admittedly uneasy on Corkery's part, as it collects key attrib-utes that have become associated with the figure of the homosexual in mod-ern Western culture. We read in Wilde a queerly *productive receptivity* at the end of the last chapter, and here we could suggest, through a subversive use of Corkery's characterization, that Synge offers an iconic and bold queer aesthetic: *untamable softness*. Both of these formulas suggest powerful alternatives to hard-edged masculinist nationalism, whether colonialist or anti-colonialist. Corkery would undoubtedly not be pleased with the styling and promotion of this image of Synge. He attempts to cut this untamably soft aesthetic into a proper nationalist passion. My reading argues that Synge shakes loose from any such attempts at domestication and that by declaring himself as a musician he aims to keep all of the dynamism and ambiguity of his aesthetic sensibility in play. We can conclude this section by directly quoting Corkery, but at the same time playfully redirecting the motivations of his claims: "[Synge] could conceive of character clouded over by a mood, but apparently not stiffened by faith. . . . We must accept what he did. The rather boyish or even tom-boyish types he chose accord with his outlook on art and life. . . . The riddle of the universe they read, as did that returned Irish girl Synge had met: Everything is queer!" (101).

THE AESTHETIC STYLIZATION OF FOLK CULTURE

Synge's engagement with the problem of aesthetic consciousness in his early writings is clearly indebted to a network of continental European writing. Two pieces of his juvenilia, *Étude morbide* and *Vita Vecchia*, reverberate with the thematics and experimentation of French decadent literature and are particularly reminiscent of J. K. Huysman's *À rebours*. Synge eventually repudiated his early works, along with the projects of French writers such as Huysman and Mallarmé, and turned his attentions to Ireland. This turn to Ireland is frequently framed as a return to the authenticity of the nationalist folk culture. Yeats's legendary advice to the young Synge, recounted in Yeats's foreword to Synge's play "The Well of the Saints," points to the Aran Islands (and by extension the West of Ireland in general) as the heart of a nationalist folk project. Finding the young Irishman in Paris, Yeats extols him: "Give up Paris. You will never create anything by reading Racine, and Arthur Symons will always be a better critic of French literature. Go to the Aran Islands. Live there as if you were one of the people themselves; express a life that has never found expression."[17] In one sense, Yeats's advice calls on Synge to fashion a project focused on the nationalist authenticity of the Irish peasant. Traveling to the Aran Islands, Synge was to turn to the most Celtic, the most traditional, the most authentic origin of Irish identity and help that origin find expression. Yet even Yeats saw that Synge's engagement with the Irish-speaking peasantry of the West could not ultimately be reduced to an expression of ethnographic authenticity. In his foreword, describing the language of Synge's plays, Yeats hesitates: "His plays have created their own tradition. . . . Perhaps no Irish countryman ever had that exact rhythm in his voice, but certainly if Mr. Synge had been born a countryman, he would have spoken like that" (63–64). Though Synge had been charged with the task of "express[ing] a life that [had] never found expression," he had not exactly managed to express the authentic voice of the peasantry—rather, he had created a stylized form of expression that implicated the peasantry and engendered its own tradition. Synge had abandoned the decadence of Parisian literary experimentation, but he did not shed the role of the aesthete in his engagement with the peasantry.

Though the peasantry of the West bore the burden of the project of nationalist expression, Synge's engagement with the representation of the peasantry hinges on the same stylized aesthetic consciousness that emerged in his *Autobiography*. To begin, there is an irreducible theatricality of the Irish peasant in Synge's work. Irish peasants are theatrical not only as they step from a century of stage-Irish buffoonery to the nationalist authenticity of the Abbey Theater, but also as they play with the propriety of their aesthetic and affective representation. Synge describes the theatricality involved in the peasantry's reception of the nationalist project:

> When a benevolent visitor comes to his cottage, seeing a sort of holy family, the man of his house, his wife, and all their infants, too courteous to disappoint him, play their parts with delight. When the amiable visitor, however, is out once more in the boreen, a storm of good-tempered irony breaks out behind him, that would surprise him could he hear it. This irony I have met with many times, in places where I have been intimate with people and have always been overjoyed to hear it. It shows that, in spite of relief-works, commissions, and patronizing philanthropy—that sickly thing—the Irish peasant, in his own mind, is neither abject nor servile. (*Prose* xxiv–xxv)

As in the *Autobiography*, this passage is organized around the staging of affect. This affect does not measure definitively the inner authentic truth of the individual but traces the subject's implication in a constellation of forces—in this case a history of cultural and religious expectations about the peasantry, and a history of interventions into their lives. The passage also recalls Wilde's discussion of the authoritarian tendencies in sentimentalist interventions into the lives of the poor from the previous chapter. Both the visitors to the Irish cottage and the sentimentalist demand forms of imitation; they demand that the people they encounter live up to their moralized expectations. Wilde takes on what he terms the tyrannical force of these expectations, and Synge reveals their subversion through a sophisticated affective performance by the peasants themselves.

Even *The Aran Islands*, the most ostensibly ethnographic of Synge's writings to address the peasantry, relies heavily on the aesthetic organization and staging of affect in its investigation of the inhabitants of the remote Western islands. The broadest frame of *The Aran Islands* is an engagement with the Irish language: the text follows Synge's learning of Irish while on the islands. Despite the pedagogical frame, the text does not follow a developmental model; rather, it is organized through textual montage. The text juxtaposes anecdotes, ethnographic observations, folk songs and folktales, first-person interior monologues, free indirect discourse, dialogue, and aesthetic, social, and historical commentary. The accumulation of such generic diversity in an attempt to explain the islanders places the text within the long tradition of writings about Ireland. In *The Aran Islands* this tradition—which normally figures England looking westward to Ireland—is folded in on itself as Ireland's gaze turns inward to the islands of its own western periphery. The insistence on montage is important because even if the text is at times dominated by the interiorized consciousness of the narrator, this dominance is not absolute. The narrating consciousness is continually exteriorized, displaced, rejected, corrected, complemented, and juxtaposed by the myriad forces of other voices and features in the text. The montage structure displaces a simplistic observer/observed binarism that had marked much writing about indigenous populations. Montage allows for some of the most striking passages in the text, in which the "natives" reach beyond the confines of their particular locale:

> There is hardly an hour that I am with them that I do not feel the shock of some inconceivable idea, and then again the shock of some vague emotion that is familiar to them and to me. On some days I feel this island as a perfect home and resting place; on other days I feel that I am a waif among the people. I can feel more with them than they can with me, and while I wander among them, they like me sometimes, and laugh at me sometimes, yet never know what I am doing. (58–59)

In some sense, this passage deploys the common colonialist notion that the observer from the metropolis ultimately enjoys a privileged point of view. This trope is first complicated by Synge's own status as an Anglo-Irish writer with deep sympathies with Gaelic Irish peoples and traditions. On another level, the passage also tracks an affect that overwhelms the distinction between Synge the narrator and the islanders he is observing: shock. Despite Synge's disavowal of French literary experiments with modernity, this passage is strikingly similar to discussions of the role of shock in modernity that appear in writers such as Charles Baudelaire. Shock produces an idea and an emotion that is partially articulate and partially ineffable; a sense of consciousness that is both shared and isolated; a type of knowledge that appears unsure and partial. Synge stages his discussion of shock in a radically different context. For Baudelaire the prototypical experience of modernity occurs in the movement of the Parisian boulevards, whereas for Synge it occurs in the wake of the English colonial project in the depopulated regions of western Ireland. As in Baudelaire's famous "A une passante," shock breaks the temporal frame of modernity with the power of an unconceivable idea ("Un éclair . . . puis la nuit!—Fugitive beauté/Dont le regard m'a fait soudainement renaître"), it opens the instant to the eternal, time to timelessness ("Ne te verrai-je plus que dans l'éternité?"), and human consciousness to the power of thought and speculation familiar to both the self and the other ("Ailleurs, bien loin d'ici! trop tard! jamais peut-être!/Car j'ignore où tu fuis, tu ne sais où je vais,/Ô toi que j'eusse aimée, ô toi qui le savais!").[18] The passages seems to strain for the fuller sense of sympathy that Wilde calls on: the shock of the modern not only marks what emotions the characters are experiencing and the shape of the world in which they find themselves; it also suggests what new and unforeseen sympathies are possible and what the world might be.

The colonialist trope would have the experience of modernity lodged solely within the consciousness of the narrator rather than the consciousness of the colonized, and on one level Synge's passage suggests as much. But the montage structure of Synge's text intervenes to allow another possibility to emerge: the consciousness of modernity can lie in the colonized, the peripheral, the abjected. When the sensibility of modernity involves the contradictory feelings of confusion and clarity, isolation and intimacy, desire and frigidity, as in Baudelaire's poem, then the circulation of this same contradictory sensibility in Synge's representation of his time with the peasantry does not simply reinscribe colonialist dichotomies but points to modernity as a condition shared by Synge and the peasants.

Following the above passage, Synge's text turns to a discussion between himself and a young woman native to the island. Like many of the islanders, she has spent time on the mainland and shows a broad curiosity, her interest ranging from men to world affairs:

> One evening I found her trying to light a fire in the little side room of her cottage, where there is an ordinary fireplace. I went in to help her and showed her how to hold up a paper before the mouth of the chimney to make a draught, a method she had never seen. Then I told her of men who live in Paris and make their own fires that they may have no one to bother them. She was sitting on a heap on the floor starting the turf, and as I finished looked up with surprise.
>
> "They're like me so," she said; "would anyone have thought that!"
>
> Below the sympathy we feel there is still a chasm between us. (59)

The passage repeats a part of the earlier colonialist dichotomies: the narrator is associated with knowledge that he imparts to the colonized. But the passage contains a surprise of its own: the young native woman cuts through the substance of the narrator's anecdote to find a point of identification between herself and urbane and sophisticated Parisian bachelors.[19] (That the young woman identifies with the figure of the bachelor, a bachelor whose social dimensions we traced in the discussion of Wilde, should be kept in view.) Always ready to undercut overly facile points of identification or differentiation, the passage ends by reinvoking the chasm that separates these two speakers. This chasm figures a chain of contradictions. It marks the distance between Synge and the peasant girl, it calls to mind the colonial "chasm" (both discursive and political) that separates Ireland from England, and it represents an experience of modernity shared by the islanders and the Irish metropolitan narrator. The aesthetic organization of the text, the insistence on textual montage and the staging of affect, destabilizes the differences between the metropolitan center and the colonized periphery. The montage structure of Synge's *Aran Islands* allows for an "intelligent sympathy" in which the peasants represented are not mere passive curiosities offered for metropolitan consumption. The affects produced in the montage of Synge's text allow for acts of intelligence through which Synge and the islanders measure their mutual implication in modernity.

Modernity in this context is akin to Foucault's formulation in "What is Enlightenment?," in which he discusses Immanuel Kant's short piece of the same title:

> Thinking back on Kant's text, I wonder whether we may not envision modernity as an attitude rather than as a period of history. And by "attitude," I mean a mode of relating to contemporary reality; a voluntary choice made by certain people; in the end a way of thinking and feeling; a way, too, of acting and behaving that at one and the same time marks a relation of belonging and presents itself as a task. No doubt, a bit like what the Greeks called an *ethos*. And consequently, rather than seeking to distinguish the "modern era" from the "premodern" or "postmodern," I think it would be more useful to try to find out how the attitude of modernity, ever since its formation, has found itself struggling with attitudes of countermodernity.[20]

Unlike the young peasant girl and Synge, who adopt modernity as an attitude in their examination of themselves, of each other, and of their historical situation, Corkery registers an intense anxiety over the possibility of such a global modernity as it threatens his sense of nationalist authenticity. Describing the dangers inherent in experiments such as Synge's, he writes:

That way of writing which produces best sellers not only in one but in half the countries of the civilized world, sanctioned it seems to be not so much by its filling of a need, as by the annihilation of distance which modern transport methods as well as wireless have brought about, one asks where it is to end? One is left wondering, for the world has never seen the like. Mr. Shaw writes a play and it is produced for the first time in a different language a thousand or more miles away. Literature designed for such ends can be nothing but brain. . . . What can such work have in common, say with the literature of the Greeks, for whom Greece was everything? (236–37)

Synge disrupts the certainty of such a nationalist model of cultural production. Though he does not simply write "best sellers," and he does not particularly rely on the modernization of technologies, Synge does work to close the distance between Irish folk culture and modernity by tracking their mutual implication. In *The Aran Islands* as in the *Autobiography*, his intelligent measurement of the affects circulating in representations of the Irish peasantry does not rest on an essentialized and reified identity; rather, it relies on a stylized social sensibility that disrupts the distinctions of colonial subject/object imaginaries.

THE PLAYBOY OF THE WESTERN WORLD

The Playboy of the Western World is the most famous of Synge's theatrical productions, most noted for having sparked riots among Dublin audiences during its first run in 1907. According to the lore surrounding the riots, conservative Catholic audiences in Dublin erupted at the reference to a "drift of Mayo girls standing in their shifts itself."[21] In one sense, what seems to have provoked the reaction was the attribution of a modern sexual sensibility to the chaste image of the peasant woman. In *The Playboy*, Synge displaces the nationalist model of peasant authenticity and replaces it with a more fluid model of the social organized around the circulation of stylized affects. Synge proposes an affective model of Irishness caught in the open-ended play of stylization.

The preface to *The Playboy* opens with what seems like a gesture toward authenticity: "In writing *The Playboy of the Western World*, as in my other plays, I have used one or two words only, that I have not heard among the country people of Ireland, or spoken in my own nursery before I could read the news papers" (96). In this sense the play presents itself as part of an authentic look at the national folk culture, a faithful ethnographic representation of peasant life. The language of the play does not simply spring fully fashioned from the imagination of the author; rather, it is worked out through what Synge refers to as the process of "collaboration" between the author and "the people" (96). This process of collaboration, however, quickly troubles any simple model of authenticity by introducing the problem of style to the representation of peasant life:

> All art is collaboration; and there is little doubt that in the happy ages of literature striking and beautiful phrases were as ready to the story-teller's or the playwright's hand as the rich cloaks and dresses of his time. . . . In countries where the imagination of the people, and the language they use, is rich and living, it is possible for a writer to be rich and copious in his words, and at the same time to give the reality which is the root of all poetry, in a comprehensive and natural form. (96)

The language of the play in this formula is organic to the people; it is a "natural form." However, language is also a matter of style, like the "rich cloaks or dresses" to be appropriated by the artist. As a stylized form, language is not authentic but is simply a mode used to evoke particular affects, moods, memories, ideas, and settings. Indeed, once the process of collaboration is introduced in the preface, the problem of authenticity turns from a question of ethnographic verisimilitude to an invocation of "the profound and common interests of life" in a broader sense. Here Synge again echoes Spinoza. Synge explains that the reality of life can be achieved through an understanding of the affects, and in particular the affect of joy: "On the stage one must have reality, and one must have joy, and that is why the intellectual modern drama has failed, and people have grown sick of the false joy of the musical comedy, that has been given them in place of the rich joy found only in what is superb and wild in reality" (96). As in Spinoza, the intensification of joy corresponds with a deeper understanding of reality. We saw earlier in Spinoza that the affects are to be understood as the traces of the human implication in the order of nature. In discussing how these affects are to be understood Spinoza explains:

> We see, then, that the mind can undergo great changes, and pass now to a greater, now to a lesser perfection. These passions, indeed, explain to us the affects of joy and sadness. By *joy*, therefore, I shall understand in what follows that *passion by which the mind passes to a greater perfection*. And by *sadness*, that *passion by which it passes to a lesser perfection*. The affect of joy which is related to the mind and body at once I call *pleasure* or *cheerfulness*, and that of *sadness*, *pain* or *melancholy*. (161)

As subjects in Spinoza act more and more in accordance with the reason of nature, as they broaden the sphere of their intellectual and physical activities, they increase their joy. Joy in this sense represents the deepening sense of reality in Spinoza because it represents the broadening of the subject's power. Similarly, joy in Synge is the deepening of an understanding of the reality of life. The style of Synge's play is no longer simply a question of ethnographic verification. The "copious" style is in fact an index or feature of the abundance of life itself, and insofar as this copious style and the affect of joy are expressive of life, they exceed the protocols of simple verification.

The play itself also opens with a gesture toward the discourse of authenticity. The scene is set in a "country public house or shebeen, very rough and untidy" (99). The shebeen figures as both the center of the peasant community and the imagined center of the national folk culture for the Dublin audience. The first character encountered is "Pegeen, a wild-looking but fine girl of about twenty, [who] is writing at a table. She is dressed in the usual peasant dress" (99). The style of Pegeen's dress suggests her implication in a discourse of folk authenticity, her implication in a repertoire of images of country life; the audience is prepared for a presentation of *vraisemblance paysanne*. Again though, Synge quickly introduces problems of the aesthetic to this image of authenticity. The "usual peasant dress" does not just express the ethnographic but introduces the problem of style, understood both as fashion and as writing. In the opening lines Pegeen is not merely a passive object for the audience's consumption; rather, she is fashioning herself through writing:

[*slowly, as she writes*] Six yards of stuff for to make a yellow gown. A pair of lace boots with lengthy heels on them and brassy eyes. A hat is suited for a wedding day. A fine tooth comb. To be sent with three barrels of porter in Jimmy Farrell's creel cart on the evening of the coming Fair to Mister Michael James Flaherty. With the best compliments of the season: Margaret Flaherty. (99)

The image of Pegeen writing out the order for her wedding dress represents a confluence of stylization: here the authenticity of the peasant dress literally is revealed as a sort of writing. If the initial images suggest the social organized around an authentic core, the introduction of the problem of style, and in particular the relation of the feminine to style, opens the world of the comedy to a certain dynamic of the aesthetic, a dynamic both vertiginous and playful. That is to say, the central activity of the play will be the social process of aesthetic evaluation: of language, characters, motives, actions, feelings, identity, and value. Unlike a model of authenticity that implies an objective standard of verification organized around a core and true identity, the farcical universe of *The Playboy* is organized around an open-ended process of stylization that defies simple models of verification. The social gestures of stylization, which trace the limits of ethnographic authenticity, happen within the realm of sexual discourse, within the social institutions of marriage, and it is precisely a queer sexual discourse that Synge will use to disrupt the orthodoxies of folk authenticity.

The image of Pegeen fashioning herself in writing and then affixing her signature figures the relation between the feminine and the problem of style. This image is set against another form of writing in the opening lines of the play. Shawn Keogh, the emasculated and cowardly groom-to-be, is attempting to obtain a dispensation from the "bishops or the Court of Rome" (100) to allow him to marry Pegeen, since the two are cousins. This form of writing-as-law will be held up for mockery throughout as the comedy opens to the play of stylization under the influence of the cast of women villagers.[22]

Between these two modes of writing—the play of a feminine stylization and the institutional gravity of the masculine law—the play is set in the dynamics of transition. The setting is outside a small village on the coast of County Mayo, and the pun of the title is caught between the peripheral and the global. Although the village is on an isolated western coast, it will serve as a lens to the entire "Western world" named in the title. Similarly, the villagers who appear at the shebeen are strangely deterritorialized: the location of the tavern three miles on any road from the village makes all visitors to the tavern "bona fide" travelers and thus not subject to liquor curfews (203). In this sense, they are both locals who are attached to the area, and travelers attached to the movements of the road. The opening scene of the comedy finds the characters poised between life and death: as Pegeen makes the arrangements for her wedding, her father, Michael James, is preparing to attend the wake of Kate Cassidy. The village shuttles between the past, present, and future, and the tension of this thematic recurs throughout: when confronted with the story of the murder of Christy Mahon's father, the villagers must weigh the importance of the past in relation to the present. Though the play gestures at the outset to the antiquity of Ireland's native patrimony in its deployment of the image of the peasantry, the village is populated mostly by the young, and in particular young girls, who live for modern scandals disseminated through popular newspapers. With the Widow Quinn's murder of her husband the village also must weigh the past and present through questions of crime and culpability. Even in the framing of the first scene, in which Pegeen orders her wedding dress, and the final scene, in which she mourns in the traditional act of keening for the loss of her "playboy," the comedy wrestles with the tension between the past and the present.

The dynamism of the location, the strange mixture of the provincial and the global, and the tension between life and death, all point to Synge's interest in movement. In the *Autobiography*, the figure that emerges to orchestrate movement is the artist-musician. In *The Playboy*, it is another of Synge's favorite figures: the wanderer. Synge explains the importance of this character in a way that resonates with Deleuze's description of the variations of affect:

> Man is naturally a nomad . . . and all wanderers have finer intellectual and physical perceptions than men who are condemned to local habitations. . . . The vagrant, I think, along with perhaps the sailor, has preserved the dignity of motion with its whole sensation of strange colors in the clouds and of strange passages with voices that whisper in the dark and still stranger inns and lodgings. (*Prose* 195–96)

As with the artist-musician, the nomad has achieved a heightened aesthetic sensibility. To the dynamic and transitory environment of the shebeen, Synge introduces the figure of the stranger fugitive. With this introduction of the stranger commences the vertiginous process of evaluation that sustains the farcical comedy of the rest of the play. The initial report of the stranger (who turns out to be Christy Mahon) serves as both a measurement of motion and an instigator of commotion:

> SHAWN [*going to her, soothingly*]: . . . and I'm after feeling a kind of fellow above in the furzy ditch, groaning wicked like a maddening dog . . .
>
> PEGEEN [*turning on him sharply*]: What's that? Is it a man you seen?
>
> SHAWN [*retreating*]: I couldn't see him at all, but I heard him groaning out and breaking his heart. It should have been a young man from his words speaking.
>
> PEGEEN [*going after him*]: And you never went near to see was he hurted or what ailed him at all?
>
> SHAWN: I did not Pegeen Mike. It was a dark lonesome place to be hearing the like of him.
>
> PEGEEN: Well, you're a daring fellow! And if they find his corpse stretched above in the dews of dawn, what'll you say then to the peelers or the Justice of the Peace?
>
> SHAWN [*thunderstruck*]: I wasn't thinking of that. For the love of God, Pegeen Mike, don't let on I was speaking of him. Don't tell your father and the men coming above, for if they heard that story they'd have a great blabbing this night at the wake. (104)

The conversation first explores the difference in reactions between curious and clever Pegeen and cowardly Shawn—who it turns out is unwilling to stay with Pegeen at the shebeen to protect her from the threat of this stranger because the local priest would object to such an arrangement before their wedding. The arrival of the stranger also sets in motion the process of storytelling that is at the heart of the comedy. As Shawn passes the story of the stranger's arrival to Pegeen with the hope of making her afraid, she quickly turns the story into a revelation of Shawn's cowardice. A similarly complicated process of narrative production and evaluation occurs when the stranger Christy first divulges his crime:

> PEGEEN [*with a sign to the men to be quiet*]: You're only saying it. You did nothing at all.
> A soft lad the like of you wouldn't slit the windpipe of a screeching sow.
> CHRISTY [*offended*]: You're not speaking the truth.
> PEGEEN [*in mock rage*]: Not speaking the truth, is it? Would you have me knock the head of you with the butt of a broom?
> CHRSITY [*twisting round on her with a sharp cry of horror*]: Don't strike me. . . . I killed my poor father, Tuesday was a week, for doing the like of that.
> PEGEEN [*with blank amazement*]: Is it killed your father?
> CHRSITY [*subsiding*]: With the help of God I did surely, and that the Holy Immaculate Mother may intercede for his soul.
> PHILLY [*retreating with Jimmy*]: There's a daring fellow.
> JIMMY: Oh, glory be to God!
> MICHAEL [*with great respect*]: That was a hanging crime, mister honey.
> You should have had good reason for doing the like of that. (105)

The presentation of Christy's deed is couched in a search for "speaking the truth." This search for the truth in a sense echoes the nationalist project's quest for an authentic Irish identity at the heart of peasant culture. However, this search for the truth occurs within a highly theatrical conversation. Indeed, the conversation emerges from the stage directions as a sort of verbal fencing: there is even the physical rhythm of lunge and parry as the characters advance, feign rage, retreat, and finally rest. The revelation of the truth of the patricide, however, does not settle the meaning of either Christy's story or his potential relationship to the villagers. Instead, the counterintuitive conclusions drawn concerning the patricide further fuel the absurdity of the comedy:

> PEGEEN: That's be a lad with the sense of Solomon to have for a pot-boy,
> Michael James, if it's the truth you're seeking one at all.
> PHILLY: The peelers is fearing him, and if you'd that lad in the house
> there isn't one of them would come smelling around if the dogs itself were lapping poteen from the dung-pit of the yard.
> JIMMY: Bravery's a treasure in a lonesome place, and a lad would kill his
> father, I'm thinking, would face a foxy divil with a pitchpike on the flags of hell.
> PEGEEN: It's the truth they're saying, and if I'd that lad in the house, I
> wouldn't be fearing the loosed khaki cut-thoats, or the walking dead.
> CHRISTY [*swelling with pride and triumph*]: Well, glory be to God!

MICHAEL [*with deference*]: Would you think to stop here and be pot-boy mister honey, if
we gave you good wages, and didn't destroy you with the weight of work? (106–7)

Rather than severing his relationship with the community, the patricide increases his worth in the eyes of the community. But it is not the fact of murder so much as it is the affect of bravery that wins the minds of the tavern.
The tension of the comedy has a camp quality in its energetic undermining
of normative values and its proliferation of desire. It is not the facts of the
situation but the particular theatrical presentation of the facts, and the circulation of affect tied to this theatricality, that forms the basis for the social
evaluation of Christy's deed. In the story of the crime there is an excess that
shatters the binarism inherent in the litigious evaluation of the facts. It is no
longer about the crime itself and the identification of the criminal; instead,
an excess, a freedom, erupts. A form of surplus value emerges that we saw
already in Wilde and that prefigures articulations of surplus value that will
appear in the next chapters.

The social approval of Christy's story is directly linked with its status as
aesthetic language and its seductiveness. Pegeen claims of Christy, "I've
heard all times it's the poets are your like, fine fiery fellows with great rages
when their temper's roused" (109). And later she flirts with Christy, saying,
"Would you have me think that a man never talked with the girls would
have the words you've spoken today? It's only letting on you are to be lone-
some, the way you'd get around me now" (121). The belief in Christy's linguistic and seductive powers even have a sort of performative effect in the
play as the awkward Christy blossoms into a lover. Christy encourages
Pegeen's affections with the beauty and ease of a lover's discourse: "Let you
wait to hear me talking till we're astray in Erris when Good Friday's by,
drinking a sup from a well, and making mighty kisses with our wetted
mouths, or gaming in a gap of sunshine with yourself stretched back unto
your necklace of flowers of the earth" (136). The affective intensity of the
language becomes more important than the facts of the deed.

The villagers do not hold the question of the truth in utter disregard,
and with the revelation that Christy's tale of the patricide was just that, a
tale, Christy's status as a wonder of the western world crumbles. In an attempt to regain his status, Christy makes a real attempt on his father's life,
which outrages the villagers even more. Though Christy pleads with
Pegeen to acknowledge his deed and to restore her respect for him, Pegeen
reacts incredulously: "I'll say a strange man is a marvel with his mighty
talk; what's a squabble in your back-yard and the blow of a loy, have taught
me that there's a great gap between a gallous story and a dirty deed" (144).
It was never the murder itself that seduced the villagers; it was the stylization of the murder in language and the powerful affects of bravery, courage,

romance, and rage. The finale of the play is the most vertiginous intensification of these dynamics. Synge explains in the stage directions for the
play that the final scene is to be an "elaborate mélange" of drama, comedy,
the poetical, the Rabelaisian, and the tragic (xiv). Although the second
attempt on his father's life also fails, Christy at the end of the play asserts
himself as the master of his household. He tells his father, "Go with you, is
it! I will then, like a gallant captain with his heathen slave. . . . I'm master of
all fights from now" (146). Then to the villagers Christy adds, "Ten thousand blessings upon all that's here, for you've turned me a likely gaffer in
the end of all, the way I'll go romancing through a romping lifetime from
this hour to the dawning of the judgment day" (146). Realizing that
Christy has finally achieved a transformation—not through the actual
murder of his father but through the vitalizing effects of language—Pegeen
rejects Shawn Keogh and starts to keen the loss of Christy: "[*hitting him*
[Shawn Keogh] *a box on the ear*] Quit my sight. [*putting her shawl over her
head and breaking out into wild lamentations.*] Oh my grief, I've lost him
surely. I've lost the only playboy of the western world" (146). Christy
leaves the scene with an understanding of affect and style that will lead
him to "romancing through a romping lifetime." In this light the ironic
comedy of Pegeen keening for the loss of her playboy acquires an added
poignancy: unlike at the wake for Kate Cassidy at the outset of the play,
Pegeen's keening does not mourn the dead; rather, she mourns the loss of
life still living. Pegeen's keening is in fact an act of "intelligent sympathy" in
which "the past [the ancient practice of keening] is living and the present
[is] so desirous to live" (*Prose* 387).

In his critique of *The Playboy*, Corkery suggests that the "normal" "flame
of love" (38) that should guide Synge's engagement with the peasants has
yielded to a queer flamboyance—"outlandish lingo" (200); "wasteful and
ridiculous excess" (196); "a verbal even more than an emotional debauch"
(196), "drenched in poteen" (185). *The Playboy's* "florid diction" even
"infects our mind" (195). (The *OED* lists "florid" as the second definition
of "flamboyant.") The shrill tone of Corkery's reaction to *The Playboy*—in a
terminology replete with homophobic resonance—contrasts dramatically
with the serenity that Corkery imagines undergirds authentic nationalist
cultural practices:

The Irishman looks in the face of his own people, hears them utter themselves with
intimacy, knows what is deep in them, what is merely fleeting, has old-time knowledge
why they are such and such. . . . Aware of himself thus advantaged, as with those
reasons which the intellect knows not of, the Irishman feels in his bones that Ireland
has not yet learned how to express its own life through the medium of the English
language. (12)

Synge's recognition of the complexity of feeling in modern Ireland at the end of *The Playboy* contradicts the simplicity of any such naturalized national identity. Pegeen as she deploys ancient folk customs to respond to contemporary life reveals an Ireland both cognizant of its historical legacy and open to the contingencies of modernity. In a sense, Pegeen figures the critical sensibilities necessary for the project of decolonization. Christy, as he takes his leave of the village and sets out to the vitality of the unknown, represents the possibility of a young Ireland that has placed its ancient past in the service of the living present. Their decoupling is itself an evocatively queer gesture as traditional gender roles are subverted and marriage, that knot of normative desire, is undone: Pegeen takes on the power and burden of critical thought, and Christy embodies a new masculinity that has shed the violence of physical conflict and has been opened to the vitality of language and desire. The silence that hangs over the question of Christy's future in a sense echoes the silence surrounding Synge's death, which occurred before the radical transformations of 1916 took place. Synge was never to see where *The Playboy* was to lead. If I have struck a positive note in this final scene, there is also a complex undertone to address in the invocation of slavery as Christy steps into the future "like a gallant captain with his heathen slave." Notwithstanding Synge's atheism and promotion of the pagan as a progressive figure, the phrase interjects the complex question of Ireland's relationship to slavery and empire. The next chapter will address these connections as it considers the Irish nationalist Roger Casement's deployment of a queer aesthetic in the struggle for universal human rights.

CHAPTER 3

✿

Roger Casement's Global English

From Human Rights to the Homoerotic

Wilde helps us to understand queer affects and aesthetics as historical forces, and Synge transforms our understanding of the Irish
Literary Revival by producing a historically engaged queer aesthetic practice. The life and work of Irish nationalist Roger Casement extends queer
representations and sentiments into the international contexts of imperialism and the fight for human rights. This chapter will argue that queer
sensibilities are dynamic elements of Casement's politics and worldview,
elements he elaborates through the comparative consideration of colonial
situations in Ireland, Africa, and South America. In particular, this chapter
explores what I refer to as *Casement's global English*. This phrase attempts
to capture the global features and usage of the English language that
emerge in Casement's writing. Antonio Gramsci's comments on the
importance of a national language offer a critical perspective from which
we can begin to theorize Casement's language:

> If it is true that every language contains the elements of a conception of the world and of
> a culture, it could also be true that from anyone's language one can assess the greater or
> lesser complexity of his conception of the world. . . . While it is not always possible to
> learn a number of foreign languages in order to put oneself in contact with other cultural
> lives, it is at the least necessary to learn the national language properly. A great culture
> can be translated into the language of another great culture, that is to say a great national
> language with historic richness and complexity, and it can translate any other great
> culture and can be a world-wide means of expression. (*PN* 325)

This chapter tracks the complexity of Casement's conception of the world as it emerges through the representational practices of his writing. This complexity will extend incipient international dynamics already examined in the works of Wilde and Synge and will set the stage for the figurations of what James Joyce refers to as the *universal* in his treatment of Casement in *Ulysses*. This chapter will examine how the politicization of language in the Irish context helped Casement make his language a "world-wide means of expression."

ROGER CASEMENT AS NATIONAL ICON

One of the most controversial figures of the Irish nationalist pantheon, Roger Casement retains his allure and glamour nearly one hundred years after his death. During his life, Casement did it all. Since his death, he has proved a remarkably durable cultural icon. As an international humanitarian, he risked his life exposing colonialist atrocities in Africa and South America. He delivered one of the most famous and rousing speeches on Irish nationalism from the English dock before being hanged for participation in the 1916 Easter Rising. Complexly queer, he enjoyed, in his global travels, the lust and love of a modern homoerotic lifestyle. Casement has also been at the center of heated controversy between Great Britain and Ireland since his execution. Indeed, in many ways, as a cultural icon he condenses the vexing and violent history of Anglo-Irish relations over the course of the twentieth century. Lucy McDiarmid sums up the richness of Casement, writing that he "has offered a means of thinking about much of Irish life, indeed much of human life, in the twentieth century."[1]

Casement was born to a middle-class Protestant family in Sandycove, County Dublin, in 1864, and spent his career working both for and against the global economic and political arrangements of European colonialism.[2] He became internationally famous while serving as a British consul heading a parliamentary investigation into alleged atrocities in the Congo Free State in 1903. Casement led a similar investigation into humanitarian abuses in the Putumayo region of the Amazon in 1910.[3] Both the Congo and the Putumayo situations involved the brutal exploitation of indigenous populations for the harvest of wild rubber. In 1911 he was knighted for his service to the Crown.

Casement's involvement in the investigation of colonial atrocities in Africa and South America led him to become increasingly sympathetic to the Irish colonial situation. In 1916, he was arrested in Ireland by the British after landing from a German submarine as part of an attempt to supply weapons for the planned 1916 Easter Rising. He was charged with high treason, and hanged in August 1916. During the course of his trial, a set of so-called Black Diaries surfaced that detailed numerous same-sex sexual adventures and fantasies over the course of his career. These diaries were used by the British to secure Casement's execution and to prevent his martyrdom among the Irish, particularly those in the United States. The origin of the diaries was suspect from the start, and their authenticity has been a subject of heated controversy. Casement has long been a point of contention between Britain and Ireland: despite numerous appeals, his body was not returned to Ireland until 1965; his diaries were held in official state secrecy by the British until 1959, when scholars were first allowed special permission to view them, and not until 1995 were they released to the public. In 1997 two editions of the 1910 diaries appeared, though they failed to end the controversy: one edition claimed the diaries to be authentic; the other claimed them to be forgeries.[4] Despite lingering conspiracy theories that point to the ambiguous provenance of the diaries, the evidence overwhelmingly suggests that the diaries are authentic.[5]

Notwithstanding the controversy, Casement remains one of Ireland's nationalist heroes. In May 2000, at the request of the Taoiseach (Irish prime minister) Bertie Ahern, and with the cooperation of the British prime minister Tony Blair, the Royal Irish Academy held a major conference on Casement titled Roger Casement in Irish and World History. The symposium attempted to define Casement's relationship to Ireland's understanding of itself at the dawn of the twenty-first century. Casement was situated at the beginning of an Irish tradition of international humanitarianism and activism that could be traced to the current human rights efforts of former Irish president Mary Robinson. This tradition of international humanitarianism, however, was not thought to have any connection to Casement's homoerotic activities and writings. The authenticity of the Black Diaries was debated at the conference, but no effort was made to understand how they were integrated with the imaginary and the practice of his political and humanitarian work.[6] This chapter not only suggests that the homoerotic diaries critically supplement the humanitarian writings by revealing their contradictory attachment to the state and the economy, but also suggests that Casement deploys in the context of his international work the affective intensities that we have traced in Wilde and Synge. Indeed, the affects that emerge in both Casement's humanitarian work and his homoerotic representations gain part of their richness from their connection to the complicated circulation of affect in the Irish struggle for independence.

Most of the volatility of the critical discussion of Casement in Ireland and Great Britain over the last eighty-odd years has been focused through the lens of the biographical. This is perhaps no surprise—the story of Casement offers everything that melodramatic biography demands: romance, betrayal, secrecy, intrigue, violence, justice, and revenge. W. J. McCormack writes that "the Irish biographical paradigm can be a snare as often as it is the means towards understanding" (196). The biographical engagement with Casement has contended primarily with the authenticity of his Black Diaries, while tending to obscure other issues, such as Casement's role in modern Irish folklore and the provocative questions raised by the constellation of Casement's political, humanitarian, and erotic writings.[7]

In terms of his own writings, the biographical focus on Casement's character has tended to eclipse his global ethical project by reducing that project to a merely particular characteristic of his personality. The homoerotic has been largely quarantined from the rest of Casement's thought and from his historical context, and thus reduced in status to merely an aspect of his individual sexuality. In this formula, the homoerotic stands as an object of moral judgment but has no value or bearing in the architecture of Casement's ethical project, as either theory or praxis. I would like to argue that the network of homoerotic activities, affects, and representations available in the Black Diaries, when read in conjunction with his international humanitarian and Irish nationalist efforts, can help recast how we conceptualize the foundations of some of the key institutions of what has come to be a globalized modernity. Specifically, the conjunction of the homoerotic with Casement's nationalist and internationalist political work serves to disrupt the one-way street of the (neo)colonialist subject/object imaginary and lays the groundwork for what we might understand as more indeterminate, potentially global structures of affect and agency. Two supplemental discourses come into focus in Casement's writings: on the one hand, his writings help inaugurate what ultimately is institutionalized as human rights discourse. In Casement's work, human rights discourse emerges as a contradictory extension of state and capitalist economic agency and sets the stage for the international circulation of politicized affects such as sympathy, disgust, and outrage. The homoerotic diaries supplement this human rights discourse by providing an immanent model of global interaction based on the circulation of homoerotic desire. This desire circulates within the global networks of European colonialism but does not simply recapitulate colonialist power dynamics. Rather, the saturating force of the homoerotic in Casement's diaries disengages the question of ethics from the state and the economy and opens a series of erotic affects and pleasures to an ethical potential. Casement provides the possibility of reading global social relations though the complex affective fabric that emerges in the constellation of his writings. As we will see in the next chapter, Joyce, in his deployment of the figure of Casement, undertakes just such a tracking of social relations through the contradictions and figurations of affectivity. In this sense, while Casement is explicitly involved in political organization, a concept of intelligent sympathy guides his efforts.

While much of the discussion of Casement has focused on his biography, attention has been paid as well to the writing of the Black Diaries. This attention has ranged from serious forensic examination of the handwriting to complicated and fetishistic hagiographic hermeneutics. *The Vindication of Roger Casement*, produced by the Roger Casement Foundation in Dublin, is a good example of the popular fetishism of the diaries. Rejecting Casement's queerness out of hand because for the "Christian people [of Ireland], freedom by a pervert would be a perverted freedom," *The Vindication* offers what is referred to as a "computer analysis" of the homoerotic diaries.[8] After a rigorous "mortar and bricks" analysis, the computer is apparently stymied. It asks: "Is this really written in English?"[9] While rejecting the homophobia fueling this response to the diaries, I would like to address this question of the language of Casement's writings and to suggest that the architecture of Casement's English is specifically marked by the global. From a historical standpoint Casement's writings were both theorized and deployed in the interstices of the global. They functioned as an instrument of the imperium, served as a novel instrument for political organization and agitation, and importantly but less obviously acted as a circuit for novel homoerotic affective ties. I would like to address the question, then, of what it would mean to think of Casement's English as a system of global representation and, in part, to think this system through the homoerotic. How does the homoerotic emerge as an intelligent affect for the critical description of the global?

"Casement's global English" is perhaps an elliptical and inexact term, but it is useful for denoting the palimpsest that is Casement's writing. The study of this palimpsest in terms of systems of representation brings into focus imperialist political structures operating in the service of a developing global capitalism and suggests that this economy also gave rise to potentials for affect and agency that were not reducible to recapitulations of that imperialist power structure. Casement's Black Diaries illuminate a homoerotic structure in this one potential model of global affect and agency. To recover the markings of this palimpsest, the chapter will track the incongruous and supplemental discourses that converge in Casement's writings. These discourses range from the now fully institutionalized discourse of human rights to the intimate and uncongealed discourse of the homoerotic. We will consider what sort of potential ethical project emerges in the encounter of these discourses. I do not argue that homoeroticism undergirds the humanitarian interventions. Instead, I will trace the differing sorts of activities, affects, and knowledge that the human rights reports and homoerotic diaries make available to ethical discourse.

The consideration of the language of Casement's writings should be seen as part of the broader problem of contemporary world language politics.

The political questions surrounding the extirpation of world languages currently have a unique urgency: by most figures, half of the world's estimated sixty-five hundred languages face extinction within the next hundred years.[10] English, while not the dominant mother tongue in the world, has become, under the historical reach of European colonialism (ultimately dominated by British sea power) and the current extension of global capitalism (driven in particular ways by the American economy and the American state), the world's primary linguistic vehicle of global commerce. English, which is thoroughly implicated in the world economy, is deeply entrenched in diverse parts of the globe and has lost much of its previous cultural or national resonance. Simply put, the English language is the residue of English colonialism, yet it no longer represents the English nation. Insofar as English has become a global institution—one that stands beside the extension of the global capitalist economy, though intimately implicated with this economy—it requires a different analysis from the racialized nationalist cultural calculus elaborated in the nineteenth century. It is no longer clear that a language represents the racial genius that finds its perfect expression in the cultural and political institutions of the nation-state. Nor is it clear what it would mean for the current economic and cultural expansion of English to represent North America, as English in the global becomes increasingly detached from its traditional geolinguistic moorings. To trace the linguistic architecture of Casement's writings, this chapter will first address the ethical project elaborated in his humanitarian and political work in Africa and South America and then consider how his homoerotic writing expands the potential of that project.

FROM INTERNATIONAL HUMAN RIGHTS TO GLOBAL EROTICS

Casement's investigation into alleged atrocities in the Congo Free State in 1903 stands as an important moment in the genealogy that leads to the International Declaration of Human Rights in 1948. This complex genealogy includes Enlightenment philosophical discussions of natural law and the nature of the human; international humanitarian law regulating warfare; reactions to the Holocaust; bodies of customary law governing the treatment of foreign nationals involved in commerce; a network of bilateral and multilateral treaties; and extrajuridical movements (such as abolition) that sought to mobilize bodies of national and international public opinion to force action on the part of state regimes.[11] In the structure of his intervention can be found many of the contradictions and tensions among the humanitarian investigator, the subject of humanitarian interest, the state, and the economy that continue to mark the international human rights movement.

The Berlin West Africa Conference of 1885, which divided the land of the Congo basin and gave exclusive control of it to King Leopold II of Belgium, set the stage for the staggering brutality that was to occur in the region. What is less well known is that the same conference constructed the model of political agency that would allow for Casement's humanitarian intervention. In an effort to quell mounting tensions among larger European powers, the conference gave exclusive ownership of the region to Leopold. L'État Libre du Congo, as it was called, constituted an experiment in international law, and the new state was to be organized around the *liberté de commerce* and the expansion of European civilization. Presiding over the conference, the first chancellor of the German Empire, Prince Otto von Bismarck, expressed the intimate connection between these principles: "In convoking the conference, the Imperial Government was guided by the conviction that all the Governments invited shared the wish to bring the natives of Africa within the pale of civilization by opening up the interior of that continent to commerce."[12]

The Congo Free State was in effect Leopold's private holding and yet was recognized as a state by the international community. This state's fundamental claim to authority, however, did not derive from models of nineteenth-century nationalism. Commerce was the organizing principle for the legal and economic structures of the Free State. As "the fundamental idea of this programme [was] to facilitate the access of all commercial nations to the interior of Africa" (129), the freedom of the Free State was organized around the circulation of capital, and the state enfranchised the nationals of the conferring powers as economic agents. The ideal citizen of the new state was the merchant: the conference agreed that "merchants shall be assured that no import dues and no transit duties shall be levied and that moderate imports only shall be placed on their goods solely to meet administrative needs." Furthermore, merchants were to be assured the freedom of residence and religious practice, as well as to trade and travel, to the use of the roads and railroads, and to coastal trade (131–32). The legal protection of the state was accorded to missionaries, explorers, and scientists, as well as to their escorts, possessions, and collections, and to the numerous geographical societies that facilitated the extension of capitalism into the region (137). As the organization of the import dues and transit duties suggests, the merchant, as the agent of capital, was figured as not merely an individual part of a larger social whole; rather, the Free State represented the complete ascendancy of the economic sector.

Speaking of the indigenous populations of the region, one British representative remarked, "I cannot forget that the natives are not represented amongst us, and that the decisions of the conference will, nevertheless, have an extreme importance for them" (131). But the conference went further than simply not inviting any native representatives; it blocked their enfranchisement as citizens in the region. The conference explained that in considering the region it had nowhere found "the presence of civilized authority, no jurisdiction claimed by any representative of white men save his own retainers, no dominant flag or fortress of a civilized power, and no sovereignty exercised or claimed except that of the indigenous tribes" (138). With the dismissal of indigenous sovereignty, both the brutality that was to occur in the region and Casement's humanitarian intervention would be subject to the terms set forth in the political and economic arrangements of the Conference Treaty.

At the time of Casement's investigation, there was no existing body of international law or tradition of human rights to authorize the intervention of foreign states into the situation in the Congo. A provision of the treaty granted England civil and criminal jurisdiction over its subjects in the region, and it was only the fact that some employees of the Free State were British subjects from other British possessions in Africa that allowed for Casement's initial intervention.[13] An examination of the structure of Casement's Congo Report submitted to the Marquess of Landsowne on December 11, 1903, reveals a careful attachment to the Conference Treaty of 1885. Casement's report can be seen as an active deconstruction of the original treaty. Casement—who at this point in his career is more of a colonial reformer than an anti-imperialist activist—begins the report by tracing the progress that the Belgians had made in what he refers to as "one of the most savage regions of Africa" (96). Casement's report is no Luddite argument against the expansion of the modern economy, but reads at first like a colonialist travel brochure: "Admirably built and admirably kept stations greet the traveler at many points; a fleet of river steamers numbering, I believe, forty-eight, the property of the Congo Government, navigate the main river and its principal affluents at fixed intervals. Regular means of communication are thus afforded to some of the most inaccessible parts of Central Africa" (98). The movement and expansion of capitalism into the region has been "admirably" orchestrated, and Casement's report, as a form of knowledge production, contributes to that expansion.

However, Casement also tracks a counterhistory to this glowing story of capital's expansion. Although the treaty had managed to bring capital to life in the region, it had also brought destruction to indigenous peoples: "Perhaps the most striking change observed during my journey into the interior was the great reduction observable everywhere in native life" (98). Casement constructs this counternarrative through a combination of testimonial evidence (from both Europeans and Africans) and firsthand observations. He attaches this story to categories set out by the Conference Treaty: movement, freedom, and civilization. Consider the following anonymous testimonial that reads as the brutal echo of his description of the regular means of communication that had come to sustain the flow of capital. In this passage a young girl explains the effects of the Rubber Wars (fought over the region's principal commodity):

> After that they saw a little bit of my mother's head and the soldiers ran quickly towards the place where we were and caught my grandmother, my mother, my sister and another little one, younger than us. Several of the soldiers argued about my mother because each wanted her for a wife, so they finally decided to kill her. They killed her with a gun—they shot her through the stomach—she fell and when I saw that I cried very much, because they killed my mother and my grandmother and I was left alone. My mother was near to the time of her confinement at the time. And they killed my grandmother and I saw it all done. They took hold of my sister and asked where her older sister was and she said: "she has just run away." They said, "Call her." She called me, but I was too frightened and would not answer and I ran and went away and came out at another place and I could not speak because my throat was sore. (146)

This passage is an inversion of the earlier narrative of capital: the admirable flow that marks the movement of capital has been replaced by the erratic and desperate movement of these women and children; the productivity of capital finds a gruesome echo in the killing of three generations of women; and the regular means of communication described earlier has been replaced by a child whose throat is too sore to speak. This structural inversion is important in at least two ways: first, it represents the trace of the existing state of international law that had no precedent for the intervention into the domestic affairs of a particular state. Casement's intervention had to be organized in terms of the Conference Treaty of 1885, which, in setting up the region as an international free-trade zone, had ironically internationalized the domestic affair of the state's economy. Second, the oppositional nature of this inversion that sought to give a voice to the voiceless reveals the place of an affective economy operating in the interstices of the economic and political arrangements organizing the region. Casement is careful in his report to track the systematic nature of the brutality in the region (in particular the system of "taxes" imposed on the natives in the form of rubber harvest and the division of the indigenous population against itself in the apparatuses of the commercial state). But the excess of affect in the report provided the rhetorical persuasion that eventually moved parliamentary and public opinion against Leopold's regime. Whether legal structures provided for intervention was beside the point; the brutal poignancy conveyed in passages like the one just cited overcame the limitations of legal agency. This affective excess can be described as a politicized sentiment that attempted to provoke and marshal feelings of disgust, outrage, pity, and sympathy.

Casement's report eventually exceeded its initial structural limits; the release of the report was key in the international debate that eventually put an end to much of the brutality in the region. However, Casement's intervention struggled with one of the key contradictions of human rights: the antagonism between the individual (who until the advent of human rights was not a recognized subject in international law) and the state (previously the only legal subject of the international). Faced with this antagonism, human rights have contradictorily emerged as a state value even as the practice of human rights theoretically seeks to limit the extent of the state's authority. As legal scholar Louis Henkin has pointed out, this contradiction even marks the founding Charter of the United Nations, which "to help justify the penetration of the State monolith . . . in effect justifies human rights as a State value by linking it to peace and security."[14] The sentimental political language of Casement's report is burdened by the same contradiction: even as it effectively mobilizes sentiment on behalf of indigenous peoples against the violence of the state, its genealogy is ultimately to be traced to the transcendent structures of the state that inscribe the oppression of the indigenous in the first place.

Unlike the situation in the Congo, which was organized through the provisions of the Berlin Conference Treaty, the situation in the Putumayo region of South America had no existing legal structure to authorize Casement's intervention. In the pages of his so-called White Diary from the period—which was meant to accompany and supplement his official report—Casement repeatedly points to the lack of legal jurisdiction as an impediment to the functioning of the investigation:

> The other [the Congo] was Slavery under Law, with Judges, Army, Police and Officers, men of birth and breeding even, carrying out an iniquitous system invested with monarchical authority, and in some sense directed towards public, or so-called public ends. . . . But this thing I find here is slavery without law, where the slavers are personally cowardly ruffians, jail-birds, and there is no Authority within 1,200 miles, and no means of punishing any offence [sic], however vile. Sometimes Congolese "justice" intervened, and an extra red-handed ruffian was sentenced, but here there is no jail, no judge, no Law. (159)

Lacking a legal structure to appeal to, he has a much more nebulous recourse to what he describes as the only institution authorizing any intervention in the region: the status of an English commercial company as an institution of civilization. Casement calls on this institution of civilization with a subtle irony throughout the diary, referencing the Company at times to describe the organized slavery (under the leadership of the infamous Julio Arana) that he is exposing, and at times to describe the ideal institution of a company as an organized system of transactional contracts freely entered into for a hypothetical mutual benefit. Casement points to this dual role of the Company: "It was immaterial who had originated it, Columbians or Peruvians—the Company was a civilized institution, it had inherited the claims of the founders of this method and it must sweep away this system and establish a lawful and civilized and humane method of dealing" (141). Even though Arana's company was nothing more than organized slavery, Casement would hold it to the standards of an idealized and human company.

The figure of the company is key to the construction of the White Diary as it continually gives Casement entrée into the systematic nature of the social relations he encounters. Consider the following passage, in which Casement uses the figure of the company as a critical lever to reveal the system of forced labor:

> Here we are confronted on every hand with concealment. When I said the Indians were slaves, then Gielgud (as I shall call him now) and Fox demurred and wanted my "proofs." I said to Gielgud "I'll prove it very soon if you, that is to say the Company, permit the test." ... Our proof lies with the Indians, your Company's "creditors," as you assert. Let me, the next fabrico, ask (I'll find the interpreters) whether they wish man by man, to take cap and pants, or whatever the things are you give them, for a further supply of rubber, or whether they would prefer to be free of this obligation? If they are "free" they have the absolute right to refuse your 3/- or 4/-worth of stuff, or whatever the goods may be. But do you ask them? You know you don't. You compel them without question asked or put, to take these things. It is immaterial whether they select them or you bestow them. And then, when they have gone off to their houses,—poor scarified devils—you follow them up and intrude upon all their home life, and force them to bring you in rubber at a rate of exchange you prescribe mind, and if they don't satisfy you you flog them, as well nigh every male stern in the district can testify, and you challenge my condemnation of this thing, and say I argue from assumption. (157)

The exploitation of the indigenous population is clearly an organized system of slavery that operates through a representational process. The forced bestowal of goods marks the Indians as debtors, and the agents of the company then act to extract the value of this debt in the form of rubber collected. When the rubber is not collected, the running tally of debt is marked with lashes of the whip. In this passage, the Indians' only "right" not to be forced into a system of slavery arises not from the political institution of a state, or from a developed conception of human rights, but from an ideal model of what a company should be. Within the ideal representational system of a company, the Indians would have the "right" to refuse the initial bestowal of debt. However, the actual practice of the company is what enslaves the Indians in the first place. To describe the process by which these Indians acquire access to representation (both in the economic relation with the company and in the arena of international politics), we need to look to Casement's writing itself as an emergent representational institution. The particular representational strategy of the investigation actually makes the language of Casement's report itself an institution that emerges alongside, though implicated with, the economic institution of the company to authorize the intervention, and ultimately redistribute power.

Casement is a systematic investigator. While not unwilling to condemn individual participants, he strives to expose the systematic nature of the relations he encounters. A rhetorical pattern governs the composition of the White Diary: the representation of the methodical probing of particular encounters to uncover the underlying nexus of social relations. There is an intensely self-reflexive impulse in this rhetorical pattern in which the biographical serves not so much as the description of an individual but as the trope for a doubled process of representation. Casement will work to represent underlying social relations, and he will double this with a representation of the process of representation itself—an ongoing self-reflection on the process of the commission's own investigation. As McCormack explains, "At once passive and active, almost in the professional style of an anthropologist, Casement was an observer of his own diaries as well as their author" (193). The result is a discourse that seeks to generate its own authority. Consider the following passage:

> As we embarked in the "batalon" to cross the river, two elderly Indian men came down with more camp equipment for us. . . . Their sterns were terribly scarred, indeed the two broad patches on one man's buttocks looked like burns. They were scars of an extra deep cutting of the lash. All of us saw them, but I broke the silence, and said, at large, "Two very incontrovertible burns I must say." These instructive backsides climbed in, and squatted beside us, their elderly owners asking me for a cigarette. "Chigarro, Chigarro" has become the greeting we get wherever we go, but especially myself, for I give cigarettes with a lavish hand. The poor souls, young and old, love them, and God knows, they have little pleasure. Whenever they get a present they stroke one's hand or shoulder affectionately, and say, "Bigara, bigara" (Good, good). They apply it now universally, and we are constantly hailed with cries of "Bigara," so I christened them this morning "the Begorrahs." It sounds exactly like an Irish begorrah. The name has stuck, and Barnes and all of them speak of our poor Indian hosts as the Begorrahs, and we made much play with the word during the day.

This passage is typical for the White Diary and shows the self-reflexive process of representation at the heart of Casement's investigation. Officially,

Casement's commission was not allowed to interview any of the local indigenous people because they did not fall under any extant British jurisdiction.
In this passage, however, Casement manages to make these silent yet "instructive" backsides speak to the systematic brutality of the region not simply by documenting their scars, but by also representing the process of that
documentation. This doubled process of representation occurs within the
generic form of the autobiographical, but this is not the psychologized
autobiography of the individual. The autobiographical is merely the form of
appearance of this emergent representational institution. The integrity of
the narrating subject is an important feature in the economy of this representational system and is secured by a process in which the witness is then
witnessed in turn. For this process of representational enfranchisement to
acquire an institutional status (as human rights discourse has managed to
do), it cannot rely solely on the moral quality of a particular individual, but
must include mechanisms that allow for future investigations. In terms of
the overall argument of this study, this doubled process of representation
that is at the heart of the emergence of human rights discourse is the political deployment of a self-reflexivity that has long existed in the representation of the Irish in English. This self-reflexivity that in Casement obtains
political institutional status repeats moments in Wilde in which the content
and forms of the circulation of homoerotic affects are traced, and moments
in Synge in which the ethical values of the community are secured by the
representation of the collective deliberation of affective dilemmas.

The passage's effect in Casement's diary is twofold: it not only allows these
"instructive backsides" to speak, but as it translates their *bigaras* into *begorrahs*, the passage calls on a long history of colonialism in Ireland and the eth-
ical/political problems of Irish representation (both in the English language
and in a broader political sense). This troping takes its place in the ongoing
reflection on the similarities between the Irish and South American situations throughout both the Black and the White Diaries. Frequently the lens
through which the comparison comes into focus is the question of language.
In this, Casement directly echoes Douglas Hyde. He writes in the Black
Diary on September 17, 1910, of an Indian who has Europeanized his Que-
chua name: "[He] calls himself Simon Pizarro, because he wants to be civilized! Just like the Irish Os & Macs dropping their first names or prefixes to
shew [sic] their 'respectability' & then their ancient tongue itself, to be completely Anglicised. Simon Pisango still talks Quichua [sic]—but another
generation of Pizarros will speak only Spanish! Men are conquered not by
invasion but by themselves and their own turpitude" (82). Casement saw
condensed in language the broader problems of economic, political, and cultural representation. Casement's sensitivity to linguistic questions is clearly
indebted to the politicization of language in the Irish context.[15] In this

passage, Casement connects quotidian linguistic decisions with the problems of political and cultural hegemony in the colonial context. Furthermore, the passage suggests that language is key to understanding the global dimensions of colonialism.

Returning to the question of the global architecture of Casement's writings, we can specify now two modes of engagement. On the one hand, Casement self-reflexively attempts to create a politicized system of representation that is implicated within existing economic and political structures, but that also stands autonomously beside them. What begin as singular reports on particular situations (the Congo and the Putumayo) emerge as important precursors to the human rights movement. Casement helped generate what would ultimately be institutionalized as human rights discourse. On the other hand, Casement attempts to speak to the specificity of a particular situation (the Putumayo) within the larger context of the history of world political order (European colonialism) and the mediation of these contexts through the question of language. By code-switching and embedding etymologies within his observations—shifting from *bigaras* to *begorrahs*—Casement attempts to index the social relations that constitute the colonial order. This linguistic iconicity requires (or perhaps, more optimistically, provokes) a critical elaboration of the dimensions of this imperial order.

Attending to the specificity of Casement's writings has focused our attention on the shifting realms of representation—in particular the economic and the political—in the historical context of European imperialism. Though we have dealt principally with moments in imperial history, I have tried to suggest that these same questions are relevant in a postcolonial context. Two features of the current global capitalist order can be described as saturation and displacement: saturation in the sense that economic mediation has penetrated spheres of life that have hitherto not been subject to capitalist evaluation; and displacement in the sense that the economic sector has increasingly been able to position itself as the principal regime for the arbitration of value, thereby displacing other domains of value, including the cultural, the political, and the social. In Casement's story of the Indians' love of cigarettes, we can read an instructive example of an inverse dynamic: the economic sphere subtending practices of value with which it is implicated but cannot entirely subsume and which do not simply recapitulate or express the politics of its power structures.

Cigarettes are sometimes rough trade: the tone and the topic of the passage clearly change when the pleasures of cigarettes are introduced. Indeed, the first instance of the Indians' speaking for themselves comes with the uttering of "Chigarro, Chigarro." It is not wrong to read in the "lavish hand" proffered by Casement, or in his subsequent theorization of the Indians' pleasure, an echo of the homoerotic representations of the Black Diaries. Consider this passage from September 28, 1910: "All of us tired, & slept most of day until nearly 5 p.m. Commission deciding on rest of route. Andokes for cigarettes at 4 & asked me to give them, looking so gently and fingering anxiously his pierced ears. He said several things to me in a low soft voice, asking questions, I thought & looking longingly. I gave him a packet of cigarettes but he did not want to go" (87). In both passages, the exchange of cigarettes suggests alternative modes of exchange and strategies of communication. The homoerotic saturates these passages: it revalorizes the request for cigarettes and introduces more open-ended questions of value.

Indeed, the Black Diaries are homoerotic ledgers obsessed with questions of value. They read literally as a detailed accounting in which Casement, the meticulous consular officer charged in his professional capacities with tracking the circulation of commodities, records a whole series of values, from the affective (his mood, his sexual desires, his health, his disgust at the depth of the exploitation he is investigating), the social (whom he encounters, his sexual adventures, where he eats, how he passes his leisure time), and the economic (how much money he spends on sexual encounters, how much money he spends on lodging and food) to the erotic (with whom he has sexual encounters, what sexual acts were performed, the shapes and sizes of his partners' bodies and body parts). The values in the Black Diaries point to the emergence of an economy on the scale of the global in which nationalities, languages, activities, feelings, ideas, and goods circulate with a surprising rapidity and variety. When reading the Black Diaries, it is essential to understand that these values are not separable aspects, but all condense and shift through the medium of a global homoerotic. The diaries represent the intersection and recoding of linguistic and capital exchanges. The commodities and pidginized linguistic icons are constituted not just economically but also affectively and erotically. Whether the participants are or are not sociologically homosexual is not the question. What is important is that the homoerotic circulates as a socialized affect that allows for communication, knowledge, and the negotiation of value. The diaries suggest a lifestyle emergent in the interstices of the global in which the homoerotic operates as the principal mediating form. Much as in Synge, the homoerotic here operates as a measurement of the social rather than as the marker of an individual identity. Reading these multiple forms of value through the lens of a homoerotic lifestyle enables us to reconceptualize the social relations these values represent. This is particularly true of the human rights discourse, seen through the homoerotic value of the Black Diaries.[16]

The Black Diaries mark a shift from a discussion of the extension of rights (whether organized around legal structures as in the Congo, or around economic structures as in the Putumayo) to a discussion of the production of value. Within this tale of the cigarette (and within the Black Diaries more generally), we can glimpse the outlines of a global structure that redirects the relations between the individual subject, the state, and the economy that marked Casement's humanitarian writing. In the Black Diaries, representation is mediated not through the transcendent figure of the state or the company that extends the parameters of its jurisdiction but through the productive force of an immanent homoerotic. The diaries do not plot the extension of rights; rather, they plot productive transvaluations. These transvaluations are productive in that they transform the hierarchized relations between the humanitarian investigator, the nodal subject of humanitarian concern, the state, and the economy and introduce a deterritorialized political and affective value proper to the global. Consider the following: "Splendid testemunhos—soft as silk & big & full of life—no bush to speak of. Good wine needs no bush. Carlos Augusto Costa—189 Rua dos Ferreiros, Funchal 7/6 Very fine one—big, long thick. Wants awfully & likes very much. João—Big £1.12.6. Internacional Hotel. Bella Vista" (63). The pun at the outset figures the changing forms of value that mark the passage: the Portuguese *testemunhos* (testimonies) playing on the English slang "testimonials" for "testicles." The entry on one level records mutual sexual pleasures, but these *testimonials* will also come to play an important role in Casement's humanitarian investigation, as eventually the testimonial form will provide much of the content of his political intervention, not to mention an important aspect of human rights work since. The move from the realm of the erotic to the political occurs within the space of a single word. The affect of the passage does not reinscribe the hierarchized relation between the European investigator (ultimately an agent of the state) and the indigenous subject of humanitarian sympathy. The humor of the passage points to the production of a mutual pleasure that destabilizes this hierarchy and forms the basis for a value of commonality. The structure of Casement's humanitarian reports figures the humanitarian agent as a mouthpiece for concerns of the object of humanitarian interest and thus ultimately maintains the distance between the two. The homoerotic in this passage values the "testimonials" as a mouthful for both parties, and thus erodes the distance between the two.

From the "lavish hand" offering cigarettes to the *testemunhos* pun, a queer flamboyance characterizes Casement's writing. Euphemistic references to Casement's queerness abound in descriptions of him that figure him as hysterical, excitable, and emotionally unstable.[17] Novelist Joseph Conrad framed his estimation of Casement through queer allusion: "He was a good companion, but already in Africa I judged that he was a man, properly speaking, of no mind at all. I don't mean stupid. I mean he was all emotion. By emotional force (Congo report, Putumayo—etc.) he made his

way, and sheer emotionalism has undone him. A creature of sheer temperament—a truly tragic personality: all but the greatness of which he had not
a trace. Only vanity."[18] Conrad allows us to see the typically derogatory
commonplaces about queerness (the heightened emotionalism, the
tragedy, the vanity) as critical features of the global. The figure of Casement
the queer—this "creature of sheer temperament"—who sees in everything
the homoerotic, and, more important, sees in the homoerotic the world,
does not so much reveal the inner truth of an individual as provide a key to
the production of a social value in the global. The affective force of the homoerotic represents the conducting limit where the personal meets the
social—where an intimate aesthetic opens into the social organized as the
ethical. The intense affective receptivity of the queer echoes capitalism's
ability to saturate and to displace. However, even as this receptivity emerges
in the circuits of global capital, it is not reducible to an expression of exploitative capitalist power dynamics. The lavish, playful, flamboyant, desiring
force of this global homoerotic affect does not aspire to the categorical tran-
scendence of the juridical, but is immanent to the global: it seems indifferent to borders, it inheres in the vertigo of exchange, its suggestiveness
saturates all spheres of activity and reflection, and its attentive intimacy
emerges both as erotica and as a deeply ethical impulse. As Casement suggests on September 9, 1910: "One half-white muchacho magnificent display & a young Cholo with an erection as he carried heavy box. Down leg
about 6–8. They are far too good for their fate" (77–78). Through the affective force of the homoerotic, Casement suggests a novel evaluative mode
for the global. In this homoerotic the problem of ethics has been detached
from the institutions of the state. The rationalist and commercial calculations of the capitalist economy reappear in the playful calculations of sexual
encounters and fantasies. Homoeroticism and affective "vanity" emerge as
a basis for social value.

It is difficult to measure the thoroughly institutionalized discourse of
human rights against the uncongealed homoerotic language of the Black
Diaries. Human rights have emerged as a necessary and frequently ethical
tool that we cannot simply dismiss. However, it is important to attend carefully to the contradictory economic and political implications of human
rights both in terms of a broader genealogy and within the parameters of
particular ethico-political interventions. The productive quality of the homoerotic in the Black Diaries should stop us from simply annexing this dynamic force to the juridical framework of human rights—the attainment of
human rights, while necessary, cannot be the only goal of global politics,
though again we cannot simply dismiss this project. England knighted Casement for his humanitarian services, indexing the state's ultimate approval of
the project of human rights. The state registered the productive receptivity

of Casement the queer as the degenerative threat of the sodomite. For his Black Diaries, England submitted Casement to the most violent of physical intrusions, concluding on examination that "of late years, [Casement] seems to have completed the full cycle of sexual degeneracy and from a pervert has become an invert—a woman or pathic who derives his satisfaction from attracting men and inducing them to use him."[19] Colm Tóibín describes the power of this moment, writing, "In all the images we have of Anglo-Irish relations over the centuries, perhaps this is one of the saddest and the most stark: a prison doctor examining Casement's arsehole a short time after he had been hanged, on the orders of the British government."[20] Understanding the productive force of Casement's receptivity figures the homoerotic as a vital mode of evaluation in the global. If Casement's human rights reports helped focus the destruction of life attending the colonialist expansion of capitalism, his homoerotic can help measure the emergent potentials for life in the global and thereby expand the contemporary project for ethics. The complexity of this conception of the world inheres in Casement's language itself, which, while it cannot provide the new universal grammar for such an ethical project, does allow us to glimpse the potential of a "world-wide means of expression" for these emergent social relations.

CHAPTER 4

⌀∿⌀

Ruling Passion

James Joyce, Roger Casement, and the Drama
of Universal Love

This chapter explores James Joyce's deployment of Roger Casement as a figure in the critique of the Irish colonial situation in the "Cyclops" episode of *Ulysses*.[1] The last chapter tracked the globalization of queer sensibilities in Casement's international work; this chapter suggests that Joyce exploits the contradictory affects that resonate around the figure of Casement to internationalize the Irish colonial context and to explore the "universal" implications of the Irish situation.

To track the figure of Casement, we must first examine Joyce's theorization of affect in relation to aesthetic expression. As with Wilde, Synge, and Casement, affect is a crucial concept in Joyce's understanding of language and in his critique of the social relations of colonial Ireland. Joyce approaches the problem of affect in terms of what he refers to as "drama." In an early lecture entitled "Drama and Life" (delivered while still a student at University College Dublin), he presents a theory of the dramatic that will guide this chapter's reading of the figure of Casement in "Cyclops." Joyce claims that "although the relations between drama and life are, and must be, of the most vital character, in the history of drama itself these do not seem to have been at all times, consistently in view."[2] Drama poses a social and philosophical question for Joyce—one that extends to human aesthetic expression writ large—and exceeds the scope of theatrical criticism, which has been distracted by the analysis of its accidental forms. For Joyce, drama stages the relation between writing and life—that is, the problems of the biographical that have developed throughout this study. As in the discussion of Wilde, Synge, and Casement, in order to understand this dramatic biographeme we must uncouple the biographical from its association with the particular historical individual. According to Joyce, drama encodes the biographical (that is, the intersection of life and writing) disarticulated from the discursive anchor of the individual; indeed, the individual is merely an obfuscation of the social dimensions of the biographical. He explains, "Drama has to do with the underlying laws first, in all their nakedness and divine severity, and only secondarily with the motley agents who bear them out" (40). Joyce thus presents drama in a way that resonates with our earlier reading of Synge and Spinoza, in which affects act as an index of the human's implication in nature and are used to measure the fabric of the social. It is not that affect emerges as the transparent representative of the truth of the social and thereby obtains an inherently moral charge, but that through the critical interpretation of the contradictory play of affects, the multiple truths of the social come into view. Joyce explains the truth of affect in terms of this critical interpretation:

> By drama I understand the interplay of passions to portray truth; drama is strife, evolution, movement in whatever way unfolded; it exists, before it takes its form, independently; it is conditioned but not controlled by its scene. It might be said fantastically that as soon as men and women began life in the world there was above them and about them, a spirit, of which they were dimly conscious, which they would have had sojourn in their midst in deeper intimacy and for whose truth they became seekers in after times, longing to lay hands upon it.... (41)

In this dramatic life writing, the inscription of the subject is secondary to the force, the passion, that subtends it. The truth of this writing does not result from the verification of the accidentals that accrue to these "motley agents"; rather, in the philosophical register, the problem of truth is a question of the substance of life itself. As we saw in Wilde's socialism, in Synge's exploration of the affects surrounding the representations of Irish folk culture, and in the homoerotic affects that mediate Casement's Black Diaries and supplement the sympathetic dynamics of human rights discourse, affects in this formula are not simply a matter of verification or of authentication but are immanent to life. The "truth" of the dramatic does not inhere on the level of the motley agents but is fundamentally and contradictorily implicated in the social. The critical emphasis on the contradictory implication of affects displaces transcendent and legalist models of judgment, in which truth functions as the authentication of an overarching principle. We have seen such a model of judgment in the institutionalized forms of human rights law discussed in the previous chapter. A similar transcendent model of judgment and authentication will appear in certain strains of reactionary Irish nationalism that Joyce takes to task in the "Cyclops" chapter. By privileging the critical role of affects, Joyce points to the implication of the truth, the judge, and the object of concern in the process of judgment. He suggests, in other words, an immanent mode of evaluation.

For Joyce the truth of drama exists between two contradictory poles: it will be predicated in particular historical situations, and in another sense dramatic truth will always exceed the historical: "However subdued the tone of the passions may be, however ordered the action or commonplace the diction, if a play or a work if music or a picture presents the everlasting hopes, desires and hates of us, or deals with a symbolic presentment of our widely related nature, albeit a phase of that nature, then it is drama" (41). Though aspiring to the grandeur of the everlasting, Joyce does not recuse himself from responsibility to the historical in the high altitudes of philosophical inquiry. On the contrary, his theory of the dramatic inserts the critic—cast as a collective figure—into the struggle for life, into the practice of freedom. As in the previous chapters, socialized affects—here figured in terms of the dramatic—support a collective critical practice:

> Drama will be for the future at war with convention, if it is to realize itself truly. If you have a clear thought of the body of drama it will be clear what raiment befits it. Drama of so wholehearted and admirable a nature cannot but draw all hearts from the spectacular and theatrical, its note being truth and freedom in every aspect of it. I may be asked what are we to do, in the words of Tolstoi. First, clear our minds of cant and alter the falsehoods to which we have lent our support. Let us criticize in the manner of a free people, as a free race, recking little of ferula and formula. The Folk is, I believe, able to do so much. (42)

Drama is cast as life at war with convention, and criticism cast as the struggle for freedom. In the context of the Irish Renaissance (particularly the efforts of the Abbey Theater and Synge), the Folk in Joyce's final allusion points to the problem of the biographical at the level of national allegory. However, much as with Synge, Joyce is not simply promoting a project of ethnographic authenticity; rather, with the emphasis on the Folk and its figuration of Irishness, he will attempt to keep the "vital relations" between writing and life in view. Drama and its criticism in Joyce's formula is not just a question of formal aesthetic practice but also points toward the ordering of human life in and through social processes of representation. Joyce's "war with convention" is ultimately meant to be a collective endeavor. The collective nature of this "war with convention" is crucial. In this sense, Joyce should be read not simply in terms of formalist innovation, but in terms of the social dimensions of all forms of representation.

Joyce stages the multivalence of this "war with convention" in the "Cyclops" episode of *Ulysses*, in which the struggle against the narrative forms of classic realism coincides with deliberation over the problems of Irish independence. The question of freedom in the "Cyclops" chapter therefore intersects both narrative conventions and political realities. Perhaps not coincidently, the "Cyclops" chapter was to form the basis of an opera that Joyce had planned with the American director George Antheil—the chapter is, in Joyce's terms, essentially dramatic. Furthermore, the chapter is peculiarly biographical, both in its obsessive insistence on historical and nonfictional names (thus biographical in the conventional sense) and in its array of "motley agents" (particularly the stylized and porous foils of the citizen, Bloom, and Casement) who stage the clash of passions and forces that characterize the struggle for freedom.

Joyce's chapter exploits the full resonance of the figure of Casement—in terms of internationalism, humanitarianism, Irish nationalism, and homoeroticism—to stage a critique of Irish nationalism and through this local critique to engage the problem of freedom in a global context. This chapter argues that Joyce circulates the figure of Casement as an affective tool—as a *poor bugger's tool*, so to speak—to track the contradictions of the Irish nationalist struggle and to open this struggle to the dynamics of the global, or to the limit of the universal. One of the shadow texts in the rich foliage of the "Cyclops" episode is the critical circulation of Casement's famous "Speech from the Dock," specifically inflected by questions of the homoerotic. In declaring "love" as the antidote to the exacerbating and self-perpetuating violence of the colonial condition, Bloom echoes Casement's solution to Ireland's colonial dilemma. Through the mingling of the figures of Bloom and Casement—and through the resonance of Wilde's theorization of love in *The Picture of Dorian Gray*—Joyce effects a queer polyvalence in the affect of love. This queerly inflected love subverts and redirects the proper love of family, country, and God that had so aggressively asserted itself in bourgeois culturalist strains of Irish nationalism. The "ruling passion" of love that emerges across an incongruous network of texts—*Ulysses*, Casement's "Speech from the Dock" and Black Diaries, and *Dorian Gray*—does not promote the regulation of identity and affection but figures freedom in the social through the perverse production of value. Ultimately, by engaging Casement's "Speech from the Dock" through its emergence in the "Cyclops" episode, this chapter suggests that Casement himself promoted a form of intelligent sympathy, an affective tool termed "love," in the struggle against imperialism. Before examining the intersection of *Ulysses* and Casement's famous speech, we must examine how Joyce stages the biography of Casement in the drama of the "Cyclops" chapter—that is, how Joyce translates Casement's life into writing.

CASEMENT: HE'S AN IRISHMAN

The plot of the "Cyclops" episode is fairly straightforward. It opens with the so-called Nameless One being overtaken in the bustle of a Dublin street. He is nearly smashed in the eye by the gear of a chimney sweep; after escaping this calamity he retreats to the safety of Barney Kiernan's pub for a drink with Joe. The Nameless One attempts then to preside over the narration of events in the bar; in some sense, this is storytelling in its most primitive popular form, with the tongue unbound by the "sacred pint" (15). However, the diegesis is quickly overtaken in much the same way as the Nameless One in the chaos of the Dublin street: The drunken patrons order a staggering number of rounds. Characters appear, disappear, and reappear in a fantastical array of guises. A montage of discourses interrupts, redirects, and recasts the narration. The narrative grounding of the episode is no more stable than the motley aggregation of increasingly inebriated patrons. This narrative complexity provides much of the chapter's comedy and more subtly points to the importance that Joyce assigns to the deliberations of popular Irish common sense. Barney Kiernan's is, after all, the court of *pub*lic opinion— bad pun intended. Kiernan's is the popular "bar" located at the "back of the courthouse," the official Bar of the colonial state (241).[3] Kiernan's is a bar that adjudicates the subaltern concerns of the colonized—a large number of contemporary and historical trials, events, issues, and characters are debated and discussed by the patrons in the chapter—outside the institutional structures of the state, and outside the narrative institutions of classical realism.[4] The bar—and here the pun should be kept in view—is a stage for the contested narration of the Irish national drama. The figure of Casement appears within this disputed narration amid a semantic confusion:

—Is that Griffith? says John Wyse.

—No, says the citizen. It's not signed Shanganagh. It's only initialed: P.

—And a very good initial too, says Joe.

—That's how it worked, says the citizen. Trade follows the flag.

—Well, says J. J. if they're any worse than those Belgians in the Congo Free State they must be bad. Did you read that report by a man what's this his name is?

—Casement, says the citizen. He's an Irishman.

—Yes, that's the man, says J. J. Raping the women and girls and flogging the natives on the belly to squeeze all the red rubber they can out of them.

—I know where he's gone, says Lenehan, cracking his fingers.

—Who? says I.

—Bloom, says he. The courthouse is blind. He had a few bob on *Throwaway* and he's gone to gather in the shekels.

—Is it that whiteeyed kaffir? Says the citizen, that never backed a horse in anger in his life? (274)

The confusion in this passage ("what's this his name is?"; "Who?") is part of the drunken web of misnomers, slippages, jokes, and allusions that characterize the conversation at Kiernan's. The patrons are faced with a constant task of adjudication and orientation as they attempt to express their own meanings and decipher the meanings of others. For the reader, confusion infuses the overall montage. The shifts in discourses, voices, temporality, and characters overwhelm the reader, who is "cast unprepared into the text (as the child before the parents' conversation) uncertain of what position, if any, is to be allocated to him or her. Experience of fear, laughter, boredom."[5] There is, however, an anomalous moment of lucidity in this citation provided by the nationalist citizen who proclaims: "Casement. . . . He's an Irishman." What could be clearer? However, matters are rarely straightforward in *Ulysses*, and this particular lucidity does not simply refer to the historical figure of Casement; rather, through compounded and subtle irony, it reveals Casement as a "motley agent" in the chapter's drama.

First, it must be shown that the citizen does not exactly *name* Casement in this passage; he *misnames* him. That the citizen identifies someone within the discursive parameters of Irish identity is not surprising—he measures everything in terms of his nationalist conception of Irishness. That the citizen would point to Casement as Irish in 1904—the time frame of the novel—is circumstantially problematic and begins to suggest the inscription of a post-1916 understanding of Casement in the chapter. Although Casement was internationally famous by 1904 for his Congo reports, he was not particularly famous for being Irish. In fact, much to his personal frustration, Casement was often mistaken for being English despite his growing involvement with Irish causes. Even by the time Casement approached Irish prisoners of war in 1916 in German prison camps to recruit them for an Irish brigade to fight for independence, his national identity was met with skepticism.[6]

The ambiguity of Casement's Irish identity also becomes evident in the comparative examination of Joyce's own works. In the 1907 lecture "Ireland, Island of Saints and Sages," Joyce mentions the Congo Free State in a way that prefigures the passage from *Ulysses*. In fact, the 1907 lecture prefigures much of the conversation in the "Cyclops" episode. Joyce's twofold aim in the lecture, broadly speaking, is to produce a history of Irish contributions to European intellectual culture while simultaneously undermining the racial and religious purity of Irish identity. When the passage on the Congo appears in "Saints and Sages," Joyce not only fails to mention that Casement is Irish; he fails to mention Casement at all. The lack of reference to Casement as Irishman is remarkable because doing so would have been in keeping with the lecture's rhetorical pattern, in which Joyce exposes the traces that "the numerous Celtic apostles in almost every country have left

behind" (157). Furthermore, Joyce apparently had a collection of Casement's writings in his library in Trieste. *Casement as Irishman* escapes Joyce's
representation in the lecture, and appears as an addition that merits critical
attention in the citizen's reference. The passage in the "Saints and Sages"
lecture in which the reference to the Congo appears is brief and introduces
an analysis of European colonialism:

> I find it rather naïve to heap insults on England for her misdeeds in Ireland. A conqueror
> cannot be casual, and for so many centuries the Englishman has done in Ireland only
> what the Belgian is doing today in the Congo Free State, and what the Nipponese dwarf
> will do tomorrow in other lands. She enkindled its factions and took over its treasury. By
> the introduction of a new system of agriculture, she reduced the power of the native
> leaders and gave great estates to her soldiers. . . . (166)

A similar analysis finds itself disarticulated from a single voice, and recircu-
lated through multiple voices in the "Cyclops" chapter. Bloom proposes an
underlying unity to the modes of international colonial domination: "But,
says Bloom, isn't discipline the same everywhere. I mean wouldn't it be the
same here if you put force against force?" (270). The citizen spends much
of the chapter heaping insults on England for its misdeeds: "To hell with
the bloody brutal Sassenachs and their *patois*" (266). J. J. introduces the
Belgian crimes of the Congo Free State specifically. The additional element
in the *Ulysses* passage is the citizen's twofold recognition of *Casement as
Irishman*. The chain of implication is subtle but suggestive: Casement
ascends to the status of nationalist hero only after the trial in 1916. The
nationalist racial coding of Casement is in a sense also a temporal marker.
The temporal identity of Casement further complicates the citizen's reference because the trial is inseparable from the homophobic scandal surrounding it. To acknowledge Casement as Irish national is also in a certain
sense to register—even obliquely—the possibility of his queerness. Casement's Irish nationalist fame is the flip side of his homosexual infamy. Joyce
exploits this paradoxical dynamic in the figure of Casement to undermine
and redirect the citizen's narration of Ireland.

Ulysses asserts but then undermines the purity of Casement as nationalist
icon by placing the recognition of Casement-as-Irishman in the mouth of
the citizen. Although the citizen's naming of Casement is ostensibly a moment of lucidity, the recognition of Casement as Irishman is embedded
within a web of misrecognition. Remember that in the passage cited above
Casement appears in a quest for clarification: "Is that by Griffith? says John
Wyse." (Arthur Griffith founded Sinn Fein in 1902 and was thus a hero in the
nationalist hagiography.) The citizen, the scribe of the nationalist hagiography,
responds: "No, i . . . iiiit's not signed Shanganagh. It's only initialed: P." After

being introduced and identified as Irish, Casement is then semantically confused for Bloom:

—Casement, says the citizen. . . .
  —Yes, that's the man, says J. J. . . .
  —I know where he's gone, says Lenehan, cracking his fingers.
  —Who? says I.
  —Bloom, says he.

In the passages that follow, yet another confusion is introduced. Much to the citizen's consternation, John Wyse reveals that Bloom originally provided Griffith with the ideas for Sinn Fein (275). The revelation of Bloom's (historically fictional) influence on Griffith follows the famous debate in the pub over the question of Bloom's nationality. In this debate the Jewish Bloom defends what the anti-Semitic citizen maintains is an untenable position: "What is your nation if I may ask? says the citizen. . . . Ireland, says Bloom. I was born here. Ireland" (272). The naming in these passages of Griffith, Casement, and Bloom indexes a failure of recognition. Pulling back further from this particular passage, the misnaming of these figures is part of the provocative roster of names that fills the chapter and clearly exceeds the boundaries of historical reference. Consider, for example, the list of "Irish heroes and heroines of antiquity" that runs from Cuchulain through the Man that Broke the Bank at Monte Carlo, to Gautama Buddha and Lady Godiva (244). That Casement would be the only historically correct referent in this chain seems unlikely. For this series of political substitutions to obtain its comical effect, Casement must be in effect misrecognized. As Casement and Bloom dissolve and meld into the same figure, the heart of the joke in this list contaminating the citizen's line of illustrious Irish nationalist heroes is the compounded toxin of the "perverted jew" (276).[7] The reference to Casement therefore does not adhere to the conventions of historical biography. Instead, this reference is a dramatic figure through which the contradictions of the citizen's conception of the world is staged.

REAL IRISH FUN WITHOUT VULGARITY

The politico-comic substitutions in the chain Griffith-Casement-Bloom-Griffith, and the intermittent uproar of drunken laughter in the pub, point to the joke as a sort of elemental figure of speech for this chapter. Following Roman Jakobsen's distinction between metaphor and metonymy,[8] we could suggest that the ontological mingling of the vehicle and the tenor in metaphor—the "similarity" on which the mingling is based—is short-circuited in the shifting comedy of the "Cyclops" episode. The drunken confusion of the jokes in the pub points to a metonymic dynamic of "splitting" and "doubling up" in which attributes, situations, affects, images, and people are shuffled in the chapter's montage.[9] Even as Casement-the-queer and Bloom-the-Jew enter the chapter, each exceeds the contours of the realist character; they are split and doubled to infuse and contaminate a series of subjects, affects, and discourses.[10] Ultimately the categories of temporality and identity are represented as effects of the chapter's montage rather than as corresponding to a priori uniformities that transcend the writing.[11] The shadow of Casement thus appears in the rich suggestiveness of Joyce's writing and provides one of the myriad points of *reconnaissance plaisante* for the cultivated reader. Casement's sexual infamy also plays a role in the vulgar humor of the chapter. If intertextual allusion is one of the calculated effects of the chapter's comical juxtapositions, the dirty joke is one of the chapter's more critically challenging elements.[12] While the subtlety of allusion may test the reader's cultural formation, the dirty joke is a dense representational knot that figures the encounter of complex and contradictory worldviews and traditions, political agendas, and ethical theories within the eloigning wake of vulgar affects. Casement is a key punch line to the dirtiest joke of the chapter and is an analogue in a series of sexually graphic figures in the novel, including Bloom's "transexualization" at the hand of a dominatrix in the "Circe" section and Molly's lusty monologue. The shade of Casement appears in the discussion of capital punishment, after the patrons have examined the grim letter of inquiry from H. Rumbold, Master Barber. In the citation that follows, the figure of Casement is humorous in the root sense of the word: the physical hierarchies of the proper subject are dissolved into the sexualized fluid body—a body of swells and excretions—and a corresponding swirl of affects and meanings. Casement appears as the unnamed in a discussion over capital punishment that "hangs" on a particular physical effect of execution at the gallows:

So they started talking about capital punishment and of course Bloom comes out with the why and the wherefore and all the codology of the business and the old dog smelling him all the time I'm told those jewies does have a queer odor coming off them for dogs about I don't know what all deterrent effect and so forth and so on.

—There's one thing it hasn't a deterrent effect on, says Alf.

—What's that? says Joe.

—The poor bugger's tool that's being hanged, says Alf.

—That so? says Joe.

—God's truth, says Alf. I heard that from the head warder that was in Kilmainham when they hanged Joe Brady, the invincible. He told me when they cut him down after the drop it was standing up in their faces like a poker.

—Ruling passion strong in death, says Joe, as someone said.

—That can be explained by science, says Bloom. It's only a natural phenomenon, don't you see, because on account of the . . .

And then he starts with his jawbreakers about phenomenon and science and this phenomenon and the other phenomenon.

So of course the citizen was only waiting for the wink of the word and he starts gassing out of him about the invincibles and the old guard and the men of sixtyseven and who fears to speak of ninetyeight and Joe with him about all the fellows that were hanged, drawn and transported for the cause by the drumhead courtmartial and a new Ireland and new this, that and the other. (250)

Clearly, Casement is inscribed in this discussion: from the point of view of the production of the novel, Casement is the contemporary in the series of the citizen's Irish patriotic martyrs. Casement, the "poor bugger," was also hanged. Casement's remainder, that "ruling passion strong in death," was— and still is—his "bugger's tool." The homophobic reception and circulation of the diaries, and the scandal that still reverberates around Casement, centers on the image of the "bugger's tool" and how this tool disrupts or reinforces competing versions of Casement's discursive image.[13] The affects provoked by this inscription of Casement are in such a contradictory swirl that they don't seem to add up to something like an ethos. They do not, for instance, reveal a shared common sense among the patrons; in fact, they seem to bring to the foreground a series of differences: in understandings of capital punishment, in the racist ranting of the narrator, and in the scientific discussion of the death of the body (Bloom) versus the political interpretation of death (the citizen). Yet the vulgarity of this image, the inappropriateness of the discussion, the clash of the inquisitive Bloom and the fanatical citizen are ultimately, one might admit, funny. The dissonance provokes humor—if not outright laughter—for the reader, and in this sense, these aggregative affects point to a certain form of "unsocial sociability."[14] After all, doesn't this humorous effect arise in part from the fact that what is circulating in the interstices of this image is a socialized—if only potential and perhaps ineffable—*understanding of something*? I would like to suggest that the sociability inherent in this joke is the dramatic truth that emerges from the critical practice of a "free people" and that the truth of this critical practice contrasts with both the knowledge production (read the "truth") of the colonial state and the alternative nationalist "truth" espoused by the citizen. This dirty joke that hangs on the image of the "bugger's tool" is part of the dramatic "war with convention" that rejects in this instance both the conventions of the colonial state and their inversion in the strategies of the citizen's nationalism. The contradictory swirl of affects that end *The Playboy* attuned our attention to the complexity of contemporary Irish history; the complex juxtaposition of affects in Casement's work added to the potential richness of global relations. The vulgar swirl of affects in this dirty joke undermines the parochialism of the citizen's definition of nationalism and represents the potentials of a free critical practice in the Irish context.

To understand the importance of the vulgar affects in this dirty joke, and the perverted and humorous figuration of Casement and Bloom, we need to examine the entanglement of the worldviews of the citizen and the colonial state. Earlier, I suggested that Kiernan's was the popular bar that stood in the back of the official Bar of the colonial state and that Kiernan's staged the subaltern concerns of the colonized. In his sustained critique of everything English, the citizen functions as a representative of the colonized. Even so, Joyce does not simply valorize the citizen's conception of the world in the face of the sanctioned and hegemonic knowledge of the colonial state. The critical edge of Joyce's chapter emerges in the clash of these two conceptions of the world and frequently relies on the destabilization of both. In fact, Joyce suggests the mutual indebtedness of these two worldviews, particularly in their litigious management of the problem of difference. In what follows, I would like to sketch briefly the management of difference in the Enlightenment theorization of the state and consider how this theorization is partially maintained in the inverted form of the citizen's anticolonial politics.

The particular concept that will reveal the litigious similarities between the citizen and the colonial state is the paradox of "unsocial sociability." The contradictions attending this paradox are part of a broader legacy of the European Enlightenment that—according to its own narratives—sought to organize the individualistic forces of free will into capitalist economic formations and liberal political structures. Immanuel Kant uses the "antagonism" of "unsocial sociability" to describe the optimal arrangement of humans in society—that is, the organization of individuals in the structures of the state. Ultimately, the management of this antagonism grounds Kant's model of international cosmopolitanism. Kant is a worthwhile reference here, as his model of the cosmopolitan as a condition among states will help to bring into relief both the inverted form of the citizen's litigious and parochial nationalism and the global subaltern quality of Joyce's "passionate" figuration of Bloom and Casement. Kant explains the emergence of the cosmopolitan condition in terms of the evolution of the state:

> Purposeless savagery held back the development of the capacities of our race; but finally through the evil into which it plunged mankind, it forced our race to renounce this condition and to enter into a civic order in which those capacities could be developed. The same is done by the barbaric freedom of established states. Through wasting the powers of the commonwealths in armaments to be used against each other, through devastation brought on by war, and even more by the necessity of holding themselves in

constant readiness for war, they stunt the full development of human nature. But because of the evils which thus arise, our race is formed to find, above the (in itself healthy) opposition of states which is a consequence of their freedom, a law of equilibrium and a united power to give it effect. Thus it is forced to institute a cosmopolitan condition to secure the external safety of each state. (20)

The "cosmopolitan condition" for Kant is the product of two stages of development. In the first moment, the savage heterogeneity of the free will is organized into the structures of the state that, as an ideal, will subject the "greatest freedom" to the "irresistible power" of the "perfectly just civic constitution." In a second moment, the "barbaric freedom of established states" must be organized into an international legal structure that will ensure their security. This "league of nations" maintains cosmopolitan diversity as it secures the peaceful coexistence of states, but not as it secures difference *tout court*. Indeed, two forms of difference emerge in Kant's discussion. The first is the "healthy" opposition of individuals or states; this difference is to be maintained in the perfect constitution of the individual state and the league of nations. The second difference is "purposeless savagery," which is truly anarchic, that is, stateless. "Purposeless savagery" marks a redundancy in Kant's model in the sense that "savagery" will always be "purposeless" because it exists outside the developmental structures of the European state. It would be easy to catalog the historical references and political agendas that linger behind this purported savagery. When savagery returns in the second moment of development, in the "barbaric freedom of established states," its meaning is, strictly speaking, metaphoric. In this metaphor, the not-fully-human barbarian/savage predicates the wasted freedom of the inhuman state; this savage waste stands in contrast to the healthy "opposition of states which is a consequence of their freedom" (16–20). The savage metaphorically marks difference from the state; the savage is other than the state. Paradoxically, through its exclusion, the savage grounds the healthy economy of interstate variation. The savage therefore both forecloses difference and ensures variation. The cosmopolitan concept as it emerges in Kant both exiles difference beyond the pale of the state and promulgates difference in the state-structured international.

The citizen in *Ulysses*, even as he wishes to cast off the shackles of colonial rule, subscribes to a similar—though inverted—form of cosmopolitanism that encourages a certain form of variation by foreclosing difference at the outset. Whereas Kant refers explicitly to cosmopolitanism, the citizen's insistence on his narrative of the Irish national struggle registers as isolationism. Nonetheless, in their fundamental dynamics, these models are two sides of the same coin. Consider how the paradoxical dynamic sketched in Kant is staged in the citizen's toast with Bloom:

—The memory of the dead, says the citizen taking up his pintglass and glaring at Bloom.

—Ay, ay, says Joe.

—You don't grasp my point, says Bloom. What I mean is . . .

—*Sinn Fein!* Says the citizen. *Sinn fein amhain!* The friends we love are by our side and the foes we hate before us. (251)[15]

In this toast, the citizen echoes Robert Emmet's famous "Speech from the Dock," in which the patriotic martyr links the memory of the dead with violent resistance to the oppression of the present. The citizen toasts to an Irish difference, and at the same time, through his glaring challenge to Bloom, he seeks to exclude the difference he imagines Bloom representing. We have already seen how Joyce ironically undermines the purity of the citizen's invocation of Sinn Fein, and the revelation of Bloom's aid to Griffith should resonate in our reading of the above passage. And Bloom eventually points out a further irony in this toast. Although the citizen invokes the importance of the memory of the dead, this memory is painfully selective in whom it chooses to eulogize, and for what motivations. The biggest blind spot in the citizen's memory is pointed out by Bloom in the finale of the chapter when he drives the citizen into a rage by pointing out, "Your God was a jew. Christ was a jew like me" (280). Joyce goes further in this section of the chapter by introducing a parody of the citizen's romanticization of the memory of the dead. Directly following the citizen's sanitized invocation of the "memory of the dead" is the parodic presentation of an execution in which the final act of killing is interrupted by the romance that erupts between the lover of the intended victim and a "handsome young Oxford graduate" (280). The "romance" of the citizen's "memory of the dead" is not the same as the literal romance that transpires on the scaffold in the parody execution. The sanitization of the execution in the parody is pushed to the limits of the absurd. Joyce, tongue in cheek, presents the execution as "real Irish fun without vulgarity," and even has the "Sisters of the Poor" invite the children of the "Male and Female Foundling Hospital" to the execution for a "genuinely instructive treat" (252). Despite the differences in the citizen's invocation of the dead and the comic absurdity in the parody, there are a number of important correspondences: both are sanitized invocations of death, whether through memory or fantasy; and each passage romanticizes execution—excluding certain factors from the scene, casting the meaning of the act in a particular light, and regulating the corresponding emotions. Joyce's montage undermines the homogeneity of each of these representations by staging the process of exclusion by which the homogeneity is achieved. Bloom exposes the selectivity and ultimate capriciousness of the citizen's memory, and the intense absurdity of the parodic execution cannot help but call attention to the exclusion of alternate narratives of the event.

The conceptions of the world that emerge in the cosmopolitanism of the colonial state and in the particularism of the citizen's narration of Irish nationalism are two sides of the same coin. They both exile difference in their foundation in order to regulate variety in their operation. Through their exclusion of difference they limit the potential practice of freedom. I would like to suggest that the sociability that emerges in the dirty joke of the "bugger's tool" has a very different relation to free critical practice. In what remains of this section, I will describe the figurative dynamics of the phrase, and in the final section of the chapter I will turn to how this phrase marks global dimensions of love, Bloom and Casement's proposed solution to the colonial problem.

Within the *"parade virile"*[16] of the "Cyclops" episode, which includes a comical number of phallic images (Bloom's cigar, the reference to Bloom as the prudent member, Cromwell's canon, even the innuendo-laden title of the chapter itself), the "bugger's tool" stands out. The figure stands out not only as it points to the persistence of a nexus of homosexual anxieties on the part of the citizen but also as it stylizes a double form of inscription that displaces the monomania of the citizen's phallic hero worship. Indeed, the term itself emerges as a figure of intelligent sympathy in the sense that the humor provoked in its deployment manages to reveal and displace the truth of both the citizen and the colonial state.[17]

The term "tool" carries a double sense: first, of an ontologically contained thing in and of itself, an "instrument of manual operation." In its figurative sense, tool exceeds its status as thing-in-and-of-itself and refers to "anything used in the manner of a tool," for example, "a person used by another for his own ends." In this figurative sense, the tool is not simply the thing-in-and-of-itself but rather the thing subjected to a process, a thing existing in relation to something else. The full phrase "bugger's tool" reinforces both of these senses: in its slang meaning it refers to "the male generative organ" (in fact, the OED cites this exact quote from Ulysses as the example of this use). However, in the complete sense of the phrase "bugger's tool" this penis is inescapably intended for, and even confused with, the receptive companion organ, the anus. Simply put, for a "tool" to be a "bugger's tool," there must be an anus. In fact, this necessity is so intense that one could argue that the real bugger's tool—the instrument that makes for the actual buggery—is the anus. The "bugger's tool" is thus not a regulatory figure of phallic homogeneity in which dominating images of patriarchal power (sword, tool, canon, cigar) are substituted for one another—rather, it is a dynamic figure of metonymic contiguity in which the erect penis not only approaches the anus but is in fact taken by the anus.

The anus's powerful receptivity becomes as important for the meaning of the phrase as the penis's insertive ambitions. So as to not amplify in one sense and truncate in the other, it should be mentioned that the fuller phrase "poor bugger's tool" reinforces this metonymic contiguity. The poverty of pathos in the phrase "poor bugger" castrates the citizen's patriarchal reverence for the phallus. The anality of the "bugger's tool" that serves as a metonymic sort of universal repeats in the banality of "poor bugger," which also in a sense can refer to anyone through the leveling effect of its sympathy. In one of its root forms, "banal" refers to that which is "open to the use of all the community." In Wakese, one might say that there is a universanality in the phrase "poor bugger's tool."

The insertion of the "bugger's tool" in the dirty joke does not foreclose or regulate difference but stages a multiplicity of affective relations—desire, anxiety, passion, fear, lust—linked through humor: for the homophobic discourse of the citizen, the ass is the threat that potentially transforms any patriot's cock into an instrument of buggery. In another sense, the "bugger's tool" is the erotic passion for life that outlasts death. For Bloom the phrase represents the giddiness in popular discussions of sexuality that should be met with the detachment of biological science. In relation to Casement, the bugger's tool is the "ruling passion" that supplements the compassion of his humanitarian efforts. The truth of the "bugger's tool" (referred to as "God's truth" in the passage) inheres in this multiplicity. The vulgarity of this figure—the root sense of "vulgarity," which is "the commonality," reinforces this multiplicity—stands in important opposition to the "proper" phrase that opens this portion of this chapter: "real Irish fun without vulgarity." This phrase implies the authentication or "propriety" of Irish identity through the purging of the vulgar. The phallic hero worship of the citizen is in this sense "real Irish fun." "Real Irish" is chaste, and ultimately is a pleasure achieved only through reformation.[18] With the authenticated chastity of Irish identity achieved, the reactionary project of cultural, ethnic, and political verification can begin—thus the citizen's fanatical inquisition of Bloom. The "bugger's tool" stages a vital multiplicity in which such verification makes no sense. Through this affective multiplicity Casement becomes a figure of intelligent sympathy, an affective tool, that allows Joyce to dissect critically the contradictions of the Irish colonial situation. Joyce emphasizes the critical role of affect both in forms of aesthetic expression and in the engagement with the legal discourses of the colonial state. In the next section of this chapter, we will examine how this vulgarity renders Casement and Bloom's theorization of love as a "ruling passion" a form of affect that does not simply regulate, litigate, and subjugate identity, but rather opens the possibility of freedom in the social through the perverted production of value.

UNIVERSAL LOVE: "LOVE LOVES TO LOVE LOVE"

In the passages preceding the direct introduction of Casement, Bloom proposes "love" as the remedy to the problems of colonialism. This suggestion crystallizes the difference in the theories of history espoused by Bloom and the citizen. In the context of my argument, the suggestion reinforces the interconnections between Bloom and Casement, as Casement's "Speech from the Dock" also promotes "love" as an antidote to the colonial situation. Despite the apparent innocuousness of the notion that we should all just love one another, Bloom's proposal provokes his drunken interlocutors:

> That's an almanac picture for you. Mark the softnosed bullet. Old lardyface standing up to the business end of a gun. Gob, he'd adorn a sweepingbrush, so he would, if only he had a nurse's apron on him. And then he collapses all of a sudden, twisting around all the opposite, as limp as a wet rag.
>
> —But it's no use, says he. Force, hatred, history, all that. That's not life for men and women, insult and hatred. And everybody knows that it's the very opposite of that that is really life.
>
> —What? says Alf.
>
> —Love, says Bloom. I mean the opposite of hatred. I must go now, says he to John Wyse. Just round to the court a moment to see if Martin is there. If he comes just say I'll be back in a second. Just a moment.
>
> Who's hindering you? And off he pops like greased lightening.
>
> —A new apostle to the gentiles, says the citizen. Universal love.
>
> —Well, says John Wyse. Isn't that what we're told. Love your neighbour.
>
> —That chap? says the citizen. Beggar my neighbour is his motto. Love, moya! He's a nice pattern of a Romeo and Juliet.
>
> Love loves to love love. Nurse loves the new chemist. Constable 14 A loves Mary Kelly. Gerty MacDowell loves the boy that has the bicycle. M. B. a fair gentleman. Li Chi Han lovey up kissy Cha Pu Chow. Jumbo, the elephant, loves Alice, the elephant. Old Mr Verschoyle with the ear trumpet loves old Mrs Verschoyle with the turnedin eye. The man in the brown macintosh loves a lady who is dead. His majesty the King loves her Majesty the Queen. Mrs Norman W. Tupper loves officer Taylor. You love a certain person. And this person loves that other person because everybody loves somebody but God loves everybody.
>
> —Well, Joe, says I, your very good health and song. More power, citizen.
>
> —Hurrah, there, says Joe.
>
> —The blessing of God and Mary and Patrick on you, says the citizen.
>
> And he ups with his pint to wet his whistle. (273)

The passage begins with the narrator's emasculation of Bloom, both by deflating his phallic power ("the softnosed bullet," "Old lardyface standing up to the business end of a gun," "limp as a wet rag") and by casting him in the transvestite drag of the "nurse's apron." The implication in this emasculation is that Bloom is doubly abnormal in the macho bravado of Kiernan's, both in terms of masculine tumescence and pertinence, and in terms of gender/sexual orientation and performance. Bloom evokes the shadows of a series of sexually deviant figures in the novel, most notably Wilde and Casement. The "perverted" Bloom then dissolves the intransigence of colonialist violence with a single word: "Love." The simplicity of the suggestion unravels the patrons. On the one hand, the Christianity to which the patrons subscribe proposes love as an answer to problems of earthly violence ("Isn't that what we're told. Love your neighbor"). In addition, a network of cultural common sense also stresses the importance of love in counteracting humanity's internecine tendencies ("Romeo and Juliet"). Ironically, it seems that "softnosed" Bloom has hit the nail on the head. Yet despite this resonance with religious and cultural directives, the solution provokes a mouthful of hateful blather from the citizen. "Beggar my neighbor is his motto," slurs the citizen, circulating the invective of the "perverted jew" examined earlier. This "motto" again unites the figures of Bloom and Casement and, as we will see, points toward Casement's famous "Speech from the Dock." Beggar-my-neighbor is a children's card game in which one player attempts to extract payment (in cards) from the other until the opponent's store of cards is depleted. Thus, the insult casts Bloom as the thieving Jew, a thematic that runs throughout the chapter. As the citizen's slur stands as a response to Bloom's call for universal love, and in light of the novel's sustained, if subterranean, interest in sodomy and the homoerotic, the phrase also echoes the homophone "bugger my neighbor." The slur thus carries its full charge of homophobic and racist meanings.

However, the critical point is not that the citizen has again displayed himself as anti-Semitic and homophobic but that his anxiety is a response to the multiplicity of love set in relief by Bloom's suggestion. Though seemingly anchored to stable cultural and religious meanings, Bloom's deployment of the term reveals an inability to discipline love, to trace its "proper" dimensions, to fit it into a unifying narrative. Love is a figure of affective excess that appears across a series of discourses and manages to expose their incompatibilities and contradictions. So whereas Bloom espouses love—a term that should resonate with his audience—his audience can only banish the suggestion as the interference of the perverted other. The paragraph that follows points to the generative nature of love, which seems both to be conjugated locally and to exceed these conjugations, to pass through them, and in its wake to expose the contradictions of its particular predications. "Love loves to love love." The generative dynamics of the passion will always overwhelm the particular agents that swoon under its influence. So while love seems to be propagated through heterosexual parings, ultimately it is the extension and vitality of the series that characterize the passion. A dyadic model of heterosexuality does not exhaust the possibilities of love, as the series exceeds these local attributes: "You love a certain person. And this person loves that other person because everybody loves somebody but God loves everybody." The anxiety that this generative capability provokes recalls Bertolt Brecht's complaint, shared with Walter Benjamin, against Georg Lukács and his allies:

> They are, to put it bluntly, enemies of production. Production makes them uncomfortable. You never know where you are with production; production is the unforeseeable. You never know what's going to come out. And they themselves don't want to produce. They want to play the *apparatchik* and exercise control over other people. Every one of their criticisms contains a threat.[19]

While Brecht is specifically addressing artistic production in contrast to criticism, the question of production can also be read in a more general sense. In this instance, the productive or generative capacities of love—which outside the properly heterosexual model of the Irish nation register as perverted—threaten the citizen's conception of the world by continually creating novel forms of social value.

The love promoted by Bloom further suggests the imbrication of Casement in the chapter. Specifically, the "perversion" of Bloom in the passage, the ongoing mutual implication of Bloom and Casement, and the deployment of love in response to the problem of colonialism point to Casement's "Speech from the Dock" as an important corollary text. Furthermore, Casement's speech is, in Joycean terms, essentially dramatic in both its content and its staging. In terms of its content, the speech confronts the historical and political reality of colonialism with the intelligent sympathy of love. Its literal staging at the dock of the English courtroom amplifies the dramatic legal metaphorics and puns that we have already tracked in the "Cyclops" chapter.

Casement begins his speech with a gesture common to condemned Irish patriots. He declines addressing the English court, and instead directs himself to a more important, if absent, constituency: the Irish people.

> My Lord Chief Justice, as I wish to reach a much wider audience than I see before me here, I intend to read all that I propose to say. What I shall read now is something I wrote more than twenty days ago. I may say, my Lord, at once, that I protest against the jurisdiction of this court in my case on this charge, and the argument that I am now going to read is addressed not to this Court, but to my own countrymen. (Black Diaries 487)

By addressing the Irish people from the restricted stage of the English courtroom, Casement locates what Jean-François Lyotard terms the *différend* in the distance between Irish and English definitions of the colonial situation. Lyotard defines the *différend* specifically in the framework of the law: "A case of differend between two parties takes place when the 'regulation' of the conflict that opposes them is done in the idiom of one of the parties while the wrong suffered by the other is not signified in that idiom."[20] The speech relies on the exposure of just such a conflict for much of its political effectiveness.

Joseph Valente's gloss of the active status of the *différend* is important for keeping in mind its potential as a site for transformative thought and action:

> Rather than constituting an injustice in the narrow or vulgar sense, the *différend* betokens a conflict whose resolution is inconceivable within the germane legal or ethical context but which nonetheless points, through the feeling of pain produced, to a more nuanced frame of justice. . . . So while the *différend* remains strictly relevant to concrete juridical situations, as Lyotard's analyses of holocaust revisionism, industrial litigation, and colonial disenfranchisement attest, it is never proper to them, never sufficiently consonant with their prevailing norms and priorities to motivate or endorse specific decisions. Instead, it reveals the impropriety of the contexts themselves, the internal tension between the sense of justice they evoke and the kinds of rules they enforce.[21]

Casement's description of the Irish situation prefigures Lyotard's philosophical definition almost term for term and also suggests the transformative power in Valente's explanation:

> This Court, this jury, the public opinion of this country, England, cannot but be prejudiced in varying degree against me, most of all in time of war. I did not land in England; I landed in Ireland. It was to Ireland I came; to Ireland I wanted to come; and the last place I desired to land was England. But for the Attorney General of England there is only "England"—there is no Ireland, there is only the law of England—no right of Ireland; the liberty of Ireland and of Irishmen is to be judged by the power of England. Yet for me, the Irish outlaw, there is a land of Ireland, a right of Ireland, and a charter for all Irishmen to appeal to, in the last resort, a charter that even the very statutes of England itself cannot deprive us of—nay, more, a charter that Englishmen themselves assert as the fundamental bond of law that connects the two kingdoms. (Black Diaries 490)

The English court cannot register the problem of Ireland properly because to do so would register the wrong that England commits in its colonial occupation and thereby unravel the authority of the English court itself. Casement exposes this *différend* theoretically here, and spends much of the speech explaining the historical results of this blindness imposed by the might of the English colonial state. This blind spot in English justice is not merely a logical lapse without real-world consequences; rather, this blindness sanctions the gruesome reality of colonialist political practices. The imposition of this *différend* will allow the British state to take Casement's life, even though the terms of his sentencing are riddled with historical and political contradictions: "Edward III was King not only of the realm of England, but also of the realm of France, and he was not King of Ireland. Yet his dead hand today may pull the noose around the Irishman's neck whose Sovereign he was not, but it can strain no strand around the Frenchman's throat whose Sovereign he was" (Black Diaries 488). Casement's response to this situation is subtle. Rather than violently opposing or reversing the power dynamics, Casement, no pacifist, suggests a third term: love. Casement links the problem of love to the question of right. In doing so he reveals his intimate and practical knowledge of rights discourse. Rights are necessarily linked in their real-world application to responsibilities. For example, to assert the right to a fair trial immediately entails questions of responsibility: Who will provide this trial? Who will monitor it and ensure its fairness? Who will pay for the trial? If there is not a fair trial, who will act, and how will this party rectify the situation? Casement realizes the mutual implication of rights and responsibilities and uses this mutual implication to redirect the charges against him. Casement was charged with high treason under an archaic statute, and according to the state, Casement's moral degeneracy threatened to contaminate others by offering "evil example to others in like case." Casement assumes the charge of this moral responsibility, but in doing so he attempts to recast his "right" to trial as the "responsibility" of the Irish community:

> That, my Lord, is the condemnation of English rule, of English Government in Ireland, that it dare not rest on the will of the Irish people, but it exists in defiance of their will— that it is a rule derived not from right, but from conquest. Conquest, my Lord, gives no title, and if it exists over the body, it fails over the mind. It can exert no empire over men's reason and judgment and affections; and it is from the law of conquest without title to the reason, judgment, and affection of my own countrymen that I appeal. (Black Diaries 490)

As we have seen throughout this study, affect in this formulation represents the fabric of the social. Casement specifically supplements the limits of the English law in this instance with a socialized affect. "Love" is the fabric of the community that would be able to adequately adjudicate Casement's moral responsibility in the case. Casement introduces love as a particularly modern mode of affiliation and contrasts it with the archaic quality of the

English law: "If true religion rests on love, it is equally true that loyalty rests on love. The law I am charged under has no parentage in love and claims the allegiance of today on the ignorance and blindness of the past" (487). Casement sets the dimensions of this socialized affect against the tyranny of colonial rule:

> Ireland has outlived the failure of all her hopes—and yet she still hopes. Ireland has seen her sons—aye, and her daughters too—suffer from generation to generation always for the same cause, meeting always the same fate, and always at the hands of the same power; and always a fresh generation has passed on to withstand the same oppression. For if English authority be omnipotent—a power, as Mr. Gladstone phrased it, that reaches to the very ends of the earth—Irish hope exceeds the dimensions of that power, excels its authority, and renews with each generation the claims of the last. (Black Diaries 493)

Casement bases the enormity and durability of Irish hope in this passage on love. Bloom, in his suggestion that love could solve the problem of colonial violence, echoes Casement's speech. The declaration in *Ulysses* that "love loves to love love" even echoes the affective excess of Casement's description of the vital dimensions of Irish hope.

Importantly, for Bloom and for Casement, this affective excess and the social values it produces are particularly vulgar in their multivalence, their homoerotic suggestiveness, and their "commanality" (bad pun irresistible). Joyce stages the vulgar multivalence of this affective response by linking this anticolonial "love" to the figure of the bugger's tool. By introducing the problem of the homoerotic, I would like to argue that Joyce is exploiting a tension that was already suggested in Casement's speech itself. Casement's promotion of love ultimately cannot be disassociated from the queer love that circulates in the Black Diaries. Indeed, as we saw in the previous chapter, the compassion of the humanitarian reports is expanded by the homoerotic passion that emerges as a basis of social value in the Black Diaries. The "queer" love proposed by Bloom offers a similarly expanded understanding of postcolonial ethics and freedom.

On one level, the emphasis on the affective affiliations of nationalism is typical of Irish speeches from the dock. The intensity of passion indexes the powerlessness of the Irish patriot against the English executioner. Passion is the patriot's last recourse. Casement's speech goes further than this. Casement defines self-government in affective terms. Considering his lifetime of practical political work, and his insistence that his speech be written so as to reach a wider audience (487), this definition is particularly striking: "Self-government is our right, a thing born in us at birth; a thing no more to be doled out to us or withheld from us by another people than the right to life itself—than the right to feel the sun or smell the flowers, or to love our kind" (498). Historically speaking, within the progress of the trial this "love of kind" has a queer inflection. The queer valence can be tracked in the etymology of the phrase "love of kind." According to the *OED*, "kind" refers to the sort of naturalized biological (read: racial or ethnic) marker that might be expected in this context. "Kind" in this sense refers to "right of birth, right or position derived from birth, inherited right" or, as a verb, "to act according to one's nature; to do what is natural to one." This biological valence points to the sexual connotations of the word that in different forms refer to "gender" or "a sex (in collective sense)," "the sexual organs," and even in a rare form "the semen." The sexual nature of the term, which is meant to mark a biological commonality, has also yielded a slang form. The term refers to "a class of individuals or objects distinguished by attributes possessed in common" and "affectionate, loving, fond . . . on intimate terms. Also *euphemistically*." This euphemism functions as a marker of the queer, as in the title of Christopher Isherwood's autobiographical *Christopher and His Kind*. Beyond this etymological suggestiveness, it also appears that Casement by time of the speech was aware that his homosexual activities had been discovered in the pages of his confiscated diaries (*Roger Casement's Diaries* 4). That Casement would at the outset of his speech insist on its being *written*, for broader dissemination, is remarkable. Casement's definition of self-government therefore is doubly inscribed (again, a rhetorical move common in other areas of Casement's writings). Self-government has both a nationalist predication and a predication in terms of modern homoerotic affective affiliations. Joyce's deployment of "love" in Bloom's speech exploits a homoerotic valence already at play in Casement's speech. Joyce dramatizes this homoerotic valence in Casement's speech by having the perverted figure of Bloom echo Casement. By highlighting the homoerotic valence in Casement's speech and introducing this queerly inflected love to his critique of the Irish colonial situation, Joyce again asserts the importance of the multiplicity of the vulgar. The problems of the Irish struggle for freedom do not simply exist at the level of the state but extend to the intimacy of the erotic and pervade the social fabric.

Joyce further emphasizes the queer polyvalence in the figure of love by linking Bloom's declaration of love to Lord Henry's theorization of love for a young Dorian in *The Picture of Dorian Gray*. Remember that the citizen claims Bloom is a "nice pattern of a Romeo and Juliet." Then the text of the "Cyclops" proceeds to the idea that "[l]ove loves to love love." When Dorian first approaches Lord Henry to convey his infatuation with Sibyl Vane, he explains that he has discovered an actress playing *Romeo and Juliet* in a "wretched hole of a place."[22] Dorian claims that he has found the "greatest romance of [his] life," and Henry warns him,

But you should not say the greatest romance of your life. You should say the first romance of your life. You will always be loved, and you will always be in love with love. . . . My dear boy, the people who love only once in their lives are really the shallow people. What they call their loyalty, and their fidelity, I call either the lethargy of custom or their lack of imagination. Faithfulness is to the emotional life what consistency is to the life of the intellect—simply a confession of failure. Faithfulness! I must analyze it some day. The passion for property is in it. There are many things we would throw away if we were not afraid that others might pick them up. But I don't want to interrupt you. Go on with your story. (49)

The appearance of "Romeo and Juliet," "beggar my neighbor," and "love loves to love love" in the "Cyclops" passage combine to point to this passage from Wilde. Henry's warning against the declaration of the "greatest romance" in his schooling of Dorian's queer sensibilities, in the context of Joyce's chapter, also reads as a warning against the violence of the citizen's nationalist romance, his "passion for property" or propriety. By deploying a figure of love inflected both by Wilde and Casement, I do not think that Joyce is promoting a gay identity; rather, he is revealing what Jonathan Arac has referred to as a "preference for impurity."[23] In fact, "deployment," though registering the militaristic metaphor of the "war with convention," is perhaps not quite the correct term to describe Joyce's inscription of the queer figure of Casement. Although he detests the hypocritical arrangements of normative modes of sexuality, Joyce is not Jean Genet, and *Ulysses* is not *Un captif amoureux*. Nonetheless, through the queer Joyce points toward the vulgar production of social values at war with convention. The "unspoken texts" of the "Cyclops" chapter, as Enda Duffy refers to the Black Diaries, offer a glimpse at just such a vulgar, or common, production of social value. In light of the importance that queer love takes in *Ulysses*, it is worthwhile recalling from the last chapter Casement's queer estimation of ethical value in the global work of his human rights campaigning. Writing on September 9, 1910, Casement observes: "One half-white muchacho magnificent display & a young Cholo with an erection as he carried heavy box. Down leg about 6–8. They are far too good for their fate" (77–78). In rejecting the productive power of the vulgar, Irish nationalists of the citizen's stripe also, according to Joyce, might be too good for theirs.

❦

CHAPTER 5

The Queer Labors of Patrick McCabe and Neil Jordan

Novel, Television, Cinema

Work! he shouted. Look at it—I should have known it'd be no good. Work!
                              —*The Butcher Boy*

With her eyeshadow laden and golden hair dyed: boy with the swirling, shiny hair—could it be Pussy? Methinks it is!—did she perhaps resemble Miss Lynsey de Paul? Let there be no doubt! Indeed often swinging her hips while working Piccadilly, to the tune of "Sugar Me!"—for services rendered, of course!
                              —*Breakfast on Pluto*

Make it work!

                    —Tim Gunn, *Project Runway*

T he opening chapters of this book tracked the circulation of queer sensibilities in Irish culture and argued that they enabled various male writers to construct a diverse array of anti-imperial worldviews. In Wilde, Synge, Casement, and Joyce, queer affects and aesthetics operated as subversive modes of national affiliation that both focused anti-imperial sentiments and critique and orchestrated fluid and inclusive ways of imagining what it means to be Irish. We have furthermore seen in all of the works under consideration an interest in the politics of value—that is to say, an interest in how political, cultural, and ethical values intersect and are articulated through the economy. In Wilde's socialism, in Synge's modernity, in Casement's global ethics, and in the playful excess of Joyce's writing, queer aesthetics are brought to bear on multiple modalities of value, revealing the entangled possibilities and limitations of Ireland's anticolonial struggle as well as its postcolonial, partitioned, modernity. The final two chapters of this book extend the conceptual engagement with the politics of value and expressions of queer sexuality to make two arguments. First, I contend that the historical dynamics of Irish anti-imperial nationalism that marked the first part of the century need to be understood in relation to the economic development of the island in the latter part of the century. Second, I argue that queer aesthetics, which offer a privileged lens through which to consider the complex articulation of Irish nationalism, also provide signal insight into the contemporary transformations of economic, social, and cultural relations.

This chapter focuses on the collaborations of Patrick McCabe and Neil Jordan, specifically on the novel and film versions of *The Butcher Boy* (1992; 1998) and *Breakfast on Pluto* (1999; 2005).[1] *The Butcher Boy* and *Breakfast on Pluto* offer queer visions of the world, an aesthetic that McCabe has referred to as the "social fantastic."[2] The works explore deeply homoerotic themes and see the homoerotic as a dynamic analogue for an array of outcast social positions, feelings, politics, and people. The queer denotes specific relations to same-sex desires and sexual practices and extends beyond these particularities to bring into focus a general, complex, and vital web of social relations. If *The Butcher Boy* and *Breakfast on Pluto* are playfully fantastical works, they are nonetheless thoughtfully historical. They explore characters, situations, and affects that on first consideration may seem aberrant, highly individualized, and nonrepresentative. Yet, as Marx reminds us, "The individual *is the social being*. His life, even if it may not appear in the direct form of a *communal* life carried out together with others—is therefore an expression and confirmation of social life."[3] In a similar spirit, the works of McCabe and Jordan reveal the sociohistorical dimensions of the intense individual psychologies they explore. These dimensions are sociohistorical in at least three ways. First, the works frame their materials in relation to Irish political history, particularly to the legacy of the struggle for national independence from British rule. This is not to say that the characters themselves openly construct their worldviews in relation to narratives of Irish political independence, or that the texts promote the same politicized nationalism as texts from the first part of the century. Rather, these works understand the broad historical resonances of the fight against imperial domination. They explore the social realities of a fractured postcolonial life—both in terms of political partition and in terms of scarred psyches—through the lens of particular characters.[4]

On a second level, the works are sharply attentive to the media through which social histories emerge into representation. Representation itself is thereby historicized. *The Butcher Boy*, for instance, takes place in 1962, the year of the Cuban Missile Crisis and also the era that television broadcasting was introduced to Ireland.[5] More than mere backdrop, both versions insist on the televisual dimensions of the situation of the main character, Francie Brady. Indeed, as we will see, *The Butcher Boy* does not simply examine static representations of national and international life and culture *on* the new space of the TV screen. More than that, it examines how social life itself—national and international—is restructured along the lines of televisuality. *The Butcher Boy*—the novel and film—suggests interesting responses to Richard Deinst's questions posed in the opening chapter of *Still Life in Real Time: Theory after Television*:

> For if there are fleeting images visible on television, there must also be persistent images of television, visible somewhere else, which may be harder to discern. What abstract images—what rules of composition, figural devices, representational structures, or conceptual frameworks—can be built into and out of the concrete images on television? How do we know what television can show us?[6]

The Butcher Boy uses television to reveal the pain, joys, and potentials of Irish national life. *Breakfast on Pluto* follows the trials and tribulations of Patrick "Pussy" ("Kitten" in the film) Braden, transvestite prostitute, specifically through her relation to the images and sounds of popular culture—film, radio, TV, and print.[7] Both versions use her story, and her dazzling self-stylized consumption of pop culture, to explore the political, psychic, and historical stakes of the Troubles in the North of Ireland. The "revolution" in Northern Ireland is framed by the "revolution" of sex, drugs, and rock and roll that was part of global 1960s youth culture; both are explored through Patrick's own personal "revolution." More than the theatrical trappings of a period piece, the engagement with multiple cultural media becomes a way to explore the historical possibilities for both Patrick and the island's political and psychic situation.

Finally, these works are historical as they track the entangled and violent circuitry of social repression in both the Irish Republic and the North since partition. The works' queer aesthetics bring into focus the abjection of myriad alternative forms of Irish identity, expression, and labor in the conservative social and religious structures of the Republic of Ireland and the neocolonialism in Northern Ireland. The recent Ryan Report (2009) on the Republic has revealed some of the brutal mechanics of this abjection. More than thirty thousand children, deemed outcasts of Irish society, were from the 1930s through the 1990s relegated to institutions run by orders of the Catholic Church, most infamously the Christian Brothers. In these institutions, children were systematically terrorized: "rape and sexual molestation were 'endemic.'"[8] A similar history of brutality occurred in the Magdalen Laundries, in which "fallen" women were subjected to beatings, harsh manual labor, and physical and psychological abuse and were confined against their will. After the release of the Ryan Report, author John Banville described in an op-ed piece for the *New York Times* the historical situation in which these institutions emerged and thrived:

> Ireland from 1930 to the late 1990s was a closed state, ruled—the word is not too strong—by an all-powerful Catholic Church with the connivance of politicians and, indeed, the populace as a whole, with some honorable exceptions. The doctrine of original sin was ingrained in us from our earliest years, and we borrowed from Protestantism the concepts of the elect and the unelect. If children were sent to orphanages, industrial schools and reformatories, it must be because they were destined for it, and must belong there. What happened to them within those unscalable walls was no concern of ours.[9]

This "architecture of containment," as Jim Smith has referred to these institutions, was not just the site for abuse; it was also a site that exploited labor. The ideological divisions and values that this architecture enforced were systematically articulated in conjunction with the economic exploitation of abjected labor. In introducing his history of the Magdalen Laundries, Smith explains:

> In the main, these institutions survived by means of a combination of charitable donations, endowments received through wills and legacies, and the operation of commercial laundries in which the penitent women worked without remuneration. In addition, many sectors of society benefitted from the religious communities' "state service." The governing burden of the British colonial administration was lightened as it increasingly ceded responsibility to the Catholic Church for areas of social welfare including education, healthcare, and institutional provision. Irish society in general, especially the emerging Catholic middle class, strengthened its identity as a nation; its sense of modernization and progress was increasingly vested in notions of moral and social respectability. The religious communities acquired significant social and cultural authority through their charitable work and, in the case of the Magdalen asylums, accumulated financial resources through the operation of commercial and presumably profitable enterprises.[10]

In brief, *The Butcher Boy* and *Breakfast on Pluto* are sociohistorical works that explore the broader postcolonial trajectories of their main characters' lives; the media of representation through which their stories are articulated; and, finally, the forms of political, social, and psychological repression involved in the production of sanitized versions of Irishness in the wake of independence and partition.

The Butcher Boy tells the story of Francie Brady and the loss of his friend Joe Purcell. Their stories are told as a flashback after Francie's extended treatment in a mental institution. The works return to the origins of the story and track the intense friendship of the two boys and the threats—real and imagined—to that emotional bond. While neither the film nor the novel explicitly portrays the friendship through acts of open eroticism, both, as we will see, conjugate the value and affect of the friendship through a queer idiom. Francie comes to see local snob housewife, Mrs. Nugent, who has recently returned from living in England, as the main threat to Joe, his family, and himself. In a frenzy of increasingly acute psychosis, Francie brutally murders Mrs. Nugent and butchers her body. Circulating behind and through the showdown between Francie and Mrs. Nugent is a cacophony of social and personal antagonisms: violent marital abuse, alcoholism, class hostilities, orphanage workhouses, neocolonial politics, threats to sanity, the Cuban Missile Crisis, pop-culture representations of cowboys and Indians and the Mafia, and space aliens threatening to invade the planet Earth. Francie functions as a touchstone for a series of abjected forms of identity, expression, and labor in the postindependence society in which the story unfolds. While Francie's actions are clearly understood as beyond the pale of acceptable behavior, the abuse that he both experiences himself and inflicts on those around him brings to light the pathologies of an entire brutalized society.

Breakfast on Pluto shares the story of Patrick "Pussy" ("Kitten") Braden as she investigates the mystery of her origins and weaves her personal story with the broader political and psychic struggles to resolve the partition of the island. The details of Patrick's story point to the compromises of Irish history and the exploitative power relations that were their legacy: her mother, Eileen Bergan, was raped by the local parish priest and then sent away to England after the birth of her son.[11] The film ultimately diverges from the novel and suggests that while the relationship between Kitten's parents was romantically and socially impossible, there never was a rape. In both versions, Patrick is abandoned to the care of a local woman, Ma Braden, who receives monthly sums from the priest for her child-rearing services. Patrick flees the village and moves to London, where she works as a prostitute (and a number of other odd jobs) and is eventually implicated as a participant in an IRA bombing of a nightclub frequented by British soldiers. Her narration of the events is fantastical, delusional, playful, hopeful, emotional, psychotic, hilarious, subversive, cheeky, critical, and on the whole not to be taken as a realistic account. In the novel, the narration is directly tied to her time in psychiatric care. The film version explores Kitten's incarceration in police custody but does not tie her narration to psychological therapy. In the film version, many issues left unresolved in the novel are resolved, and the film traces a longer journey to what might be thought of as a stable and productive state—a productivity invoked as Kitten, in full drag, wheels a baby in a stroller in the opening sequence and narrates her life story to the baby.[12] The queer figuration of maternal and feminine productivity stands as a visual synecdoche for the full force of cinematic, narrative, musical, and affective productivity that the film sets in motion. Kitten and her friends index a whole tribe of outcast positions in the social structures of the small southern border town, in the British-controlled North, and in England. In one scene, the fabulous foursome, dressed all out in the explosive androgyny of 1970s glam rock—Kitten (Pussy), Charlie (played by Ethiopian-Irish actress Ruth Negga), Lawrence (fan of *Celebrity Squares* and child with Down syndrome), and Irwin (frustrated young Republican)—are barred entrance from a town dance only to be picked up by the Border Knights, a wild motorcycle gang of philosophical, pot-smoking, astral, pansexual, hippie druids. While the foursome see themselves as members of the town, in this sequence, the doormen certainly don't, and their rejection unites the misfits with the broader forces of the counterculture.

More violent than the social rejection experienced in the village is the military repression of the British state. Representatives of the state aggressively deride Patrick: at a border crossing in the film, where Kitten meows her name, "Paddy Kitten," to a soldier, who replies, "Yeah, you are a Paddy"; in the language used and beatings by the British authorities, who refer to her as "'a facking cow!'" and "'Irish bitch!'" (142); in the authorities' insistence on her cleansing her story of its queer elements, that is, insisting that she hammer her verbal playfulness into a confession. Both film and novel, disturbingly, at different moments, represent Patrick's collusion with this abjection—she comes to love Terence the psychiatrist, who asks her to write her story out (in the novel), and she begs the cops (in the film) to keep her in detention because it offers a security she seems to find nowhere else.[13] As troubling as the adoration of Terence and the desire to remain in police custody are, both versions of *Breakfast on Pluto* represent a main character who articulates herself beyond the violent cycle of reprisals that were characteristic of the Troubles. The works do not take up an exclusively partisan line of critique, nor do they cleanse history of its violent political realities. Instead, the strength of both the film and the novel is that Patrick is offered as a character in search of some kind of alternative way of being, an interrogative and not a dogmatic character, a character who must face the violence that erupts in her life and yet go on living. As Pussy herself asks:

> But will it all be so easy for him, this fragile, flamboyant self-styled emissary, or shall he prove nothing more than another false prophet, ending his days in a backstreet apartment, sucking his thumb and dreaming of Mama, a silly old hopeless Norman

Bates of history? Or will he triumph, making it against all the odds through the gauntlet of misfits, dodgy politicians, errant priests, psychos and sad old lovers that is his world, laying his head beneath a flower-bordered print that bears the words at last: "You're home"? (xi)

Patrick's story is therefore staged as a complex personal engagement with a complex social history. Neither version shies away from representing IRA and UVF violence. It is clear that Patrick comes from the social milieu in which the IRA finds its support—Irwin is a recruit, for instance, and the IRA soldiers refuse to shoot Patrick because she knows Irwin. Patrick herself seems opposed to all these manifestations of violence and operates as a lens through which to work through historical violence that has already occurred. Patrick brings into focus the violence of the British state, the violence of military resistance against occupation, and the violence associated with the production of normative and sanitized versions of identity. She is, as Neil Jordan says in the commentary that accompanies the DVD of the film, both an intensely "naive" and "brave" character.[14] In discussing Jordan's film *Michael Collins*, Marcia Landy offers a description that applies equally well to *Breakfast on Pluto*, claiming, "Certainly the film works heroically to banish many myths and perhaps to create some new ones along the way."[15]

Perhaps a more apropos cinematic reference than Norman Bates is a different kind of film: Charlie Chaplin's *Modern Times*. Like Patrick, the Tramp from *Modern Times* faces the violence of capitalized modernity, becomes obliquely involved in political agitation, finds himself incarcerated and begs to remain so, looks for love in the most cliché expressions, and ultimate seeks a certain kind of happiness dubbed "home." In the film version of *Breakfast on Pluto*, Kitten even refers to herself as a "gamine," which is the name of the female lead in *Modern Times*. Finally, in both *Modern Times* and *Breakfast on Pluto* the main characters, as they work within the historical structures in which they find themselves, produce forms of affect that exceed the inscriptive forces of those structures. Following Matthew Tinkcom, we can think of the signature of this excess as a kind of camp, insofar as "camp forms a philosophy of how one can and cannot (or must and must not) participate in the labor of humans to produce the world for themselves, famously under conditions not of their own making."[16]

The chapter focuses on specific forms of what I term "queer labor." Despite the different contexts and very different stories, the main characters of these works engage the world around them specifically through forms of labor. To invoke *Project Runway*'s Tim Gunn, as best they can, they *make it work*. Francie takes on the housework—and housecoat!—of his deceased mother; he is sent to a Church-run work school; he takes on the eponymous role of butcher boy; and, in the jargon of psychology, he must also "work through" the motivation and consequences of his actions. Pussy starts the section "When I Was a High-Class Escort Girl," which opens the novel, by explaining that she's "afraid [she doesn't] get too many clients these days!" The novel then proceeds to track the series of jobs that she undertakes in order to fashion herself and her world—singer, escort, writer, and even the labors of motherhood. The film version, as I have already suggested, invokes forms of labor in its opening sequence, in which Kitten, wheeling Charlie's baby in a stroller, passes by a construction site of Irish workers in London. The workers catcall: "How's about you, darlin'? What's the chance of a bit tonight then?" To which Kitten responds: "Why yes! Of course, boys! I'll leave the door open tonight and you can all troop in and give me a jab! Why not?" The confusion on the workers' faces, as these two modalities of Irish labor recognize and misrecognize each other, opens the narrative space in which Kitten proceeds to tell her story. The films and novels all represent various traditional forms of labor, and furthermore, as I have begun to suggest, they also examine the more abstract labor involved in various processes of representation, specifically the new kinds of social labor organized in cinema, popular music, and television. The careful attention to popular culture does not just record a passive history of consumption, a history of tastes and fads, movie stars and chart-topping hits. These narratives reveal the productive powers of consumption that create and re-create the historical imaginaries of the texts as well as the history within which the texts circulate for the readers and viewers.

Figure 5.1. Work

McCabe and Jordan explore the productive power of consumption as a particularly queer activity. In *The Butcher Boy*, cinema and television offer Francie and Joe a vehicle for the expression of a queer connection to each other that is unspeakable through other cultural idioms or technical media. In *Breakfast on Pluto*, Patrick's drag re-presentation of popular culture is manifestly queer both in its expression of alternative gender and sexual identities and in its power of super-adequation, its power to produce new values through its employment of the mechanisms of popular representation. The engagement with particular media shows that these forms of abstract and collective affective labor are conjugated through specific representational mechanics. To address the specific forms of queer labor in these works, I divide the remains of this chapter into two sections: "Queer TV" and "Queer Cinema." The first section thinks through queer televisual labor in *The Butcher Boy*, and the second examines queer modalities of cinematic labor in *Breakfast on Pluto*.

This chapter represents an important development in the historical argument of *The Poor Bugger's Tool*. The opening chapters of the study all explore various productions of excess value. The final two chapters consider, in addition to forms of excess, modalities for engaging that excess through alternative forms of labor. Examining queer labor through its specific articulations, we will be able to answer the question "What does queer labor do?" The general response to this question suggests four things:

1. Queer labor produces and circulates forms of value: economic, cultural, political, ethical, and psychic. As I argued in the book's introduction, critical work influenced by Michel Foucault has done much to explore the productive nature of queer sexuality but has not done as thorough a job of tracing that production as it circulates within and against capitalist economy. Queer labor as a critical lever in this chapter brings into focus the productive forces of queer sexuality as well as their intersection and circulation both with and against other forms of value.

2. Queer labor is historical. Queer labor both produces and circulates relations between the past and the present. Bringing history within the realm of human activity, the concept of queer labor will enable us to examine how the characters and texts act, as Marx says, to create history but not in conditions of their own choosing nor with the outcomes they might wish for.

3. Queer labor reveals the social distribution of contemporary power relations. By revealing the politics of access, distribution, exploitation, and production, the queer labor of these works enable us to trace a complex picture of the power struggles both within the imaginaries of the texts and within the historical situation in which the texts circulate.

4. Queer labor opens the historical lines along which the autopoesis of both the individual and the collective becomes possible in these works. Queer labor emerges as a vital and philosophical creativity through which the past, present, and future come into being as activity, thought, and life.

Before examining our specific modalities of queer labor we need a brief introduction to the "social fantastic" imaginary of these works, which share a sense of historical disjunction. The queer labor practices undertaken by the characters and the works themselves emerge as complex responses to this elemental disjunction. To set the stage for our critique, we need first to follow the incredible Francie Brady through—

THE WASTES OF SPACE AND TIME!

In both the novel and the film, as Francie is wheeled away for a round of electroconvulsive therapy in his first stint in psychiatric care, he shouts gleefully that he is "off to travel through the wastes of space and time!"[17] Francie's invocation of the phrase is an instance of his playful adoption of the language and sensibilities of popular culture, in this case science fiction movies, to interpret the world around him and to guide his own actions. On closer consideration, and on a more serious note, the sci-fi cliché appears as an entirely apt way to describe the worlds of *The Butcher Boy* and *Breakfast on Pluto*. Both works introduce imaginaries in which the sense of space and time has been severely disrupted, disoriented, and disconnected.

The novel *The Butcher Boy* opens with an adult Francie recalling a key place from his childhood:

> When I was a young lad twenty or thirty or forty years ago I lived in a small town where they were all after me on account of what I done on Mrs. Nugent. I was hiding out by the river in a hole under a tangle of briars. It was a hide me and Joe made. Death to all dogs who enter here, we said. Except us, of course.
>
> You could see plenty from the inside but no one could see you. Weeds and driftwood and everything floating downstream under the dark archway of the bridge. Sailing away to Timbuctoo. Good luck now weeds, I said. (1)

Leaving aside for now the temporal complexities of this passage, we can note that the hide is positioned as a very queer place. It is a strangely liminal space: it is down by the river that flows near the small town in Ireland but is also the next stop on the way to Timbuctoo. While it has a specific location "in a hole under a tangle of briars," it is invisible, a secret location, off the map, known only to Francie and Joe. It is a location suspected but unknown by the townsfolk hunting Francie down. Despite its obscurity for the people of the town, it is a panoptic place for the boys, who are able to see out and to contemplate the panorama of village life and the complexities of their situations.

As we will see later in the section titled "Queer TV," this social organization of knowledge and visuality that characterizes the hide is deeply marked by television's transformation of social space. While the hide takes its place in the particular story and memory of Francie, it is further situated on a literary map as the language of the passage recalls the feelings and landscape of Mark Twain's *Adventures of Huckleberry Finn*; the opening scene of Joseph Conrad's *Heart of Darkness*, in which the Thames rolls darkly into the inhuman world of empire; and finally the schoolboys from James Joyce's "An Encounter," who also play at cowboys and Indians. Spatial liminality is likewise invoked in the opening sequence of the film. The voice-over of an adult Francie recalls the same temporal disjunction as in the novel: "When I was a young lad twenty or thirty or forty years ago I lived in a small town where they were all after me on account of what I done on Mrs. Nugent." The shots show Francie and Joe on opposing mountain precipices with a lake in the distance. The two Irish schoolboys are dressed with Native American face paint and feather headdresses. They call out to each other in the cliché war cries of TV westerns. The war whoops echo and bring into relief the depth and textures of the mountainous landscape. The playful invocation of the American West brings to the foreground the equally imaginative framing of the Irish landscape—after all, the Irish scene looks nothing like the American West. The shots of the mountains recall the cinematic Ireland produced in the lush images of John Ford's *Quiet Man* and the nostalgic Ireland in the postcard images of John Hinde. The scene in this sense does not document the make-believe play of boys in a realistic or natural setting so much as it frames the interplay of multiple stylized visual aesthetics. In the novel and the film, the voice(-over) of the adult Francie also points to a spatial disjunction—after all, in scenes with such a rich spatial sensibility, from where exactly does Francie's adult voice emanate?[18]

Spatial dislocations radiate, intensify, and repeat.[19] The fantastical world of pop culture increasingly saturates Francie's sense of space, and it becomes progressively unclear what space Francie thinks he occupies. With the Cuban Missile Crisis on TV and sightings of the Virgin Mary, the town becomes a manically apocalyptic site awaiting the manifestation of Our Lady and/or nuclear holocaust. While these spatial disruptions are variously playful, violent, psychotic, religious, and paranoid, the novel and film also suggest that they have historical dimensions. The fantastical threats to the sense of space, after all, have their historical analogues: the United States and the Soviet Union were engaged in a battle for world hegemony; British imperialism had wiped away a longer memory from the island in its decimation of Gaelic culture and language, a sense of loss suggested in Francie's misrecognition of the street signs and statues in Dublin; and, finally, emigration had historically made *home* a painfully vexed notion for generations of Irish people.

The novel *Breakfast on Pluto* opens with a similar sense of spatial disjunction (we again leave aside the temporal complexity for the moment). The title invites us to take breakfast on another planet, and the "Prelude" traces a long history of spatial disruption:

> *The war begins, Battle of the Boyne,*
>> *Ireland, July 1690*
>
>> William of Orange, with an army of some thirty-six thousand men, including English, Scots, Danes, Germans, and Huguenots, met James the Second with an army mainly of French and Irish, numbering about twenty-five thousand. Despite the gallantry of the Irish cavalry, James was put to flight and William was triumphant.
>
>> *March 1955; Two hundred and sixty-five years later.*
>
>> Into the village of Tyreelin (pop. 1500) on the southern side of the Irish border, a young boy is born.
>
>> Approximately one mile from there is a place that looks mysteriously like his yet is a separate state, its terrain zigzagged with roads that seem to go everywhere and nowhere at all, across which cattle and bombs and butter and guns seem to travel with dizzying and bewildering rapidity. Customs officials daily have their status reduced to that of Keystone Kops when their huts are not being blown sky high, that is. Conspiracies seem to thread the most innocuous conversations. (ix)

Spatial disruptions are part of both the island's long history and its contemporary reality.[20] McCabe has said that the novel is "about politics and borders and gender borders."[21] Vexing and disruptive figurations of borders run throughout the novel and the film: the political border between the north and south of the island; the border traversed by emigration to England; the international borders seemingly dissolved by the circulation of pop culture, such that the musical *South Pacific* is more of a personal touchstone for Patrick than the Battle of the Boyne; metaphoric borders of gender and sexual identity; the temporal border invoked by the Border Knights ("that border that runs between where you've just been and where you're going"); what we might call the technological border of the camera as the free movement of the film's aerial shots—figured playfully at certain moments by red-breasted robins—traverse with absolute ease the spaces within which particular characters find themselves so painfully entrenched; and, finally, that historical border that runs between the conditions of the world in which Patrick finds herself and the world that through her queer labors she struggles to create.

The works are also temporally queer. In *The Butcher Boy* (both novel and film), individual and collective trauma is largely experienced in temporal terms.[22] The intimate consideration of trauma's relationship to time is one feature that opens the novel particularly well to cinematic rendition. Two polarized examples: time can be marked by either repetition or absolution, a time that has been morbidly fixed or a time that has been set free and transformed into the eternal. Francie's mother experiences her psychiatric breakdown and violent marriage temporally as endless repetition. Francie describes his mother's initial visit to psychiatric care in the novel in temporal terms: "Right, I says, I'll just stay here and watch the telly and off she [Ma] went I didn't notice the time passing until I heard Mrs Connolly at the door with da and some other women she said ma'd been standing for two hours looking in the window of the fishing tackle shop with the bag on the ground and a tin of beans rolling round the footpath" (8). The film stages the morbid repetition of the mother's condition in the fantastic mania of the Christmas party sequence, in which she fills the house with sweets to celebrate Uncle Alo's return. She plays the *Butcher Boy* song continuously on an old phonograph. Her movements mimic the spin of a broken record as she beats batter and whirls platters of cakes around the house. During the party itself, the toasted and monumentalized memories of courtship and honeymoon, of emigration and success, of love and home, all clash with the lived reality of daily ignominies.

There is, on the other hand, a kind of transcendental or planetary time in the novel and the film, a time that escapes the quotidian degradation and violence that mars the characters' lives. Take, for example, the opening of the novel as Francie describes his time in the hide:

> Then I stuck my nose out to see what was going on. Plink—rain if you don't mind!
>
> But I wasn't complaining. I liked rain. The hiss of the water and the earth so soft bright green plants would nearly sprout beside you. This is the life I said. I sat there staring at a waterdrop on the end of a leaf. It couldn't make up its mind whether it wanted to fall or not. It didn't matter—I was in no hurry. Take your time drop, I said—we've got all the time we want now.
>
> We've got all the time in the world. (1–2)

Unlike the time of repetition that is haunted by guilt and violence and is trapped in the reprisal of particular sequences, this planetary time, *all the time in the world*, has been absolved. Keeping with the religious connotations of the term, this is an absolute time, forgiven its connections to particular events; it has, at least conceptually, achieved perfection. This absolute time is an important motif in both the novel and the film, anchoring the characters' sense of hope in a brutalized world. So in the novel Francie is able to say absolutely of his time with Joe that "they were the best days" (97). Similarly, Francie's mother says of Francie that *he will never let her down* (5). In the film version, Sinéad O'Connor playing the Virgin Mary invokes the eternal quality of Joe's friendship as well as God's love.

Breakfast on Pluto likewise presents an imaginary in which time is out of joint. Patrick's journey toward selfhood in both the film and the novel also investigates the temporal aspects of trauma, *troubled times*, both personal and national. She returns again and again to the rape of her mother by the parish priest (her "father"). She disrupts the temporal logic of the rape, a logic that would set the event in a sequence of assault, violence, trauma, memory, and either revenge or justice, by narrating the event through the images and themes of popular culture. An entirely different temporal affect emerges. Take, for example, the cinematic representation acted by Liam Neeson as the priest and Eva Birthistle as Patrick's mother, Eily Bergen. The scene adopts the perspective of the mother, who looks like the glamorous 1950s star Mitzi Gaynor. While it is clear that the priest rapes her in the scene, and it is clear that the rape and its aftermath have an intensely traumatic effect on Patrick, the rendition of the event follows the bubble-gum logic and tone of 1950s Hollywood culture: Eily is dressed as "any priest's drudge" in a uniform of blue housecoat, hairnet, and stockings "the color of stale tea," so as to, as she admonishes with wagging finger, keep any priest's naughty "dicky doodle peepsters" in his black serge pants. The rape is clearly traumatic for both Eily and Patrick in the scene. But the rendition of the event in the camp terms of popular culture disrupts the temporal power of the trauma. It suddenly, because of the humor, becomes something that Patrick can contemplate without a complete breakdown. Patrick's investment in the images also gives a kind of power—in a scene in which female power is so violently assaulted, to emphasize the irresistibility of the perfume and the bubble-cut curls, and the resemblance to film star Mitzi Gaynor, certainly ironically invokes the irresistible appeals of commodity culture but also suggests a power to which Patrick, who is also sporting fabulous curls, has access. Finally, Patrick's rendition of the scene disrupts acceptable historical notions of Ireland and Irish creativity. The schoolteacher giving the assignment, a cameo part played by McCabe himself in the film, suggests that the students are invited to write about anything: *I was Dracula's girlfriend, I fought in 1916,* and so on. However, to invoke actual local historical trauma, even in the camp manner that Patrick does, violates this seemingly open invitation.

Like *The Butcher Boy*, both versions of *Breakfast on Pluto* also present idealized temporal moments, moments that seem to transcend the violence of cause and effect that beset sequential time. Consider, for example, the fantasy of motherhood that Pussy concocts while reading old copies of the gossip magazine *Loving, True Confessions*:

> If If somehow I did get a vagina, one thing I was certain of, and I didn't care who it was with, was that I wanted at least ten of a family. . . . You can just imagine it, lying there on your deathbed, the cancer of whatever it is, literally rampaging through you, and, from every corner of the world, in aeroplanes, ships, long-distance trains, all the children for whom, through thick and thin, you have broken your back, together now braving the elements, withdrawing savings, fighting bitterly with employers, simply in order to be by your side. And there you are with your lank and tired hair, a few bad teeth perhaps but behind your eyes, that thing they know, and always have, which through this life sustained them, the thing we all call love. "Always you used to say to us, Mammy," they'd say, "like tooth and nail together fight but outside stick together! Do you remember that, Mammy?" And would I remember it?
>
> My eyelids closing in a gesture of recognition—a small smile playing upon my lips.

Certainly, as she herself admits, a major aspect of this fantasy is about Pussy's desire to have a vagina and to produce for herself the kind of family and home which circumstance has denied her. Nonetheless, an important aspect of this melodramatic daydream is related to the organization of time: the fantasy is first fashioned during a moment of leisurely consumption, and the details of the vision pit a temporally transcendent value—motherly love—against the temporal contingencies of disease, death, travel, employment, and sibling relations. Just as in the expressions of absolute or absolved time in *The Butcher Boy*, this temporally transcendent love is cast as an antidote to the violence and trauma of lived historical reality: "And as my eyelids closed and the first tears pressed their way into the world, I'd clasp each hand and say goodbye, to each adieu bid, safe in the knowledge that baby one and baby two, right up to baby ten, had all their lives been given it, and to the very end received it, that wonderful thing called love" (41).[23]

Fittingly, this last example of the production of a temporally transcendent affect is framed in the language of organic reproduction: the *labor* of affect as "the first tears pressed their way into the world." Why is this pun on maternal labor fitting? Because the characters of both *The Butcher Boy* and *Breakfast on Pluto* respond to the complexity of their respective historical situations—the wastes of space and time that we have just sketched—through queer forms of labor. Both Francie and Patrick work to bring some coherence of thought, activity, and life to the chaotic worlds in which they find themselves. The queer geographies and temporalities that we have traced that shuttle between the historical and the fantastical, the personal and the national, the local and the global, and the momentary and the eternal, set the stage for the queer cinematic and televisual work that the characters undertake. We now can turn to the specific forms of queer labor through which Francie and Patrick attempt to reshape their world.

QUEER TV

In his final act of psychotic housework, after murdering Mrs. Nugent and escaping from police custody, Francie sets out to burn the entire contents of the abandoned Brady home:

> What's this ma used to say? I've so much tidying to do I don't know where to start. . . . Everywhere you looked there was dog poo! In the corners, smeared on the walls. I gathered as much of it as I could and put it in a big pile in the middle of the kitchen. . . . There was a heap of clothes lying in the corner. A handful of earwigs fell out of the pocket of Al Capone's coat. There was skirts and odd shoes and sorts of things. I threw them all on. Then I went out to the scullery and got plates and knives and any other things that were lying around. I wiped my hands. Dear oh dear this is hard work I said. And I haven't even touched the upstairs yet! . . . Then the Sacred Heart with his two fingers up and the thorny heart burning outside his chest. Do you remember all the prayers we used to say in the old days Francie? He says. Oh now Sacred heart I says, will I ever forget them? May the curse of Christ light upon you this night you rotten cunting bitch—do you remember that one? . . . I do, He says, raising his eyes to heaven, then off he goes what about this I says John F. Kennedy the man himself. What about me says Pope John the twenty third do I have to be dumped too? I'm sorry Holy Father I have to or else I'll get into trouble with the rest so on you go it'll not be long now. I had a hard job carrying the telly over I wanted it on the top but I managed it. The guts was still hanging out of it, wires and bulbs all over the place. (206–7)

In the novel, Francie selects the *Butcher Boy* record, which obsessed his mother before her suicide, to accompany the inferno. In the film, the trumpet song from the TV show *The Lone Ranger* scores the scene. In both, Francie tops off the pile of shattered domestic memories with the defunct television set. However, the television is not simply another item added to the pile of waste. The passage suggests that, even dismantled and disemboweled, television projects a transformative power in the scene. After all, despite the destruction of this particular set, the abstract power of television still inflects Francie and his actions. It may no longer transmit images of the world, but it still produces the world as image: Francie functions in this passage not as the distinctly human agent asserting himself over the world of things but as himself a particular kind of image interacting in particular ways with other images.[24] Francie, who acts through the image of his mother, sets upon the "props" or images of domesticity that have turned to waste with the failure of the household. He speaks openly with the other images, and they respond. All along he addresses the absent studio audience projected through the staging of his language. Francie is produced as image through the complex televisual organization of social labor that the novel explores. While on the one hand Francie experiences this new world of images as part of a psychotic episode, on the other hand readers and viewers confront the scene as fully congruent with the world of mediated images that has become the norm but was only beginning to take a technological foothold at the projected time of Francie's story in the early 1960s. From a contemporary perspective, given our saturation by new media, one need not be psychotic to think that mediated images are demanding live interaction, because frequently they are.

Television—that machine that sits squarely in the living room yet transcends any particular apparatus in its abstract coordination of energy, images, desire, and social time—is a key object of thought and reflection for *The Butcher Boy*.[25] Both novel and film present images of television and explore how the images on television have transformed the social and historical landscape. To begin with, the television has replaced the hearth as the organizing icon of domestic labor in the novel: "There wasn't many about they were all having their tea. I could see the grey glow of the tellies in the living rooms" (42). In an early sign of domestic turmoil in the Brady house, the television goes out: "It was all going well until the telly went. Phut! That was that then, a blank grey screen looking back at you. I fiddled with it but all I got was a blizzard of snow so I sat there looking at that in the hope that something would come on but it didn't and there was still nothing when da came home" (9–10). His father, unable to fix it, puts "his boot through it, the glass went everywhere. I'll fix it, he said, I'll fix it good and fucking proper" (10). When Francie takes over domestic duties in the novel and the film, he restores the broken television to its spot in the living room: "When I was cleaning out the coalhouse what did I find only the old television. I put it sitting on the table in the same place it used to be" (120). Television is also a key feature of the Nugent household. When Francie sneaks into the Nugent's during the infamous poo scene, he announces himself in his "telly voice" (68): "Dant-a dan! Welcome to Nugents Mr Francie Brady! Thank you I said, thank you very much. It gives me great pleasure to be here . . ." (56). As he explores the house, he turns on the television:

> I helped myself to some bread and jam and turned on the television. What was there
> only Journey to The Bottom of The Sea, Admiral Nelson and his submarine gang they
> were getting a bad doing off a giant octopus that was hiding inside a cave. . . . He was a
> cute sucker sending out these big curling tentacles with suckers on them knocking the
> sub against rocks upside down and everything. . . . *Kill the bastard!* I shouted, I was
> getting excited too, *harpoon him that'll shut him up!* (57–58)

Television inflects Francie's defecation scene both as he continues to
address a virtual studio audience and, in the novel, as the description of
the shit itself, "a big one, shaped like a submarine" (62), recalls Captain
Nelson's ship.

Television is not just an inert content of the novel or film or a newfan-
gled apparatus introduced to the town—it is a machine that transforms the
world it represents. The broad power of transformation is suggested when
Francie visits the shop of Mickey Traynor, the "holy telly man" (10), who
sells TV sets and religious images:

> I went to Mickey Traynor's shop. There was a big picture of Our Lord hanging on the
> wall. It said: *Buy a television or else you bastard!* No it didn't it said Our Savior looks after
> us all. . . . Well Mickey I said will you ever forget the days of the old television? He stuck
> his pencil behind his ear what television would that be now he says. . . . I don't remember
> your da coming in at all now he says and goes back to his work, poking away at the inside
> of another telly. Without the back on it looked like one of these cities of the future you'd
> see in Dan Dare. (100–110)

The passage suggests two things: First, television represents a transformation in visuality; it has usurped older regimes of the image, indexed here by
religious iconography. Television is the highest development of a world of
capitalized consumption organized around the image. As a disseminator of
capitalized images, television both commands the vision of the viewer-
consumer and projects its productive trajectories of visuality and vision
outward. Second, television both represents aspects of society on its screen
and has in a sense absorbed the whole of modern society. With its production of proximity and distance, live transmissions and recorded loops, and
its electric broadcast grid, television presents a new organization of social
relations, the city of the future that is already present.

In this light, Francie's snorted admonition to Phillip Nugent as they
wrestle in the broken glass of Mrs. Nugent's wedding photo, "Watch yourself with the glass" (55), not only iterates menace but indexes a new social
order of the image. Indeed, from the opening scene in the hide, the novel
suggests a queer kind of social visuality that is markedly televisual. Take, for
example, the many references to polish throughout the novel. In these

references we see the articulation of a feminized domestic labor and the
general extension of the televisual: when Francie first breaks into the
Nugent house, he remarks: "Polish too there was plenty of that. Mrs.
Nugent polished everything till you could see your face in it. The kitchen
table, the floor. You name it if you looked at it you were in it. You had to
hand it to Mrs Nugent when it came to the polishing" (57). When going
through Phillip Nugent's clothes, Francie finds

> a pair of grey trousers with a razor crease and black polished shoes could you see your
> face in them you certainly could. I thought to myself, this could be a good laugh and so
> I put it on. I looked at myself in the mirror. I say Frawncus would you be a good sport
> and wun down to the tuck shop for meah pleath? I did a twirl and said abtholootely
> old boy. I say boy what is your name pleath? Oo, I said, my name is Philip Nuahgent!
> (59)

Fr. "Bubble" at the reform school is described as polished: "I never saw
such a bright white polished head as that old Father Bubble had" (66).
When Francie's father visits him in the school, the room "smells of wax polish" (83). When Francie returns from the school, as he tries to explain to
Joe the abuse he has experienced, he recalls "the old days and hacking at
the ice and whose turn it was to toss the marble and all that, that was what
I wanted to talk about. They were the best days. You could see through
them days, clear as polished glass" (97). When Francie gets Joe to relive the
old days with him,

> . . . he said OK it was the best day yet you'd think Nugents or the school for pigs or Tiddly
> and all that had never happened. We spun stones across the lake and when I looked at
> Joe doing that I nearly wanted to cry the feeling I got was so good. Everything was so
> clear and glittering and polished I said to myself: Those days in the lane. We didn't
> imagine them. They were just like this. (109)

When Francie returns from the psychiatric hospital and sets the Brady
house in order he explains: "I walked around the house I don't know how
many times I liked the smell of the polish that much. Flowers and everything on the mantelpiece. I could see my face in the sink too" (158).

In all of these examples, the intensification of domestic labor, figured
in the associatively feminine work of polishing, produces an idealized
image of the home, and more than that, it produces the self as an image
primus inter pares. The human is produced here not as absolutely distinct from the world of images but as sharing the same substance. The
power of television to represent everything on its screen has in a sense
been externalized and generalized in the novel as everything becomes

televisual. The televised world of things addresses Francie and shows him to himself as image. We see this transformation of substance into the extension of images in a variety of contexts in the novel. The sky, for example, is transformed:

> I left the town for behind me and came out onto the open road. The white clouds floated across the clear blue glass of the sky. I kept thinking of da and Alo standing outside the gates of the home all those years ago. How many windows do you think are there says da. Seventy-five says Alo. I'd say at least a hundred says da. (36)

Francie's body and physical objects are transformed: "But if you listened carefully you could still hear the song. Down By The Salley Gardens that was what it was called. I wanted to sit there until all trace of it was gone. It was like I was floating inside the colored shaft of evening sunlight that was streaming through the window" (40). "The marble rolled along the hard clay in a trail of light" (70). "I was glowing with all this excitement" (141), Francie exclaims while robbing the bakery. The distinction between the world and the world as it appears on TV is jammed. This jammed signal does not suggest the dissolution of the material world in the light of the televisual so much as it suggests the productive materiality broadcast by the visual regime of TV.

Even sites of organic reproduction are restructured along the lines of the televisual, so the descriptions of the chickenhouse also read as descriptions of television's mechanics:

> I closed my eyes and breathed in it was like breathing in the whole cold fresh and crunchy town. I could hear the chickenhouse fan droning away steady as ever down in our lane behind the houses. One day Joe said to me: It's the best sound in the world, that fan. I said why. He said because you always know its there. And he was right. If you weren't thinking of it you wouldn't hear it. But once you listened, it was always there humming away softly like a quiet machine that kept the town going. (104)

> I climbed in the back of the chickenhouse and just stood in there in that woodchip world listening to the scrabbling of the claws on tin and the fan purring away keeping the town going. When we were in there me and Joe used to think: Nothing can ever go wrong. But it wasn't like that anymore. (131)

> I slept for a while in the chickenhouse a thousand eyes wondered who's this sleeping in our woodchip world chick chicks I was going to say its me Francie but I was too tired. (167–68)

The electric transmission that recalls the "brr . . . in my head like the noise the telly used to make" (162), the ideological comfort that sets these mechanics at the heart of town life, the collective and abstract organization of visuality and vision—these chick chicks have been as absorbed by the powers of television as thoroughly as Francie and the town.

The world of *The Butcher Boy* has been transformed by television, and this new regime of visuality is repeatedly tied to forms of labor. Engaging this televised world through forms of queer affective labor, Francie productively extends and recirculates televisual images to express, craft, and experience his relationship with Joe. Francie and Joe's desires completely infuse these images and their circulation, combination, deployment, extension, repetition, enjoyment, and consumption. For example, Francie, after returning from the "school for bad bastards," as he tries to rekindle his relationship with Joe, works to reestablish a televisual circuit:

> I always met Joe at the bottom of Church Hill. . . . I got things for him, not comics he didn't read them much any more, fags or sweets maybe. I got the fags from behind the bar in the hotel I knew the barman went out to change the barrel at the same time every day. I got the sweets in Mary's but I paid for them I'd never lift anything on her. Then we'd head out to the river. I told him I could get him anything he wanted. We had some laughs out there. It was no different to the old days. It was just the same only better. Isn't it Joe? I'd say. He said it was. I says its better than the school and exams and all that shite isn't it Joe. I'd ask him to put on the cowboy voices like he used to. He said he couldn't do them anymore. Go on, try Joe I said. I can't do them he said, that's a long time ago. I know it is Joe I said but I'll bet you can still do them. No, he says I can't. But I knew he could. Try it Joe I says. Then he said it—OK fellas we're ridin' out!
>
> You see Joe, I said, you can do it!
>
> It was just like John Wayne. You'd swear it was him. I was over the moon when he did that voice. He used to spin his silver colt and say it just like that—OK fellas we're ridin' out! Say it again Joe I said, say it again! I couldn't stop asking him to say it again. But I had to in the end for I could see him getting red under the eyes and I didn't want to annoy him anyway he's said it enough he was tired he said he had to get back. I left him in town and then I came back out myself. I'd try doing the voice but I could never get it as good as Joe. I'd lie there on the flattened yellow grass where he had been but no matter how I tried it always got arseways. It didn't sound like John Wayne at all. It sounded more like the bird what do you call him—I taught I taw a puddytat. (108–9)

This passage displays the queer televisual circuitry through which Francie and Joe articulate their relationship. As an attentive and loving friend, Francie buys Joe sweets and steals him cigarettes. Away from the pressures of life in the town, they rehearse the language and formulas that express their affection.[26] It is not that these words operate as a cover of a more authentic expression of same-sex desire but that the performance of these visual and sound images is fully congruent with queer desire—as Francie says, he "was over the moon when he did that voice." To act out these scenes is to circulate the desire they articulate; the desire and affect are immanent to the movements of their bodies. In the scenes in the hide, in which the boys find an adolescent respite from the routinized structures of modern work, they produce an alternative set of social values through the reprisal and rehabilitation of TV performances. This rehearsal is both part and parcel of the production of TV audience and creates values, relations, and forms of knowledge not reducible to market metrics.

This particular passage also suggests the social dimension of televisual labor: the production and circulation of these images is collective and not simply individual or esoteric. If the first part of the passage shows the congruent and fluent circulation of the boys' queer desire, the second part suggests the incongruities, the transmission interferences, that alienate the circulation of desire. If queer labor produces value as images, we can also see that the quality of those images will move differentially between the generative and the psychotic. The queer televisual labor in the novel will produce both alternative and progressive social values—for example, in the queer affections of the boys—and psychotic values, newly visualized forms of alienation in alcoholism, suicide, and murder. These two potentials are poignantly displayed by Francie after his emergence from psychiatric care when he returns to work in an attempt to set his relationship with Joe right once again. First Francie attempts to reform his image in order to produce a different version of himself with new psychic and social coordinates:

> Then what did I do only get myself all dressed up there was a white jacket in the window of the drapery shop like what you'd see Cliff Richard wearing and a shirt with one of these bootlace ties. I looked at myself in the mirror. The tie was real John Wayne style but I says there's to be no more about John Wayne or any of that, that's all over. Everything's changed now its all new things. Then I brushed the jacket and headed down to the café. (158)

Even as he resists it—"no more about John Wayne or any of that"—Francie again produces himself as a kind of televisual image.[27] This image of John Wayne that Francie sees as fully congruent with his queer affection for Joe becomes increasingly dissonant, particularly as it encounters other visual expressions of labor:

> I kept thinking I was going to meet Joe or the blondie one or some of them on the street so I didn't want to take the jacket off just in case. Leddy started into me over it—for the love of Christ he says and all this but I says what do you care what I wear all you care

about is me collecting the brock as long as I do that what do you care if I come in in a cowboy hat! Oh for fuck's sake! He says and in the end he just threw the fag into the gutter and says: do it then do what you fucking well like I'm past talking to you God's curse the day I took you in in the first place!

I said: Don't worry, I'll work twice as hard now that I'm back you won't have any complaints about me Mr Leddy!

. . . I worked until the sweat ran out of me. Then when I was finished I'd be away off to see if I could see Joe. . . . There was one thing Leddy was right about and that was I had ruined my good jacket all right for when I was heeling a bin into the cart stew or some stuff went all over me. I was wondering should I go back down and clean it before I went near Joe's for that was what I had decided to do I couldn't stick the empty streets and the waiting any more. Then I thought: What would you want to clean it for—do you think Joe cares if your coat is a bit dirty? What are you talking about Francie—Joe Purcell? He's your friend for God's sake! He's your best friend! (161–62)

The image of John Wayne the queer lover and the image of the butcher boy clash in this passage first because of Leddy's sense that the visual and affective labor of one image detracts from the visual and physical labor of the other. Even as Francie vows to "work twice as hard," it is clear that his labor is alienated as he fights to charge with significance and to circulate images that have been increasingly drained of meaning. Indeed, despite his assertion of Joe's friendship, it is evident that Joe no longer participates in the circulation of these images the same way Francie does. Francie experiences alienation not as he steps into the form of these images but when these images fail to circulate, when they have been stripped of their social value. Consider, for example, Francie's description of his trip to break Joe out of boarding school. Joe fails to respond to Francie's call "Joe! Where are you Joe Boy? I'm here! saddle up! We're riding out!" (187):

Then he said: Do you hear me. What do you want me for? I never thought Joe would ask that I never thought he would *have* to ask that but he did didn't he and when I heard him say it that was when I started to feel myself draining away and I couldn't stop it the more I tried the worse it got I could have floated to the ceiling like a fag paper please Joe come with me that was all I wanted to say dumb people have holes in the pit of their stomachs and that's the way I was now the dumbest person in the whole world who had no words left for anything at all. (189–90)

The queer affective labor that produces Francie as televisual image does not alienate him from an authentic core. There is not an authentic personality opposed to an alienated simulacrum. It is when Joe refuses to complete the queer televisual circuit that labor has been stripped of value and is no longer able to circulate affect and meaning. Joe steps into other visual circuits, inflected by the neocolonial and *arriviste* images of the Nugents. Francie's *breakdown* is at once psychic and technological. The image of Francie, the butcher boy, dressed in a white jacket smeared with grime, sporting a John Wayne tie, captures the hope and the alienation of his queer labors. Driven to work twice as hard to achieve the world he desires, he nonetheless finds himself at that liminal space between life and death, sanity and madness, the human and the animal, food and shit, love and loss, a colonial past and a televised modernity, with only the queer promise of friendship to make sense of it all. Readers and viewers are asked to complete the circuit of this televised modernity by consuming the image of Francie and producing through this consumption their own history.

QUEER CINEMA

While *The Butcher Boy* offers a picture of a brutalized world in which the promise of friendship seems a distant, even if glimpsed, hope, *Breakfast on Pluto* portrays a character who navigates a perilous and violent world and finds in the end some kind of emotional, social, and historical resolution. In the commentary that accompanies the DVD of *Breakfast on Pluto*, Neil Jordan notes that both films move between brutality and comedy but that *Breakfast on Pluto* offers a comedic resolution for the main character, one not achieved in *The Butcher Boy*. Like its precursor, *Breakfast on Pluto* is a film with a sustained interest in representations of labor. While *The Butcher Boy* examines new forms of social labor particularly through the screen of television, *Breakfast on Pluto* emphasizes cinematic modalities of labor. Obviously, these are not mutually exclusive forms. Rather, it is a question of which mode predominates and inflects the actions and accents, the sounds and images, mind-sets and motions, within the world imaginary of the texts. In this final section, I focus on three cinematic sequences in particular: the first tracks Kitten's career in show business, when she becomes a singer for the (fictitious) band Billy Hatchet and the Mohawks (Billy is played by real-life Irish rocker Gavin Friday); the second sequence shows us Kitten's encounter with her father, Fr. Bernard, while working in a neo-Marxist collectivist peep show in London; the third proleptic scene (the film is shot as a retrospective narration) introduces the film and suggests the historical productivity of queer cinematic labor. These scenes reveal Kitten's active involvement with the labor of cinematic representation and how through this involvement she engages the complexity of her historical situation— both personal and national. Kitten's queer sexuality, articulated through a vibrant relation to the cinema, produces forms and expressions of value that critically engage the legacy of colonial antagonisms with the British state and social antagonisms within Irish and English society. Furthermore, this queer aesthetic practice literally brings her history to life in the Nietzschean sense as she glamorously fashions herself and the scintillating possibilities of a whole new world.

Early on in the film, Kitten's flamboyant sexuality and transgressive gender identification are tied to alternative relationships to labor. She is expelled from school because she refuses to stifle her sexuality and insists on expressing it in all of its fabulous energy and dynamic innocence. During a creative writing exercise she writes a short story in which she imagines the rape of her mother by the local parish priest. She asks where she might obtain a good sex change during a schoolwide retreat meant to address the transformations of puberty. She hits on fellow students. She wears makeup and fingernail polish and even announces herself to her classmates as "Miss Kitten" as she is hauled off to the disciplinary office. Along with her alternative sexual orientation comes an alternative relationship to labor. In the decisive creative writing scene, she asks that she be allowed to take home economics and sewing instead of physical education. While in sewing class, she claims to be making outfits for her foster sister, although clearly they are really meant for herself—as she explains to the teacher, "Don't we all need a bit of glamour?" In what Jordan refers to in the DVD commentary as her first decisive moral action in the film, she leaves school, foster family, and her small hamlet and meets up with Billy Hatchet and the Mohawks. Kitten becomes Billy's lover and joins the band as a rock-and-roll "squaw." The sequence is fittingly titled "My Career in Show Biz."

For the "macho" and "deeply homosexual" Billy, Kitten's allure is immediate.[28] As he first questions her, his seductive growl hints at erotic intimacy and invokes the fires of Republican political passion. Kitten's feigned concern about the Troubles in the North entices Billy, who hears sexual and political sympathy in her coy responses. Despite grumbled misgivings, Kitten literally works herself into the band by hand sewing a "squaw" outfit to complement the group's glam-rock Native American image. Billy and Kitten take their love to the stage. The material imaginary of the band—its look, sound, attitude, music, politics, and lifestyle—provides a vehicle for the expression of their homoerotic desires. Beyond this, her performance transforms the social values that the band circulates. The duet sung by Kitten and Billy, "Sand," tells the story of a European stranger wandering in a foreign land who becomes the lover of a young Native American woman. Billy and Kitten sing the lyrics into each other's eyes, gently swaying in front of a packed house at a Republican Prisoner's Welfare Association show. The camera moves through a dance floor full of couples, two-stepping in country-western outfits, and zooms in to focus on Kitten and Billy singing to each other. The band, the only group not coupled, even though on stage, acts as a surrogate audience and expresses a humorous disbelief at Kitten and Billy's affections. The lyrics and the camera draw the viewers into the erotic play of gesture, look, voice, and movement and also reveal the public nature of these intimacies as they are staged at a political benefit concert. This dual nature of the couple that is both intimate and affective as well as public and political is a cinematic concept—one that organizes the camera, sound, gesture, affect, and meaning—that plays through the entire film. (Other examples include Billy and Kitten's slow dance in front of the band's van; the confession scenes between Kitten and Fr. Bernard; Kitten's dance with the British soldier before the bomb goes off in the nightclub; and Kitten's interrogation in the hands—or fists—of the British authorities.) The visuals of the "Sand" performance are twice interrupted: first, with a cut to a roadblock mounted by British soldiers over which the lyrics "I am a stranger in your land" play on the soundtrack. The soldiers insult Kitten— who presents herself as "Paddy Kitten," a name that plays with the charged gender and sexual meanings of imperialist slurs—and Billy, whom they hail as "Geronimo" and who claims himself as "just a Mick." Second, the audience interrupts the performance by throwing beer bottles and booing the band off stage. The queer performance proves too transgressive for certain purified nationalist notions of Irish identity. Kitten's image circulates and critiques multiple forms of alienation and expression, and it is precisely her production of self as image that allows her to do so. She expresses her own sense of alienation as she longs for a world in which she can love and be loved. Her image invokes, even if through a camp idiom, Native American decimation in the face of European aggression. Her image also suggests a link between this Native American history and a history of occupation and domination in Ireland. She emerges as a target for the social violence that occurs in Irish society. Finally, even if it only endures for the length of her performance, she works a rock-and-roll attitude that finds in the look and rhythms of the counterculture a way to express the possibilities of a different world.

Rock bands and film share a long history, and *Breakfast on Pluto* emphasizes that the queer role of band squaw is a cinematic rendition of a rock lifestyle. In a brilliant scene in which Billy must explain that Kitten has to leave the band, we see the transformation of Kitten and Billy into cinematic images. Standing outside the pavilion's canvas wall, the two are caught and projected as silhouettes by a distant light. Still dressed in the glam clichés of Native American garb, Billy breaks it to Kitten that the band wants her out. To ease Kitten's disappointment, Billy explains, "I have a proposal," to which Kitten coos, "Oh, a ring perhaps?" Billy must respond in the negative and leads her out of this cliché—we should think of cliché here both in literal terms of the shot and in figurative terms of meaning and identification—and, in the next scene, into another as he introduces Kitten to the small caravan that he offers as a home. Kitten steps from one cliché imaginary to another: from rock-star squaw cast as a silhouette to campy housewife taking on the duties and dreams of domesticity. She wants to inhabit the affects and idioms of popular culture—Jordan says that she wants to live her life "in the lyrics of a pop song"—yet she introduces a difference, a camp excess, in her reprisal of popular formulas. She produces herself as the complex interplay of multiple images and does not conform or contain herself into any purified or rigidly authentic expression. The labor of sewing and singing produces both an intimate and a public self, charged with emotional and political meaning, just as in the scenes that follow in her shabby caravan, the euphemistic labor of "serious spring cleaning" provides Kitten the ethical energy and determination to throw the stash of guns hidden beneath the floor of her new home into the dead water of the quarry.

In the second sequence, Kitten joins a unionized peep show located on London's famed Old Compton Street in Soho. The scene is framed by the search for a new job: Kitten is picked up by the officer who brutally interrogated her after the club bombing and is brought to work with the group of performers off the street. Jordan explains that the scenario is based on what was an actual unionized peep show, what he playfully refers to as "a neo-Marxist cooperative of strippers." In a series of events that do not take place in the novel, Charlie provides Fr. Bernard with Kitten's address in London. He then travels to London to give Kitten the address of her mother. In a reversal of the previous confessional scenes, in which Kitten enters the confessional box to interrogate the priest about the origins of her birth, Fr.

Figure 5.2. Occupy the cliché

Bernard in this scene pays for a peep show and talks to Kitten through the microphone in his small cubicle.

The onsite location is of particular importance, as the crew filmed in one of the few remaining peep-show clubs in the area. The location is a site of congealed forms of visual labor—and, according to the DVD commentary, a site loaded with traces of other bodily congealment—as well as a socially articulated architecture of desire. These capitalized visual trajectories and architectural spaces arrange viewers in small booths around the performers, who are separated by one-way mirrors. When customers pay, a small door slides open to reveal the sexual performer. The space of the peep show inflects the production of the cinematic image. In front of the camera, the mirrors cease working in a mimetically derivative manner and actually become productive. Jordan explains: "Mirrors are great. You are often presented with something, you know, something you never expected. Whereas if you try to construct an image through mirrors, or in this case a one-way mirror, as a half reflection, if you actually said, 'I want to see this and this,' you'd never find it, you know. . . . It's amazing." The functioning of mirrors has in a sense been turned on its head in this formulation. In looking in mirrors, one typically sees exactly what one expects; mirrors are derivative in that they return an existing image of reality. The peep-show mirrors in this scene, as constructions that congeal the labors of desire, bring to light new images and new realities when activated by the work of the camera.

Kitten and Fr. Braden harness this productivity in the scene as they both become images and use the newfound freedom of this becoming to interrogate the complexities of their shared traumatic history. The visuals and the language of the scene emphasize the "screening" that occurs in the production of identity, aesthetic expression, and forms of knowledge. The characters address each other through the screen of formulaic expression: Kitten blandly steps into what she imagines the customer's fantasy to be. The customer, Fr. Bernard, refusing the cliché of these fantasies, addresses Kitten through a kind of fairy tale, a story that addresses the problems of desire and repression, violation and violence, guilt and redemption, that each of the characters must work through: "Once upon a time, there was a boy who never knew his father and mother. . . ." The audience watches Kitten work with two customers before the camera cuts to an overhead shot that looks down on Fr. Bernard. A bare red light bulb burns at the top of the shot, and to the left of the priest is a microphone. He slips his coins into the slot, and the camera cuts to his point of view and looks to the side window that slides open to reveal Kitten, who, seeing that a new customer has paid, begins to lick her lips. As the camera moves back and forth from each character's point of view, staring intensely into the one-way mirror that separates them, each of the characters is produced and reproduced as a vibrant and dynamic complex of images. In the same way that Kitten and Billy activate and in-habit their silhouettes against the pavilion's canvas, in the peep show con-fessional Kitten and Fr. Braden are transformed, and transform themselves, into cinematic images. The work of these images reveals the distance and proximity, love and betrayal, violence and care that connects the characters. The camera (again) presents for contemplation a couple that organizes an intimate and affective private space and simultaneously points to a broader political and historical context. Kitten's queer labor at the peep show and Fr. Bernard's queer determination to work things out has made this cine-matic thought possible.

One of the most significant differences between the novel and film ver-sions of *Breakfast on Pluto* lies in the fact that in the novel Pussy writes her story as a form of therapy while in psychiatric care, whereas in the film Kitten narrates her tale to Charlie's new infant. The psychiatric storyline is entirely absent from the film. In the novel, it is within the institution of the psychiatric clinic that Pussy *works through* the personal and political violence that has so aggressively marked her life, including the rape of her mother, the murder of Lawrence at the hands of Protestant paramilitaries, the execution of Irwin by the IRA, Silky's attempted strangulation, the bombing in the nightclub, and the violence of incarceration and interro-gation by the British authorities. Long after her doctor, Terence, has left her, Pussy continues to think about the project of writing her life story in relationship to his care: "Maybe one day taking" the time to write it down for Terence, what my fondest wish would be (he asked me to—even though he'll never see it now) . . . (199). As a concluding thought, I would like to suggest that the film replaces the individual articulation of

Figure 5.3. Working through it

psychological care with a public form of queer cinematic labor. Certainly, the novel exposes the social dimensions of Pussy's particular psychological situation. However, the *working through* in the novel is carried on by a different kind of *work* in the film, which is framed by the opening sequence itself. Scored by The Rubettes' version of "Sugar Baby Love," the camera opens to Irish laborers on a work site. The film's story is told in retrospect, so we watch the workers construct a building sequentially before, yet narratively after, the nightclub bombing that occurs later in the film. In a figurative sense, although on first viewing the audience is unaware of it, the workers are putting things back together again. The agents of this material reconstruction directly confront the psychic and organic labor through which Kitten has remade herself and her world. In full drag, strolling Charlie's newborn, playfully taking on the worker's catcalls, and starting the work of the film's narrative, Kitten suggests cinema itself as a kind of reproductive labor. This is perhaps the history lesson: the ample materiality and life of this image, caught in the playful encounter of workers and their work, that opens to the circuitry of the film and its audience.

CHAPTER 6

ⲟⲃⲟ

"Sinn Feiners, me arse. I'm A Socialist, Never doubt about it"

Jamie O'Neill's At Swim, Two Boys *and the Queer Project of Socialism*

The most strongly guaranteed mark of their own stronger health is to be precisely the fact that they, I mean these youth, themselves can use no idea, no party slogan from the presently circulating currency of words and ideas, as a designation of their being, but are convinced only by a power acting in it, a power which fights, eliminates, and cuts into pieces, and by an always heightened sense of life in every good hour.
> —Friedrich Nietzsche, *The Use and Abuse of History for Life*

The mode of being of the new intellectual can no longer consist in eloquence, which is an exterior and momentary mover of feelings and passions, but in active participation in practical life. . . .
> —Antonio Gramsci, *Selections from the Prison Notebooks*

It's at the same level of repressive work as the judge in the Angela Davis case who affirmed: "Her behavior can only be explained by her being in love." And what if, on the contrary, Angela Davis's libido was a social, revolutionary libido? What if she were in love because she was a revolutionary?
> —Gilles Deleuze, "Chaosophy"

"Are we straight so?"
"Aye we're straight," said Jim.
"Straight as a rush, so we are."[1]

When Doyler Doyle asks Jim Mack if they are straight—a question that is a minor motif in Jamie O'Neill's magisterial *At Swim, Two Boys* (2001)—the reader's response, if this reader is caught in the spell of the novel's central romance, is some version of a gleeful, knowing, excited, very queer "No!" The question, from this perspective, is self-evidently ironic, its irony structured by the broad projects of historical recovery that began in the wake of the Stonewall riots of 1969, the specific marketing of the novel as a gay romance set in the events of the 1916 Easter Rising, the sentimental aspects of the narrative code, and the increasingly expressive queer sexuality enjoyed by the principal characters: Doyler, Jim, and Dermot MacMurrough. A problem arises, however, because, as Doyler himself reminds us, from a certain historical standpoint the proper response to the question, despite the irony that structures its contemporary circulation, is in the affirmative.[2] He explains to Jim that the phrase comes from the days of Wolfe Tone and the United Irishmen: "No, you gaum. I mean that's where it comes from. It was their test for to join. Are you straight, they asked. I am says you. How straight so? Straight as a rush. Go on then, say they. In truth, in trust, in unity and liberty, says you. That was the United Irishmen . . ." (195). This positive response to the question, rather than negating alternative sexualities, endorses the Enlightenment political project of Tone and the United Irishmen—truth, trust, unity, and liberty—and their fight against British colonialism and casts the boys' friendship as an extension of that project: "'Well, [the phrase] 'tis ours now. For you and me,' and his arm came over Jim's shoulder, 'aren't we straight as a rush together?'" (196).

Even as the novel itself endorses both a progressive queer politics and Enlightenment Irish republican politics, its reader finds it impossible in this case to articulate an adequate or coherent response to Doyler's query. Indeed, the *proper* response, the response that would endorse both of these political projects, would be both *yes* and *no*: *yes* to the values of Enlightenment progress and the Irish anticolonial struggle and *no* to restrictive normative modes of sexuality. The differential of this incoherent response points from the limits of this specific grammatical conundrum to the limits of the historical conditions that the text both represents and reproduces. What emerges first as a moment of textual catachresis in which the metaphorics of queer sexual identification (*No, they are not straight!*) fail to coincide with the coded political rhetoric of Enlightenment republicanism (*Straight as a rush! In truth, in trust, in unity and liberty*) ultimately reveals in the vexed historical legacy of the Enlightenment project of universal emancipation and reason a moment unable to articulate this promised universality. The reader thus assumes in the contradictory pull of this textual situation the weight of a historical condition of modernity—that of modernity promised but unfulfilled.

Moved by both the ideals of Enlightened freedom and rationality and the politics of sexual liberation, this reader faces a historical situation in the engagement with the text in which the eloquence, as Gramsci might call it, of these revolutionary projects formulates only a fleeting and, as we have seen, ultimately inarticulate reply. This does not mean that the novel is dismissive of these projects. Indeed, Doyler's question and its potential responses are shot through with revolutionary "feelings and passions"—both directly, from references to the 1798 Rebellion, the Paris Commune, and the 1916 Easter Rising, and obliquely, from the broad influence of the 1969 Stonewall riots—whose immediacy and force translate contradictorily into the textual edifice. In other theaters of enunciation, say those of Enlightenment, anticolonial, or sexual revolution, versions of these potential responses—*No, they are not straight!* and *Straight as a rush! In truth, in trust, in unity and liberty*—might operate fluently as calls to action, but here in O'Neill's novel they mark an aporia in the act of reading. The reader's situation is therefore at once literary-critical and politico-historical as it brings into focus the trajectories of revolutionary passions from their violent emergence into history to their inscription and reproduction within the structures of the literary and the social text. The variegated temporalities and the drama of that inscription—which invoke at once the joys of the revolutionary moment, the tragedy of retrenchment and defeat, the weight of memory and nostalgia—run throughout O'Neill's novel and lend it much of its literary force. Thus despite the compelling representations of revolutionary forces, the reader in a sense is still faced with Lenin's famous question—"What is to be done?"—and, perhaps more pointedly, with the vexed legacy of responses to this question.

In interviews, O'Neill has described the historical situation in which he wrote the novel in precisely these revolutionary terms by referring to the lost potential in the politics of modern gay liberation:

> In the late 1960s and '70s, when there was such a thing as the Gay Liberation Front [GLF], I really think it is a shame that they didn't shoot anybody. Because you get people going up in pulpits, or politicians, and they denounce people. I don't mind being denounced myself, because I am older and strong enough to deal with it. But kids listening to this and just coming to terms with their sexuality [are harmed by] being denounced from pulpits and television screens. It costs these people no courage to do that. They're not risking anything. If we'd shot a few people back then when the time was right, when we had a very socialist call to revolution and arms, these people would be a bit more wary of what they're saying.[3]

The terms of description here recall the admonishment of Doyler's superior in the Citizen Army who rebuffs him at one point, saying, "When will you learn, Doyle, that there is such a thing as a revolutionary moment" (423). O'Neill too sees that there is a revolutionary moment, but that this moment—at least in one form—has passed. Henry Abelove has argued that the GLF was not "predicated on a commitment to a supposititiously stable or definite identity. It was rather predicated on a commitment to a worldwide struggle for decolonization and its potential human benefits."[4] O'Neill shares an expanded sense of queer politics.

The novel does not articulate a revolutionary call to arms, then, but does inscribe itself within the wake of the events that responded to that call.[5] This inscription is explicitly literary, as it is not only the complex legacy of these political revolutions that the novel attempts to make its own, but also what Colin MacCabe has called the "revolution of the word" achieved by Irish modernism, most spectacularly in the work of James Joyce. Indeed, the conundrum that we have unpacked in Doyler's question to Jim replays key features, under different guises, of the pivotal scene in which Stephen, on the brink of his flight from Ireland, has a "long talk with Cranly on the subject of [his] revolt" in the final chapter of *The Portrait of the Artist as a Young Man*:

> Cranly, now grave again, slowed his pace and said:
> —Alone, quite alone. You have no fear of that. And you know what that word means? Not only to be separate from all others but to have not even one friend.
> —I will take the risk, said Stephen.
> —And not to have any one person, Cranly said, who would be more than a friend, more even than the noblest and truest friend a man ever had.
> His words seemed to have struck some deep chord in his own nature. Had he spoken of himself, of himself as he was or wished to be? Stephen watched his face for some moments in silence. A cold sadness was there. He had spoken of himself, of his own loneliness which he feared.
> —Of whom are you speaking? Stephen asked at length. Cranly did not answer.[6]

In this talk, the homoerotic both figures the sentimental codes of identification through which the shifting and ambiguously charged pronouns reveal the entangled nature of the boys and their friendship ("His words seem to have struck some deep chord in his own nature") and opens the liberatory revolt of the signifier that will form the basis of Joyce's subsequent textual practice, as Stephen seems to have flown from the nets of identification ("Of whom are you speaking?"). The disjuncture of meaning and expression that marks the language and concept of friendship in this talk, as in O'Neill's novel, marks a productive aporia in the reading of the text. In response to this aporia—represented by Cranly's silence—writing, in this specific case that of Stephen's diary, emerges as praxis. O'Neill's novel will come to terms with its own historical conditions through the products of that praxis, the language of Joycean—and more generally Irish—modernism. Doyler's question situates the reader in relation to the vexed revolutionary legacy of the Enlightenment through the materiality of Joycean language.[7] In this way, O'Neill's reader emerges as a historically engaged intellectual through the active participation in the practical life of the text.

As both the campy invocation of the lost moment of GLF assassinations within the pages of a local gay rag and the engagement with the materials of Joycean literary language suggest, the modality of historical praxis is a central concern for O'Neill. This chapter will examine this practice and argue that the novel opens the possibility of a queer socialist project, a queer practice of value—production, consumption, and redistribution—both on a characterological level (and, by extension, an individual psychic level) and in the dynamics of its own construction (which point to collective forms of sociality beyond the purview of individual consciousness). *At Swim, Two Boys* undertakes the queer aesthetic reproduction and redistribution of both revolutionary political energies and Irish cultural capital within the textual—and social—edifice. The novel does not just represent a recovered historical drama in the events of 1916; it produces and reproduces specific historical conditions through its textual mechanics. Within these textual mechanics, the act of reading emerges as a circuit of value production that reveals contemporary social relations subject to particular struggles for hegemony.

The central struggle, both at the diegetic level of the characters and at the metacritical level of the reader, pits what we might call the institutions of moral abstraction against both politicized materialism (socialism) and forms of organized affect, of queer sentiment. The terms of this political contest are at once sociohistorical and literary-critical. On the one hand, are the forces of the Church, the colonial state, the nation, the family, and the sovereign subject, which seek to interpolate the allegiances and desires of the various characters in terms of abstract values and ideals (a restrictive Christianity, purified nationalism, or normative sexuality). These forces of moral abstraction are clearly targeted by the novel as it attempts to construct alternative forms of collectivity, historical understanding and memory, and aesthetics. On the other hand there are the forms of organized affect in the emerging queer sentiment and culture which the characters construct and with which the reader—as we have already seen—participates. The organization of this queer culture emerges with the practice of a politicized redistribution of the literary and cultural values of Irish modernism. It is not dogmatic and universal forms of abstraction that organize this counterhegemonic queer culture, those abstractions dismissed as "so much foolosophy" by MacMurrough (456), but, instead, what we might call a form of affective labor that reorganizes the social relations that emerge from the text and that the text represents. This materialist textual practice is literally a touching sentiment, a metonymic undertaking, a shared affect, so the touch of this materialism is at once physical and sentimental—touchable and touching, so to speak—and this affective materialism inflects many features of the novel, from the playful textual substitutions, to the physicality of queer love, to swimming in the ocean, to the contemporary affective consumption of the text's historical romance. This *touching materialism* offers an alternative form of the universal or the collective in that it does not organize through idealized abstraction but instead operates through an immanent form of practice in which the "universality of things" (391) is organized by alternative forms of labor. Before we can address this alternative universality, we need to consider the theorizations of history that have thus far characterized the novel's critical reception.

QUEER NATIONALISM AND THE DISCOURSE OF HISTORY

Joseph Valente's analysis of the novel in "Race/Sex/Shame: The Queer Nationalism of *At Swim, Two Boys*" is by all measures a welcome improvement over the early review by Kimberly McMullen in "New Ireland/ Hidden Ireland."[8] McMullen largely dismisses the novel's critical importance. Her key complaint is that it lacks the irony of the best postmodern work and instead merely offers "derivative characterizations [that] seem deliberately to evoke earlier texts, not with the parodic intention of subverting them, but seemingly to capitalize upon their familiarity" (133).[9] Valente's analysis goes to the heart of this problem of "familiarity" and argues that O'Neill's novel undertakes a serious historical and literary project of resignification as it unpacks in all its complexity the "historically incisive ethnic-erotic analogy" (59) that connects the depiction of the political events of the 1916 Easter Rising and the central love affair between Jim Mack and Doyler Doyle. Relying on recent psychoanalytic discussions of the critical importance of shame, Valente's project brings into focus the connections among emerging queer sexualities and the abjected colonial racial identity of the Irish.

Rendering the complexity of antagonisms in the text into the confrontation between sex and nation—indeed, identifying this as "the underlying master trope" (59)—and casting both as dissident, Valente is able to read both queer sexuality and Irishness as active deconstructive critiques of one another. Neither mode of identification is able to express any sort of fully present or pure identity in the way that, say, Daniel Corkery had hoped religion, race, Catholicism, and the land might have (see chapter 2). Instead, as dissident forms of identification, both organized around forms of shame, each is able to express the importance of difference not as a form of victimhood but as a productive site for the creation of alternative and progressive forms of political and cultural representation. In particular, shame is seen as operating as a form of expressive collectivity rather than an individuated and isolating experience, and shame is seen as a way to rethink the representational practice of speaking for others that guides the at times undertheorized exclusionary and coercive tendencies in the populist politics of pride. Valente's analysis seeks to harness this disruptive complementarity of queer and Irish modes of identification as an instance of Lacanian "exceptionality":

> Indeed, "queer nation" represents the underlying master trope of *At Swim Two Boys*, which endeavors to extend or "resignify" the idea along two interrelated tracks, the analytic and prescriptive. . . . In this regard, queer sexuality instances what Lacanian psychoanalysis calls "the logic of exception." As colonized Europeans, metropolitan subalterns, racially denigrated "whites," participant subjects and subdominant objects of the British empire, the Irish under the Union occupied a position of historical exceptionality that likewise rendered their ethnic status the central, all-consuming element of their subject formation and its profoundly destabilizing property, that which determines their sense of identity and that which disturbs its coherence, inhibits its self-enclosure. It is this unusually schismatic Irish condition that necessitates O'Neill's corollary, prescriptive resignification of the concept "queer nation": the articulation of an Irish nationalism that, far from reifying some ethnically proper spirit, orientation, or form of life, would fulfill the queer mandate of instituting "an oppositional relation to the [social/sexual] norm" or "resistance to the very idea of norm as such." (59)

The complementary exceptionality that operates between queer sexuality and Irishness will come to a zenith in the garden party episode, which Valente claims ". . . deploys the vision, the trial, and the reputation of Oscar Wilde, along with related Irish figures of scandal—Casement and Joyce—to analyze how Irishness came to be a privileged site for articulating racial and sexual forms of abjection during this period and to propose how such overdetermined abjection could be transvalued and its revolutionary possibilities mined" (67). The episode depicts a volunteer rally at the MacMurrough mansion, focusing in particular on Dermot MacMurrough: first on his mentoring of young Doyle, then on his confrontation with old schoolmate Tom Kettle, and finally on his shameful witnessing of Doyle's expulsion from the nationalist boy's flute band. Valente brings into focus the early importance of Wilde in the episode (67–68) as MacMurrough invokes him during the mentoring of Doyle. The episode is organized around dynamics of pride/shame and out/in. So, for instance, it is while *out* wandering the garden that MacMurrough tells Doyle to wear his badge proudly. Valente writes:

"MacMurrough further emboldens Doyle to display his badge of member-
ship in the Irish Citizen Army, the Red Hand: 'I hereby grant you the freedom of my garden to wear your badge with pride'" (67). Conversely, it is
back *in* the confines of the mansion that Tom Kettle launches his shame-
filled rant (shame about his own middle-class Catholic roots, shame of his
lazy submission to the culture and politics of West Britonism, shame about
his boyhood homosexual activities). The key moment for Valente, the moment at which the pressures of the regulatory tensions of pride/shame, out/
in, are exposed and potentially redirected, if not breached, occurs in the episode's "coming out drama" (69). In this drama MacMurrough addresses
himself to Kettle:

> "You know, what my aunt said—about the charges being trumped up against me."
>
> "Water under the bridge."
>
> "Not exactly." MacMurrough wondered was he going to say what was on his mind,
> and after a while discovered that he possibly was.
>
> . . . "It's quite true, I was guilty as charged."
>
> Kettle swayed on the soles of his feet. He appeared to waver between outburst
> and conciliation. An indignant compromise prevailed.
>
> "You can't imagine I didn't know? . . . I am informed you have since—how we say—
> put away the things of a child."
>
> MacMurrough's eyes lifted, "Truth for instance?"
>
> "You're telling me there is a flaw in your character?"
>
> "I am telling you that I don't think it is a flaw."
>
> The empty glass went down on the table. ". . ." There's nothing more to be said . . . .
> Damn it all MacMurrough, are you telling me you are an unspeakable of the Oscar
> Wilde sort?"
>
> "If you mean am I Irish, the answer is yes." (268)

Valente unpacks the historical resonance of this figurative substitution
by tracing the genealogical relations between abjecting racialist discourses
of the mid-nineteenth century that saw the Irish, and a host of other ethnic-
ities and nationalities, as racially degenerate, and the emergence of what
Foucault refers to as the "species of the homosexual" at the end of the century, particularly as this emergence coalesced around Wilde's trial. In this
argument, shame operates as a form of physiological sociality whose dynamics have implications both for the subjectification of the racialized and
sexualized individual and also for the broader political collectivities in
which and through which norms as such are established. Indeed, shifting
projections of shame in MacMurrough's "coming out" allow for moments
of identification—both as Irish and queer—without having either of these
operate as *the* normative mode of identification.

Certainly, the immediate gist of this scene is, as Valente claims, in its figurative playfulness:

> With MacMurrough's final decisive retort, the mounting coordination in this episode of sexual and ethno-national identity-formation, sexual and ethno-national abjection, sexual and ethno-national deviation from the hegemonic norm suddenly slides into figurative identification; where one logically anticipates a homosexual reference, MacMurrough substitutes, with conjoined violence and aptness of a metaphysical conceit, the term Irish. (69–70)

If this analysis tells us much about the deeply imbricated historical modes of subjectification through which MacMurrough and Kettle are represented, it tells us less about the historical situation of the contemporary reader or about the representational mechanics of the text itself. That is to say, Valente's characterological analysis looks to the history of the past—1916 and the pressures on sexual and national identity experienced historically at that moment—as opposed to the present in whose history the novel is read. This does not mean that he is unaware of the historical present. Indeed, the present is key to unlocking the genealogy of relations that he traces. His argument hinges on the present in which the reader anticipates the development of the narrative: "Where one logically anticipates a homosexual reference, MacMurrough substitutes, with the conjoined violence and aptness of a metaphysical conceit, the term Irish." It is the contemporary reader who anticipates the unfolding of the text in this way. Valente focuses on the pastness of history, however, and does not take up the full contemporary historicity of this reader.

This contemporary and anticipatory reader is historical in at least two ways that the characters of MacMurrough and Kettle are not: first, he or she is a function of the text that unfolds in the present of the act of reading, a sort of narratological present. As we have seen, this narratological present is an important aspect of the functioning of the text and will become even more important as we unpack the value of history and the history of value that the text plays with. The second historical feature of the reader is that he or she is necessarily a reader with a certain historical culture. After all, only the reader who has absorbed a certain level of queer culture, who knows the dynamics of the coming-out drama in the first place, is able to anticipate MacMurrough's "coming out" in the scene. The characters themselves, unfamiliar as they must be—within the realist codes of the novel's description—with the history of queer culture in the twentieth century, cannot anticipate what is about to happen in the scene in the same manner. The text points to the distance between this queerly cultured contemporary reader structured as an extradiegetic narratological function and the characters represented in the diegetic movement of the narrative. We read: "MacMurrough wondered was he going to say what was on his mind, and after a while discovered that he possibly was." MacMurrough, the character whose consciousness is anchored in 1916, must wonder about his potential expression because his acculturation predates the emergence of the fully scripted coming-out scene, even as he finds himself involved in the unfolding of just that drama. Technically, then, it is not MacMurrough who substitutes . . . the term "Irish" where the reader anticipates some variant on the term "homosexual," so much as it is O'Neill who does so, acting as the reader's queerly cultured contemporary. There are thus at least two historical trajectories projected through the passage: One points, as Valente shows, to the genealogy of racial and sexual discourses that intersect in the subjectivities represented by MacMurrough and Kettle. And a second is the history of sexual politics embedded in our own moment, for this complex has produced a text that demands a reader first capable of anticipating a coming-out story and then capable of enjoying the textual pleasure effected when this coming-out story is both fulfilled and denied.

Rather than finding ourselves faced with the psychoanalysis of historically projected characters shaped by complicated genealogies of racial and sexual identification, we now have before us a problem of textual dynamics and in particular how these dynamics produce and engage specific historically formed subjectivities and values. The passage, as McMullen would have it, "capitalizes" on a familiarity with the patterns of disclosure and visibility orchestrated in the "coming-out drama." The passage leverages a cultural capital, or literary value, that can be unlocked or transformed into the pleasure of reading only by a subject who has been socialized in particular ways—culturally, historically, politically. As Marx explains, "Production thus creates the consumer. Production not only supplies a material for the need, but it also supplies a need for the material. . . . The object of art—like every other product—creates a public which is sensitive to art and enjoys beauty" (G 92). The exchange that takes place materially in the text as a racial/national term ("Irish") is substituted for a sexual term ("queer") both effects a certain kind of historical sociality in the queer sensibility that the passage demands and produces in order to be properly read, and invests that sensibility in the historical past, which becomes a site for the production of contemporary values. We have, then, not just a situation in which the past weighs on the shoulders of the present but, more than that, a situation in which the present turns to the past with an actively transformative hand.

The critical unpacking of the genealogical connections between discourses of race and queer sexuality largely imagines historical development as unfolding from the past to the present. According to the logic of this analysis, the middle of the nineteenth century saw race established as a category and site for political, cultural, and psychic abjection in the fields of anthropology, ethnology, and biology. As this discourse took shape and coherence, it provided a context within which the discourse of homosexuality (with its own institutions, such as criminology, psychology, and sexology) could produce yet another abject species/race. As Valente shows, forms of Irish sexuality at the outset of the twentieth century became a privileged site to bring these complex dynamics into focus. As a form of analysis, this argument emphasizes historical influence: racialist discourses influenced sexual discourses, and both of these continue to shape the contours of contemporary politics within which movements such as Queer Nation, O'Neill, and Valente operate. This trajectory is clear in Valente's argument: "It is this unusually schismatic Irish condition [that exceptional ethnic condition of being colonized Europeans] that *necessitates* O'Neill's corollary, prescriptive resignification of the concept 'queer nation'" (59; my emphasis).

But what if the playful substitutions also operate as material exchanges in the productive functioning of the text? What kind of value does the exchange circulate? What kind of subjectivities does this exchange produce? What does history understood through these relations of textual production look like? We see that the exchange does circulate values already sedimented within the past—values articulated within the discourses of race/nationality and sexuality—but that it also produces, calls into existence in the materiality of its language, a novel form of sociality in the queer sensibility of the text's reader. The historical trajectories of the passage do not simply proceed from past to present, because this novel sociality, although produced through contexts that bear the mark of the historical and discursive past, is able to turn actively to history and transform that history into a contemporary value. The historical past then becomes not simply a site for the delineation of influence or events, or even for the excavation of discourses, but also a site that can be "capitalized," that can be transformed in the textual circuits of contemporary value production. Because this transformation in O'Neill's text is effected through material modes of textual exchange, because the values and subjectivities this exchange produces are self-reflexively reinvested in the dynamics of the textual production, his project suggests more than simple resignification or reimagination of the past. His novel suggests, rather, that the historical past is not just an inert inheritance but is actively produced and reproduced in the efforts of contemporary social relations. As Marx reminds us, "Men make their own history, but they do not make it as they please; they do not make it under self-selected circumstances, but under circumstances existing already, given and transmitted from the past."[10] O'Neill's text similarly employs circumstances or discourses "transmitted from the past," but then literally proceeds to "make history" as it turns with a transformative and critical hand to those layers of sediment.

To return to how the novel capitalizes on a familiarity with Irish modernism, we can say that Valente admirably unpacks one aspect of this formula, the historical familiarity in the intersection between abjected forms of Irishness and queer sexuality. And we can now address the capitalization of that familiarity—that is to say, the production of that history—within the textual dynamics of reading. As we have seen, the moment of textual exchange at the heart of Valente's discussion both calls on and produces a specific historical subject in the form of the anticipated reader. As the invocation of Oscar Wilde in the scene makes clear, the novel does in some sense capitalize the value "Irish modernism." The production of the historical reader happens in the exchange and redistribution of literary value—inscribed in this instance by Wilde. The key to the novel's engagement with history lies in its relation to value.[11]

To understand the problem of value, we must first consider how the text itself introduces problems of value thematically and structurally. To begin, we should note that a significant motif records in a series of analogical moments the intersection of forms of language and forms of value. These analogous inscriptions run the gamut from the complete conflation of the linguistic and the economic, to the use of language and diction to reinforce class status, to general questions of the worth of language, to the circulation of authorial value just seen in the inscription of Wilde. These analogous intersections do not resolve the differences between economic and linguistic representation; instead, they open up the rich relationship between the two. The opening paragraph of the novel sets these relations in motion:

> At the corner of Adelaide Road, where the paving sparkled in the morning sun, Mr. Mack waited by the newspaper stand. A grand day it was, rare and fine. Puff clouds sailed through a sky of blue. Fair-weather cumulus to give the correct designation: on account they cumulate, so Mr. Mack believed. High above the houses a seagull glinted, gliding on a breeze that carried from the sea. Wait now, was it cumulate or accumulate he meant? The breeze sniffed of salt and tide. Make a donkey of yourself, inwardly he cautioned, using words you don't know their meaning. Where's this paper chappie after getting to? (3)

The connections between language and value operate on multiple levels in this paragraph. Mr. Mack's literally tries to "account" (3) for the value of words as he searches for the etymology of the term "cumulus" (3). The passage introduces a series of terms that connote value, particularly in terms of rarity: "sparkled," "rare and fine," "glinted" (3). It also introduces Mr. Mack's petit bourgeois class anxieties in linguistic terms. He is obsessed with finding the paper chappie and purchasing the relatively expensive *Irish Times* because—we eventually learn—of the social class status that this purchase secures. He does not want to come off looking like a donkey by asserting an improper etymology because he associates proper linguistic usage with heightened class status. In all of these examples, we find analogous connections between forms of language and forms of value.

As the text unfolds, these connections proliferate. To cite but a few examples: Mr. Mack is obsessed with the cash value of language: he mulls over clever phrases to send in to the papers, which, as he says, "pay for catchy items like that" (10). Furthermore, Mr. Mack is a believer in the burgeoning business of advertising, an explicit conjugation of text and value. He explains to his son: "'I want you to deliver some advertising-bills round the local populace. What do you think? They're hot off the printer's press.' He showed one to his son, running his finger along the words at the expected rate of reading. 'It's the modern way of drumming up trade'" (30). Even his ultimate petit bourgeois social analysis of class is summed up linguistically in the difference between the "smells" and the "swells" (17). Class standing—and thus socially secured value—is also readily apparent in the language of the aristocratic Eveline MacMurrough (whose "illustrious and priceless name" is "worth its weight in gold" [102]) as she moves effortlessly from English to French "for dramatic effect" (260). At least one of the dramatic effects is precisely the verbal performance of her own aristocratic standing. Her father's good name was literally bought from the Church: Father Taylor, the local Gaelic League priest, praises the memory of her father, and Eveline MacMurrough registers what that memory cost: "He was a great man and a good. Any number of windows I have seen, painted windows in chapels wheresoever in the province, with his name in dedication.' Yes, she idly thought, her father had been scrupulous in providing for the Church. The rate of one glass winder per bastard born, if she did not mistake" (100). Doyler, our devilishly handsome socialist, unpacks the politics of value behind the language of jingoism when he offers his assessment of the "loyalty" of his municipal employers: "Most the men they laid off. Employed a rush of boys in their place. Half the wages and the same blow they proves their loyalty to the Crown" (40). Finally, it is also Doyler who "reads" a ten-shilling note after a negotiated sexual encounter with Dermot MacMurrough: "The boy took the ten-shilling note. A week's, two week's wages, MacMurrough calculated. Not so very long ago and the least smile should have earned a sovereign. He watched him read the note like a morning paper, turn it over and read the back page" (159).

All of these analogous moments explicitly inscribe forms of value and forms of language and point to the problem of value as a broad concern of the text. As the comments from O'Neill that we examined earlier already have suggested, this engagement with value will take on a political valence, particularly as the novel addresses the legacy of revolutionary socialism associated with James Connolly and the Citizen's Army. The novel addresses this revolutionary political legacy, however, from within a literary-critical horizon—that is, the problem of the production and circulation of literary value. The analysis of the politics of value emerges, therefore, in literary terms, and as we have seen already, the novel uses these terms to amplify the full resonance of its historical conditions. On a more specific level, the text is concerned with the value of language as it accumulates or dissipates between the poles of *cliché* on the one hand and *literary language* on the other. The next two sections of this chapter will address these poles.

CLICHÉ

Eveline MacMurrough poses the problem of cliché during her first visit with Fr. Taylor, in which she contemplates the contradictory effects of his discourse on the history of Irish nationalism: "The formula was stale, let alone the notion, but it had sounded singular on the lips of a priest" (23). As Eveline's observation already suggests, cliché is a key moment in the critical reception of language, either as verbal communication or as written text, because it marks the intersection between that which is already known by the listener/reader and the unfolding effects of meaning. Ruth Amossy, explaining this critical intersection, suggests that cliché in a fundamental way structures the reading process:

> Although regarded as the height of stereotype and the very mark of triteness, clichés play an important role in the most varied kinds of textual strategies. So-called "literary" discourse makes extensive use of clichés. A threadbare figure can help direct the reading; it shapes the receiver's attitude towards the text it belongs to, as well as to the social discourse it exemplifies. Its ability to condition a text's reception provides a necessary complement to the cliché's essential precariousness. Indeed, the cliché, with its *"deja-vu"* effect, cannot exist outside of the reading process: it must always be recognized by the reader. (In the apt words of Michel Charles, it is simply a "reading hypothesis.")[12]

On the one hand, at the level of the language itself, cliché appears as dead metaphor, as inert linguistic expression, as worthless insight or utterance. Cliché thus matters less for the value of its own expressiveness and more for its critical function in the process of reading. Within the reading process (and the larger social processes within which reading figures), cliché operates as an opportunity for critical elaboration that either results in the articulation of a critical sensibility of the reader or contrarily emerges as a site at which the critical sensibilities of the reader have been neutralized, rendered unconscious and automatic. In the context of our discussion it is important that Amossy links both of these contradictory possibilities to the literary value the cliché represents:

> The cliché no longer has its canonical value. By becoming as automatic as possible (which is a sign of its loss of value), it calls for two reversible and complementary types of deciphering. A trite metaphor or stock figure may be denounced for its faded stylistic effect: in that case it prompts a sudden awareness coupled with critical assessment. Precisely because of its mechanical nature, however, it may also be immediately assimilated before its triteness is even noticed. (35)

As we shift the frame of analysis from the metaphors and phrases themselves to the question of the function of cliché in the reading process, we see that there is potentially much at stake with these empty utterances as they either invigorate or anesthetize the critical sensibilities of the reader. We also see that cliché articulates these potential sensibilities specifically in relation to regimes of value; cliché marks both a temporal and a critical feature of the circulation of literary value.

Although for Amossy value in this context refers chiefly to canonical literary value, in *At Swim, Two Boys* the value of cliché is expanded so that the cliché points to the broader articulation, maintenance, and circulation of a hegemonic common sense, that power-laced sense of what is true and false, what questions are legitimate and illegitimate, and what escapes the horizon of representation.[13] Rather than appearing as simply a narratological question, cliché marks sites where the struggles over political meanings and social values leave their trace. From one perspective, the establishment of the cliché suggests that these struggles have seemingly been resolved; after all, cliché points to the already known. However, as Amossy suggests, the cliché is in a precarious position: its borders require vigilant surveillance or else they run the risk of becoming—perhaps once again—sites of instability, ambiguity, or contest.

A key struggle for hegemony that undergirds the circulation of cliché formulations of common sense in the narrative world of *At Swim, Two Boys*—the world anchored in the events of 1916—sets the petit bourgeois, Catholic West Britonism of Mr. Mack against the emerging expressions of queer sexuality and the socialist politics of Jim and Doyler. Mr. Mack in this sense becomes a voice for a constellation of three specific blocs of power operating in the historical moment of 1916 Ireland. First, he promotes and supports the colonialist economic order, refusing the political analysis of this order offered by the novel's diverse chorus of nationalists and socialists, and understanding his own class status only through the ideological notions of hard work, order, dedication, propriety, and progress. Next, he emerges as a defender of the imperial political arrangement. Figuratively conditioned by a youth as an orphan, shamed by his flight from combat during the Boer Wars, Mr. Mack clings to a neurotic idealization of the values of the British Empire. Finally, Mr. Mack, who projects only limited power outside his own household, functions as a Gramscian legislator within his own domestic confines and defends a doctrinaire Catholic sexuality. The text's representation of this hegemonic constellation of values takes advantage of their cliché formulation on the lips of Mr. Mack and presents them with a range of irony, distance, humor, horror, and dismay. The critical consciousness of Jim takes its first foothold in response to the unorganized and capricious worldview expressed through Mr. Mack's circulation of cliché formulations. The affective complexity of this literary engagement with the cliché also creates a space for the potential elaboration of the critical consciousness of the reader as this reader is offered both a critical analysis of the power arrangements that Mr. Mack promotes and an ironized portrait of Mr. Mack, whose bumbling, and ultimately tender, persona hardly seems an adequate spokesperson for the ominous forces that he nonetheless supports.

An important instance of this struggle embedded within the form of the cliché occurs early in the novel. Here young Jim presses his father on a seemingly delicate subject:

"Papa?"

"Are you holding tight there?"

"There's been something on my mind."

"There always is when you calls me papa." Mr. Mack took a grip of the shelf and looked down at his son's upward face. Sallow skin on him. One or two spots coming. Trouble in his eyes. Oh begod, Gordie gone now, oughtn't I—kipping on his own now, oughtn't I—would they not learn him against that at the college? "Don't do it," he let out.

"Do what?"

"Say a prayer instead. It will go away, the urge will." His son was mouthing words so he quickly added, "Say no more about it now." He thought a moment. "Sleep with your hands like so." He crossed his breast with his arms and the steps tilted under him. "Didn't I tell you to hold tight?" He regained his balance. "Let the word Jesus be the last on your lips. Or Mary. A prayer to the Blessed Virgin would often be most affectacious. We'll say no more now. Save it'll leave you insane in the end."

"What will leave me insane?"

He scratched his head, then felt his moustache. The boy's eyes, having deeply blinked, were doubly troubled. "How old is this you are?"

"I'm turned sixteen."

A cheek dimpled in calculation. "Show me up them candles like a good boy. I was older than you at your age."

"Da, it's about socialism."

"Socialism?"

"It's been on my mind to know what it is." (110–11)

From the invocation of "Papa? . . . There's been something on my mind," the passage suggests a cliché moment between Jim and his father in which the son asks for his initiation into the coded adult world of sexual knowledge. Mr. Mack fears that his precocious son is on the verge of asking about masturbation and can only respond with a trite solution: "Don't do it. . . . Say a prayer instead." The reader, attuned both to the stereotypical signs of sexual initiation and to the already suggestively homoerotic friendship between Jim and Doyler, reasonably anticipates that Jim is about to ask about something sexual—if not homosexual. However, the text interrupts both of these expected developments, and instead Jim explains, "Da, it's about socialism." The disruption of the cliché in this instance opens both a diegetic space for Jim to question his father's worldview and a space for the reader's critical projections and identifications. Jim clearly develops a critical understanding of the limitations of his father's worldview as he comes to work openly with Doyler on the swimming lessons, which figure a range of counterhegemonic activities and values. The queerly cultured reader of the text finds a similar clarification of the limitations of Mr. Mack's worldview, particularly as the stumbling answers seem provoked initially by the scene's invocation of, and implicit challenge to, normative modes of sexual knowledge.

As the scene unfolds, Mr. Mack's anxiety increases as he fights to reestablish the authority of his petit bourgeois common sense in the response to the invocation of socialism. The intrusion of socialism in a scene in which he already finds himself prepared to defend repressive sexual norms drives Mr. Mack into a mildly paranoid rant in which he deploys the edicts of Catholicism to combat the red menace:

"What it is primarily is, what it is is wrong."

. . .

"Well it's, basically it's, what it is is greed. Oh yes, there's greed there. Greed and envy. A heap of envy involved. Then there's pride. Greed, envy, pride—sloth. Sloth there, too. Oh, all the sins. Every man-jack of them. The entire boiling, the hopping-pot, the whole kit and caboodle. I know what it is," he added wisely. "You was listening to the sermon last Sunday. Well, 'twas all there. Three-quarters an hour the father spoke on the subject and you can't ask fairer than that." (120)

In the same way that prayers to the Virgin Mary offer a trite remedy against the evils of masturbation earlier in the passage, here the Seven Deadly Sins serve as the expected weapons in an argument against the specter of socialist politics. For the reader, Mr. Mack's response to his son's sexual and political education registers as humorous. By spouting nothing but well-trodden forms of religious dogma, he literally manages to say nothing substantive about the subjects at hand: the effect of the passage lies in its performance of Mr. Mack's tongue-twisted anxiety. This performance clears the space for Jim's own critical assessment of his father's worldview. He will explicitly return to the critique of this worldview with Doyler when he asks, "What would you think would leave you insane?" (123). This humorous performativity also presents the potential for the critical intervention of the reader as it reveals the inadequacies of Catholic political and sexual doctrines in the misfit of the stuttering formulations.

Contrapuntal to the humor of this scene, the novel also presents the forms of physical violence—therefore the attempts at direct physical domination—that complement Mr. Mack's clumsy persuasion of his son:

> "Who's this been spreading notions?"
>
> "It's well known."
>
> "I asked you a question."
>
> "Doyler told me."
>
> The till slammed home. "Now, look at here, young fellow-me-lad. Amn't I in trouble enough without you palling up with agitating corner boys? Is it him spreading them notions in you? Lord save us, you haven't the sense you was born with. I'm your father. Your father's in peril of a prison term. Your father's name is muck in the street. My name is in the paper for sure. Piece of blackguardism in letters high as your hand. That's talking about your father, that is. And you want to be trumpeting Larkinism? This is where you want it."
>
> He tapped his son's head, not intending to strike, but the tap in the event came out a blow. The lad recoiled. "That's where you want it," he said. Consistency required he drive the blow home. "And that's where you'll get it if I hear another word." (112)

We see here the father's use of physical force in the domination of his son. The violence is not driven by his tyrannical nature, which is largely nonviolent, despite his obsequious attachment to military service. Instead, the violence erupts as Mr. Mack lends voice and fist to the antagonisms contained within the structural positions he occupies as father, Catholic, and petit bourgeois shopkeeper. The physical violence that erupts represents the occluded antagonisms simmering beneath the seemingly benign forms of cliché thought and expression.

In opening up this question of cliché we began with the notion that cliché represented a particular form of the problem of value and language. In this light, O'Neill does not just provide us with insight into the social antagonisms embedded within forms of cliché, but also brings into focus how cliché circulates particular kinds of social and economic values. Note that as the verbal confrontation between Mr. Mack and Jim escalates, Mr. Mack, the general manager of the corner store, not only takes up the defense of a hegemonic common sense; he also literally attends to the management— the rehabilitation, representation, and recirculation—of commodified forms of economic value. At the outset of the discussion we find that Mr. Mack is ". . . putting the new candles at the back and bringing the old ones forward. He had already dusted the old ones and now, truth to tell, it was hard knowing the other from which" (111). Then, as the tension mounts, he attempts to set both his son and the store till in order: "He pulled out the till drawer. 'What did I tell you? Herself is going dark as well as cranky. Coins all over the place, in the wrong place, you'd be all day grubbing for the correct change.' With delighted hands he set about the till's rearrangement" (111). Finally, before the striking of Jim, we read: "The till slammed home" (112). The passive construction of the phrase, in which the till seemingly slams itself, downplays the act as emanating from the will or nature of Mr. Mack and instead reinscribes the structural position that Mr. Mack embodies. The phrase also brings "home" (112) to a single phrase the conflation of the ideological management of the common sense of the Mack household and the management of material forms of economic value in the shop.[14]

Given the conflation of economic and sociopolitical values secured by Mr. Mack's formulations of common sense, it is perhaps no surprise that his struggles to quell his son's curiosity, to reestablish dominion over the household and the shop, and to maintain the unspoken norms of sexuality are all orchestrated into the quotidian gesture of sweeping: "What are you standing for? Haven't you sweeping to do?" (113). From the novel's perspective, sweeping is admittedly a light touch. The loss of Jim's mother and the assumption of traditionally feminized form of domestic labor both suggest a cliché that is precarious and open to reformulation. Nonetheless, Mr. Mack has recourse to the gesture. Once he senses that the threats to his conception of the world have been held at bay, that he has successfully reasserted the various forms of authority and submission that constellate his social position, Mr. Mack literally takes the cleaning into his own hands:

"No no finish up what you're at first. If a job's worth doing. Sweep it out in the road, can't you? The road is where it belongs. Arrah, give it here to me."

> At last he could let go. He swept away, scraping and scrubbing the floor, scratching the boards with the bristles of his broom, his side tugging with jerks, till a cloud of dust had risen to envelop him. Then out the door with it, out in the road where it came from, out in the street where the muck belonged. He closed the door on the returning dust while the remaining dust settled about him. "If a job's worth doing," he said, "'tis poor Brother Ass had better seen it done." (114)

In this passage Mr. Mack attempts to set in order three distinct, though imbricated, levels of value. First, he attempts to reestablish the difference between viable forms of economic value and the excess of "muck" or waste. The shop is to display its wares with all the brilliant sheen of the commodity fetish, while the street is to recycle the muck, waste, dust, and excess, which no longer represent fungible forms of value. This "cleaning up" of commodified value has the more generalized effect of setting back in place the social distinctions of class that Mr. Mack works to hard to maintain. The shop will now appear proper, and its owners that much more securely above the lower classes that inhabit the local slum, the Banks, where, for example, Doyler, local muckraker, lives. On a second level, it is clear that the already rattled Mr. Mack takes up the sweeping of the store with a certain mania: "scraping and scrubbing the floor, scratching the boards with the bristles of his broom, his side tugging with jerks, till a cloud of dust had risen to envelop him." He is not just attempting to sort the contradictions of the commodity form; he is also trying to set the psychosexual dynamics of the house back in order. The impropriety of the boys' relationship has already been glossed in homoerotically coded economic terms—Jim's inappropriate possession of Doyler's flute, his pilfering of cork grease and almond oil (113)—and here the maniacal cleaning of the store manifests Mr. Mack's anxieties about the psychosexual dynamics of his household. The scene is perhaps not as intense or campy as Faye Dunaway's famous cleaning scene in *Mommy Dearest*, but the insistence that the "muck" belongs in the street and not in the shop/home reinforces the notion that Doyler, who again, given his job, is associated with muck, has violated the heterosexual codes that govern the household. Finally, the passage also sets back in order the political power of the domestic sphere, as Mr. Mack—adult, father, and shopkeeper—takes power—at least in the form of a broom—back into his own hands.

Tellingly, this reestablishment of order is tied together with a cliché: "If a job's worth doing . . . 'tis poor Brother Ass had better seen it done." As we saw earlier, Mr. Mack is in a sense not saying anything particularly profound with this phrase, but the unfolding of the entire scene brings into focus the complex orchestration (articulation, maintenance, and defense) of values (economic, psychosexual, political) that the invocation of this phrase then inscribes. The distinctly cliché nature of the expression is brought into even sharper relief by the end of the confrontation between father and son. This occurs two pages later, after the pair argues over the looming possibility of Jim's vocation as a Christian Brother:

> "Look, Da, if I'm not to be a brother, what am I to be?"
>
> "You're to follow me in the shop of course. There's your vocation. To learn to be a better shop-keeper."
>
> It surprised what the boy said then. It surprised the way he said it.
>
> "Well it may so be a vocation isn't like that. It may so be a vocation is like a friend you might make. You don't choose a friend. A friend would come to you. And you don't turn him out, no matter what others would say. You're only too thankful you found him." (116)

Jim challenges his father in at least two ways. First, he opposes the social and economic values that his father struggles to defend. He refuses to look at a future position as shopkeeper as a vocation. He refuses to "turn out" a friend that has come to him—the language here both invokes Doyler and recalls his father's earlier chant, "Tis muck to the street so it is" (113). On a second level, Jim challenges his father's formulaic turn of phrase: "It surprised what the boy said then. It surprised the way he said it." This surprise at the language in terms of both content and form introduces the second pole in the text's understanding of language and value, which is the value of literary language.

LITERARY LANGUAGE

As with forms of the cliché, the novel itself presents a broad interest in the value of literary language both in the imaginaries of particular characters and in the dynamics of its own construction. The literary emerges as an articulation of a complex interaction of social relations, and as a linguistic mode, it also operates in a complicated web of power relations. The examples of this interest and these webs of power are myriad and diverse: the phantom Scrotes and Dermot MacMurrough construct a genealogy of philosophy and literature that points to a same-sex erotic tradition that might provide a point of collective culture for queer youth. Fictional figures such as Father Taylor and historical figures such as Douglas Hyde (through the citation of his *Loves Songs of Connaught*) promote the vanishing history of Irish-language literature. Brother Polycarp propagates Latin literature for the Catholic Church. The novel itself openly constructs its own literary genealogy and includes both direct and indirect references to an impressive list of authors, including James Joyce, Padraic Pearse, Thomas Moore, William Shakespeare, Oscar Wilde, William Blake, Charles Dickens, and Percy Bysshe Shelley.

In keeping with its socialist sympathies, *At Swim, Two Boys* explicitly introduces the problem of the literary through a transvalued socialist terminology, particularly through what we might think of as a queer practice of *redistribution*. Consider the following passage:

> A bat squeaked past. Hush, said a wave. Rush, said its fellow.
>
> Where goes the tide when comes the ebb?
>
> Where goes the night when comes the day?
>
> He was musing on these lines, seeking their provenance, when a patter of feet behind, a tap on the back of his head and his cap tilted forward over his eyes. He turned wildly.
>
> "There you are, pal o' me heart."
>
> Jim blinked. It was Doyler. Dowdy suit and cap at a rake. Teeth flashing in the gloom.
>
> "I say," said Jim and immediately felt foolish for it.
>
> "Say what?" said Doyler, clambering onto the wall beside and clapping his hand on Jim's shoulder. He had a bunch of flowers with which he waved in front. "What cheer, eh?"
>
> "Tulips?" said Jim.
>
> "Aren't they brave? They will be brave in the morning, anyhow. They're for the ma. You know there's hordes in the garden behind."
>
> "You're after stealing them?"
>
> "Stealing, me arse.[15] Redistribution if you must know." He leant forward and spat into a rock-pool below. "What kept you at the brothers'?"
>
> "You were waiting on me?"
>
> "Wanted to say hello was all."

On a diegetic level, this passage represents the text's socialist agenda through the actions and dialogue of the characters: Doyler conceptualizes his picking of the tulips as a form of redistribution. This is perhaps not as serious an example of the politics of redistribution as, say, Doyler's own analysis of the hiring of young workers for muckraking cited earlier, but the instance nonetheless represents the motivated redistribution of wealth within the economy represented in the narrative. Specifically, Doyler effects a redistribution of an economic *quantity*, the tulip. The selection of the tulip as a figure of economic quantity is not without historical resonance, as the phenomenon of *tulipomania*, an early market-speculation crisis in the Netherlands during the period of the Thirty Years' War, attests. Indeed, the dialectical image of Doyler, the local muckraker, holding a bunch of tulips, the aesthetic inscription of value, sharply captures the deep economic and psychic contradictions governing the organized production, consumption, and distribution of wealth in the projected world imaginary of the plot.

From this ironic juxtaposition of Marxist theoretical claims and the brave bunch of flowers waved by flirtatious hands, however, it is also clear that the passage effects a redistribution of *qualities*, specifically a surplus of affective literary qualities inscribed as forms of value. This redistribution of affect transforms the text from a moment of socialist instruction to a tongue-in-cheek seduction, and it also shifts the focus from the character-ological realm of the individual subject to the redistribution of the broader codes that inscribe collective forms of value production, consumption, distribution, and circulation. Marx explains that there is no such thing as labor in general, but only specific forms of labor that carry within them the resonance of social labor. So, too, the forms of affective value redistributed in the passage, even as they exceed their particular frames, emerge through the assemblage and encounter of particular value codes. The redistribution of these codes is readily apparent: the passage mediates literary versus visual—or nascent cinematic—value coding: even as we read that the flowers are for Doyler's mother, the visual codes of the passage frame a flir-tatious Doyler sitting next to an inquisitive Jim, who is also clearly an intended recipient.[16] The lines of verse play with the distribution of pres-ence and absence; more specifically, the musing over the provenance of the lines redistributes the presence and absence of the figure of Stephen in the novel's prose. The passage thus mediates Joyce's project, which comes in and out of focus, through the codes of sentiment and identification that fuel the same-sex romance. Finally, "Pal o' me heart" is a translation—read: redistribution—of an Irish phrase, *a chara mo chroí*, in English. The histor-ical resonance of this mediation extends to the whole of modern Irish liter-ature in English, especially as punctuated by the Famine. As Seamus Deane explains, "I . . . In Ireland's case, the language of the real, in all its rigor, is Irish—and that emerges as silence; and the language of the possible is English—and that emerges in eloquence";[17] the robust vitality of Irish eloquence in English is thus marked, haunted, by the silencing of the Irish language. The multivocal eloquence of this particular passage emerges through a practice of writing that plays with the aesthetic redistribution of these varied value codes.

Doyler's decision to redistribute the tulips conjugates the problem of value within the language of characters, their decisions, and their actions—thus in the framework of the sovereign subject. This is the same framework Kant invokes in the opening of his famous essay "An Answer to the Ques-tion: What Is Enlightenment?"[18] In this essay, critical Enlightenment is a coordination of an attitude, a personal awakening, and a gesture: "The motto of the Enlightenment is therefore: *Sapere Aude!* Have the courage to use your *own* understanding!" (54). Doyler's ability to cast his actions as a form of redistribution in this sense amounts to a kind of individual eloquence, a proper coordination of critical awareness, deed, and language. Doyler's resignification of the meaning of this gesture produces a space for the critique of his economic situation, his family and sexual situation, as well as the national political situation. The practice of writing that emerges in this passage, however, effects an affective redistribution of surplus values beyond the framework of the Enlightened subject. The coordination and assemblage of codes that cut through the passage suggests forms of collectivity and agency that exist beyond the purview of the individuated consciousness and subjectivity, even as these are important relay points in their production and circulation. The affective excess that emerges in the redistribution of codes inscribed in this passage—the folding together of Joycean modernism, the sentimental codes of gay romance, the haunting presence of the Irish language, and the political codes of queer and Marxist theory—emerges as a socialization of values both beyond and through the sovereign consciousness of the subject and the institutions that produce it. What emerges is a socialization and assemblage that is immanent to the practice of writing itself. This practice opens the flow of qualities, intensities, movements, relations, and thought over which and through which the deeper struggles for hegemony in the text occur. I would like to call this practice the text's project of *touching materialism* and to understand the articulation of this practice as the text's challenge to the moral institutions, both formal and informal, that govern the world imaginary within the narrative and the coded forms of reception within which the text circulates and unfolds.

The radical affective power of this touching materialism—perhaps first emblazoned by the Red Hand pin that Doyler sports on the inside of his lapel—that emerges as immanent to the practice of writing is vividly figured by Doyler's guerrilla remapping of the city of Dublin. In his survey of the city for the Citizen Army, the capitalized empire of the "universality of things" (391) is transformed by a practice of writing that does not just answer abstraction with abstraction but sees itself embedded in the intense crisis and potential of particular situations: "Every now and then he stopped to make a note of a problem in the way and its workaround, or of a particular vantage, say for sniping" (402). In Doyler's notes, the cityscape is transformed and made available to revolutionary action not simply in the literal sense of enabling the armed forces of the Volunteers and the Citizen Army to mobilize, strike, and recede, but also in the sense that the abstract organization of the city—through the state, the empire, the economy, and so on—is disrupted, short-circuited, and left open for multiple practices and tactics not organized by the abstracting forces of the colonial state and economy. This is why it is important that Doyler's survey is intertwined with the story of "the boots" (401), the other young queer that Doyler both mentors and confronts, because it opens the spaces for these queer transformations of the cityscape. In O'Neill's writing, the materials of modernism—in particular, its literary languages—are surveyed in relation to contemporary pressures to both produce and reproduce the queer as an open practice of representation (what Valente calls "the queer mandate of 'an oppositional relation to the [social/sexual] norm'" that resists "'the very idea of the norm as such'" [60]), and the need to think or rethink a socializing practice for the redistribution of diverse forms of social, cultural, and economic value. It is across and through the literary that the text not only imagines but, more than that, actually assembles the dynamic and open counterculture that challenges most robustly the hegemonic organization of culture and politics secured by the forces of moral abstraction.

As with the cliché, the survey of literary language in *At Swim, Two Boys* is imbricated with the production of hegemonic and counterhegemonic conceptions of the world. More than this, though, the affective power of the novel's touching materialism appropriates and transforms the social and historical conditions it encounters. This transformation expands the individual and collective forms of agency available in and through the text. Consider the following passage, in which Jim contemplates the quotidian struggles within the Mack household. In particular, consider how literary language operates in relation to the critique of hegemonic common sense:

> He should not have provoked his father that way. It was unfair provoking him with the court hanging over. Would he truly have belted him Jim wondered. It was a long time since his father had chastised him that way. His clumsy feet and the chair all wobbly looking liable to collapse from under him. The lour of his face and the intimidation of his hand raised to strike. Then his great thick fingers on the scrawny strip of leather. The way he made a menace of uncoupling the buckle. He had looked foolish; and in a cold way Jim had felt ashamed of him. He remembered the time Gordie stole Aunt Sawney's pipe. His father bate him with a ha'penny cane from out the shop. The cane broke but only because he kept missing Gordie and striking the leg of the table by mistake. What brutality he had in him he could not purpose. Impulse only gave it vent.
>
> He was pleased with the way he had formed that. That was an acute way of thinking. He repeated it to himself, moving his lips to the words. What brutality he has in him he cannot purpose. Impulse alone gives it vent. (124)

The passage presents the violence endemic to the maintenance of the hegemonic organization of power in the Mack household, even as Mr. Mack can only awkwardly take up the execution of this violence. The awkwardness of gesture that he projects in the beating of his sons is brought into relief by the perceived elegance and novelty of Jim's phrasing. As in the passage considered earlier, where Jim's language surprises the hackneyed verbal sensibilities of his father, here literary wording in a sense surprises Jim and the reader as it brings into focus both the mundane brutality of petit bourgeois family life and conversely the absurdity of that brutality, which is able to secure neither the consent of all the members of the family nor its own sense of justice or grandeur. Jim's phrasing thus emerges—as it does in previous encounters with his father—as both elegant in a literary way and as critical of prevailing ideological values. This is not to set a fetishized or intrinsic value of literary elegance against an equally fetishized sense of awkwardness or uncoordinated vulgarity. The increased coordination of literary elegance on Jim's part, and the increased eloquence of the queer characters on the subject of their desires and political situation, correspond to a more deeply philosophical and sharply rational understanding of the world around them.[19] Unlike Mr. Mack's early concerns with the class connotations of language (seen in the opening paragraph of the novel), the queer characters' increased literary elegance recalls the Spinozist expansion of sympathy that we have traced through Wilde, Synge, Casement, Joyce, McCabe, and Jordan. Furthermore, this increased coordination of literary sensibility will not produce either institutional or commonsense measures of abstract judgment—like those called upon by Mr. Mack—but will instead open a practice that defamiliarizes the terms of these abstract measurements and will open them to new meanings, associations, and pleasures. The expansion of literary affect is directly tied to the expansion of agency in the text as the elegance of the literary comes to figure in the project of swimming. The power of the text's touching materialism emerges as the writing comes to figure a socialization of agency both in and beyond the world of the novel.

This passage also suggests in miniature a particular kind of historical temporality for the literary organized around repetition. If the cliché points to the sedimented acculturation of the attentive reader who, like Amossy, sees in its "déjà vu" effects the loss of "canonical value," Jim's careful attention to the literary quality of his phrasing, as he mouths the words to himself, points to the forms of repetition that underlie the establishment of canonical literary value in the first place. Literary value in this sense bears a contradictory burden, as it must both surprise with its innovation—and thus avoid the risk of the cliché—and enter into a chain of repetition, be returned to just as Jim returns to it, in order for its literary quality to circulate, in order to be appreciated. Thus there is no intrinsic quality of novelty or innovation that divides the cliché from the literary. Both the cliché and the literary inscribe forms of repetitive historicity and in this sense operate through modes of familiarity, and both the cliché and the literary are forms of textual value that inscribe the dynamics of social relations in their encounter with the reader. They are in this sense complementary even if seemingly antithetical evaluations. The difference between the two in *At Swim, Two Boys* emerges between the potential rational critical dynamics of the cliché, which push the reader and characters to either embrace or challenge the familiarity of its formulations, versus the enhanced affective practice of the literary, through which a multiplicity of qualities, desires, memories, thoughts, texts, and actions are organized and reorganized beyond the purview of individual consciousness. From the enlightened critique of the cliché to the transformative power of affective labor, these two modes of literary value mark out the historical horizon of the text.

The layers of this argument are complex and warrant our careful unpacking, particularly in relation to Joyce. Consider the following passage, in which we again find Jim contemplating language, though this time it is the sexual language introduced by his brother:

> In his pocket he found some sweets; Lemon's, he remembered. The crinolined lady on the wrapper looked light and gay with her parasol, very much like Nancy would look if she wore Aunt Sawney's drapes. Nancy made him blush and he believed she always would now. His brother had rarely mentioned her before he left for England, but on the last night at home he said, Nancy's a bit of—jam, he called her. When Jim remonstrated, he grew coarser still. Don't come the green with me. I know the sniff of the glue-pot. Then—Is it Nancy you think of when you fetch yourself off? How could his brother say such a thing? How dared he utter those words. Jim couldn't look at Nancy since without the blood rising, and the blood rose now to his ears as he thought of it.
>
> He crushed the wrapper and let it fall behind.
>
> The breeze died and the heat was suddenly material, like a cloak that dropped on his back. The wall made him conspicuous. What might a watcher suppose was his purpose? He counted the clues to his identity: school cap, shop name on bike, bills in the pannier. His availability to interpretation intimidated him. He saw his arms were around his knees. He sniffed the muggy flocculent smell, then let go his legs. In his mind a formula impersonally repeated: he has never swum in the Forty Foot, he has never swum in the sea. Of a sudden he leant forward to check the Muglins, but the rock of course was obscured by the point. (36)

This passage contains quantifiable inscriptions that point to the mediation of the scene through the language of Joycean modernism: The lemon candy recalls the lemon soap in Bloom's pocket in the opening chapters of *Ulysses*. The sexual charging of the seemingly nonsexual word "jam" recalls the similar charging of terms throughout Joyce's work. The exposure of the latent sexual dynamics of the family recalls the relation between Bloom and Stephen as well as key passages from both *Portrait* and *Ulysses*. In the phrase "His availability to interpretation intimidated him," we read the echo of Stephen Dedalus's belief in the "ineluctable modality of the visible," through which he imagines a world thoroughly available to his own interpretative powers. On one level, these invocations of Joyce establish the literary ambitions of the passage's project: that the emergence of a historical queer consciousness at the turn of the twenty-first century, the moment of O'Neill the author, finds its roots in the emergence of Irish modernism, in the language, politics, psychology, and material relations that Joyce helped to bring into history.

However, as the passage collects these "clues to [its] identity" we can see that the reader is again faced with a moment in which the modes of identification contradict each other: the passage clearly suggests that *yes*, this is the Joycean schoolboy, whose connections to the categories of class, religion, nation, and empire are defined by the politics of language and sexuality through which his subjectivity is constructed, but also that *no*, this is not Joyce's schoolboy, this is not the subject who fetches himself off to the image of Nancy, instead this is the queer schoolboy knowingly hailed by the queer reader. In this second sense the clues amount to a negation of the allusion to Joyce insofar as we imagine Stephen's desires organized around manifest cross-sex drives. Things become even more complex, though, as this negation of the identifying clues also strangely amounts to an invocation of a Joycean practice of writing. As the passage reminds us, it is in fact Stephen whose dream is the "ineluctable modality of the visible" that secures his own critical knowledge, and not Joyce, whose textual practice works to disrupt the authority of representational modalities. For Joyce and O'Neill, literary practice, exchange, and repetition is "a formula impersonally repeated" (O'Neill 36)—that is, a practice neither directed nor understood simply through the restricted lens of individuated consciousness or the critical awareness of the bourgeois subject. Rather, it is within the practice of writing itself that the contours and qualities of both individual and collective forms of social being take shape and coherence—and this practice involves destruction, creation, recirculation, and a continual renewal that meets each situation as event. Writing thus both calls on the past and destroys it, both surveys known coordinates and forges new paths, as MacMurrough lovingly thinks to himself while burning Scrotes's writings, the abstract philosophical work that sought to secure a moral reason to justify same-sex love, harnessing the power of the Joycean allusion, "*We shall now begin, over again, anew*" (456).

The passage under consideration, therefore, is more than simply the self-reflexive examination of the value of Joycean value. It marks out the horizon within which the investment in, and circulation of, Joyce takes place: Jim's learning to swim in the sea. This powerful central activity of the novel inscribes and assembles the most directed critical and affective under-taking both for the characters and for the reader. That is to say, an entire complex aesthetic and political project emerges as the boys learn to swim: one that challenges hegemonic modes of sexuality, hegemonic national and colonial politics, hegemonic notions of language and beauty, and hegemonic relations to capital and class. All of these levels appear in this passage that inscribes Jim over the Joycean palimpsest. In particular, the passage circu-lates Joycean literary value through the emergent sexual consciousness and activities of Jim—the invocation and circulation of literary value is coter-minous with Jim's awakening to the world of sexuality through his swim-ming at the Forty Foot. The writing of the emergent queer sexual consciousness with which Jim contemplates and trains for the Easter swim figures a directive project—one that is collective and connective beyond the individuated subject—both for the characters, who will route the mul-tiplicity of their experiences through their various forms of involvement with the swimming lessons, and for the reader, who values and transforms the language of Joycean modernism through the lens of this practice. In Gramsci's terms, the "active participation in practical life" (10) here points simultaneously to the diegetic project of swimming and to the textual dy-namics that take up and circulate Joyce as a form of literary value.

The contest between the institutions of moral abstraction that produce both the sovereign subject and its political life in the structures of the na-tion-state and the affective power of the touching materialism that emerges in the practices of swimming and writing is explicit. Consider Jim's pivotal position between the two regimes:

"It is a shame, for a vocation is often easier with a mother in the home."

The brother shifted from his chair, heaving himself up and round, and Jim closed his eyes as resiny black linen enfolded his neck. The brother's arm wrapped around him, bringing him down, on to his knees, the brother kneeling beside.

"Don't worry you feel confused. It is only natural you feel confused with your mother taken from you."

A finger rubber on his cheek, down his chin-bone, to the collar of his shirt. Far out to sea, Jim registered the touch.

"Believe me, Jim, this world without a mother's care is a parlous place indeed. I know this because mine too was taken from me at a tender age. But I found solace in the words of our Lord. Do you know the words I intend, Jim?"

"I do, Brother." (54)

Here the discourse of shame, as it attempts literally to "enfold" Jim, is part of a larger abstract universalism, the discourse of the Catholic Church, that through the call to a vocation attempts to organize Jim's understanding of language and thinking ("Do you know the words I intend?"), body ("The brother's arm wrapped around him, bringing him down, on to his knees, the brother kneeling beside"), family (Jim orphaned by the death of his mother is open to the reorganization of the family by "Brother" Polycarp), and, finally, purpose (as the Brother tries to mold Jim's will).[20] That Jim registers the touch "far out to sea" on one level operates as a defense mechanism against the Brother's molestation, but on a deeper level registers the alternative form of touch, the alternative affective power, that organizes Jim's relation with Doyler and the sea. Jim registers the importance of this alternative affective practice, and the desires, expressions, and activities this practice assembles, when he later claims that he is less disturbed when the Brothers fondle his genitals than when Brother Polycarp touches his neck—the arm around Jim's neck attempts, through coercion and domination, to produce an entire worldview that Jim and the novel reject.

Later in the novel, Brother Polycarp's molestation and his attempts to bring Jim to a vocation with the Brotherhood again introduce the problem of abstraction:

> His collar pulled and his tie strained against the intrusion. He blinked. He was irresistibly aware of the oddness of moving things.
>
> "At that time I had discovered in myself a certain sin. It is not necessary I tell what sin that was, save that it was a solitary vice."
>
> Thumb-grope and finger-creep. How oddly things moved and strangely unmoved him, they fumbling over the chain of his medal, they playing with the medal on its chain and on his chest.
>
> "As fouler I grew and deeper in my misery, the temptation rose to share that vice with others."
>
> Out over his windpipe, along his throat, pressuring his apple, which made Jim gulp and swallow. The physicality of that reflex surprised him from abstraction. He felt a blush rising, mottling his cheeks.
>
> "Who those others were it is not necessary to tell, save that my schoolfellows were shocked and repelled by my solicitations."
>
> The hand held now in its span the round of his neck.
>
> "Do you understand solicitation?"
>
> "I think I do." (118–19)

The scene literalizes the contest between the institutions of moral abstraction, here cast in the discourse of sin, and the counterhegemonic regime of touch, what I have termed a touching materialism—an alternative affectivity that shakes Jim from this abstraction. This moral abstraction attempts to organize at the level of the story a hierarchy of social power—relationships to history and language, relations to the self and the body, and relations to other selves and other bodies. The attempt to consolidate this hegemonic constellation at the level of the story—say, at the level of the projected represented history—is also an attempt to organize the writing of the novel as it attempts to safeguard the effects and dissemination of meaning ("Do you understand solicitation?" "I think I do"). In both of these passages, in fact, Brother Polycarp, as a representative of the institutions of moral abstraction, attempts to instill a didactic relation—and ultimately therefore a cliché one—to language that the practice of swimming and the queer affects of literary writing openly challenges.[21] In the concluding section of this chapter we must consider the transformative power of this queer affective practice.

AT SWIM

The introduction to this chapter suggested that the political revolutions that *At Swim, Two Boys* charts—from the 1798 Rebellion to the Easter Rising to Stonewall—have left a contradictory legacy, one that is textual as well as fully historical, in which the call to freedom is heard, yet the articulation of freedom seems incoherent, contradictory, impractical, and violent.[22] Indeed, the eloquence of the revolutionary call hardly seems like eloquence at all by the final paragraph of the novel, in which Doyler's ghost looks one last time on Jim—who is dying in MacMurrough's arms after a decade of strife in the Irish Civil War—only to repeat, "What cheer, eh?" (572). I have also argued through the course of the chapter that in response to the failure of this revolutionary eloquence the novel produces a practice of writing that assembles an alternative to normative forms of universality through an immanent form of labor. In conclusion, I would like to turn to this transformative labor through which the boys produce their own kind of freedom. The project of swimming is framed by the characters as a kind of labor that will transform themselves and their world to produce a new sort of knowledge. To quote Doyler:

> "I reckon if we worked hard, every morning, say, we worked on your stroke, before I went to work, before you went to college, out to the raft here and back while the raft is out, every day we'd do it, rain or shine, till you find your feet, or your fins I should say, I reckon come Easter next we'd swim out there together, and I'll show you the place and you'd know, I don't know, what I meant like." (139)

The boys literally work "against nature" as they train and sexualize their bodies, their understanding, and forms of expression—in particular, as nature and knowledge are controlled by the discourses of the Church, the state, the family, and the nation. Much like Stephen Dedalus, who will try to fly by the nets of nationality, language, and religion, Doyler and Jim see their swimming in terms of freedom:

> "Come swimming with me," said Doyler.
>
> "Swimming?" It was the last thing on his mind.
>
> "Forget your baths, come swimming in the sea. It's different in the sea, don't ask me why, but you don't find the same anywheres else. There's a freedom I can't explain, like your troubles was left in your pile of clothes. There's how many waves to wash you, sure they wash right through your head. Will you come?" (127)

This passage reads as the inverse of the passages in which Brother Polycarp attempts to coerce Jim into a life with the Church: the passage sounds an open call as opposed to forced consent ("Come swimming with me"); Jim is asked to rethink language and his daily practice ("Forget your baths, come swimming in the sea"); the social abstractions of dress and subjectivity are pushed aside for a new freedom ("your troubles was left in your pile of clothes"); and the new freedom cannot be described in a "party slogan" (Nietzsche) or even in the realm of the sovereign subject as the materiality of the waves and waves of materiality "wash right through your head."

> Pleasant to swim in the rain, they say. It would be too. The sea would lower your temperature already so the rain wouldn't feel so cold. It would be hard getting in, you'd have to push yourself, but were you in already, that would be pleasant. That would be freedom, to be out in the rain and not to trouble. Your trouble in your pile of clothes.
>
> Confess a sin, is it possible, before committed? (131)

Swimming, both as an activity in the plot of the novel and as a coordination of the multiple codes that run through the text, transforms the boys and their bodies, identities, and language. The freedom that the text imagines happens in this affective expansion of the writing that appropriates and transforms the history of both the characters and the readers.

We come now full circle to question that began this chapter—"Are we straight so?"—and see that the touching materialism of the novel, the queer affective labor of the writing, has transformed this question so that it is no longer a problem of eloquence. Instead, the novel poses the question as a question of practice. It is a practice, an assemblage, forged during the swimming, that is not only fully possible but also fully practical. Through the affective labor of writing and reading, the novel presses beyond the dialectical problems of contradiction, the problems of eloquence, and articulates a simple and powerful affirmation as praxis:

A flash of his grin. "I'll see you won't fall in," he said and the arm went round Jim's shoulder.

Gently this time, though still the touch shot through Jim's clothes, through his skin even. It was this way whenever their bodies met, if liming he brushed against him or laughing he squeezed his arm. The touch charged through like a sputtering tram-wire until it wasn't Doyler he felt but what Doyler touched, which was himself. This is my shoulder, this my leg. And he did not think he had felt himself before, other than in pain or in sin.

"Are we straight so?"

"Aye we're straight," said Jim.

"Straight as a rush, so we are." (82)

Alive to both themselves and each other, alive to the natural world around them, alive to the human labor that electrifies their touch, alive to the language that affirms both the characters and the readers, alive to the full resonance of the historical moment. The text does not unravel in the contradictions of the revolutionary call—instead it affirms a power of life through and beyond that call: *so we are.*

NOTES

INTRODUCTION

1. The concert is still available online: www.youtube.com/watch?v=UHTAMss9tQM. The *Los Angeles Times* also quoted the Irish singer in "Inspiring Song, Spirit at Lincoln Memorial Concert," by Robin Abcarian and Jill Zuckman, January 19, 2009.

2. Siobhán Kilfeather, "Erosion of Heterosexual Consensus, 1940–2001," in *Field Day Anthology of Irish Writing, Volume IV: Irish Women's Writing and Tradition*, ed. Angela Bourke, Siobhán Kilfeather, Maria Luddy, Margaret MacCurtain, Gerardine Meaney, Máirín Ní Dhonnchdha, Mary O'Dowd, and Claire Wills (New York: New York University Press, 2002), 1039–41; quote on 1040.

3. Tóibín suggests that Irish, Jewish, and gay writers all enjoy a certain difference that enables them to be cultural innovators. Furthermore, he claims that the "tragic and the unfulfilled" are important themes in both gay and Irish writing. See *Love in a Dark Time: Gay Lives from Wilde to Almodóvar* (London: Picador, 2002), 5, 25–26.

4. Joseph Valente, "Race/Sex/Shame: The Queer Nationalism of *At Swim Two Boys*," *Éire-Ireland: A Journal of Irish Studies* 40.3–4 (2005): 67.

5. Sally Munt, *Queer Attachments* (Burlington: Ashgate, 2007), 12.

6. Kathryn Conrad, *Locked in the Family Cell: Gender, Sexuality and Political Agency in Irish National Discourse* (Madison: University of Wisconsin Press, 2004), 4.

7. Margot Backus, *The Gothic Family Romance: Heterosexuality, Child Sacrifice, and the Anglo-Irish Colonial Order* (Durham, NC: Duke University Press, 1999), 4.

8. Declan Kiberd, *The Irish Writer and the World* (Cambridge: Cambridge University Press), 12.

9. Fabio Cleto, "Introduction: Queering the Camp," in *Camp: Queer Aesthetics and the Performing Subject: A Reader*, ed. Fabio Cleto (Ann Arbor: University of Michigan Press, 1999). Further references to this work will be made parenthetically in the text.

10. Michel Foucault, *The History of Sexuality: Volume 1: An Introduction* (New York: Vintage Books, 1978). Further references to this work will be made parenthetically in the text.

11. Lynne Huffer, *Mad for Foucault: Rethinking the Foundations of Queer Theory* (New York: Columbia University Press, 2009), 75.

12. Foucault's influence on queer theory is evident. For Marxist engagements with Foucault, see Antonio Negri, "Value and Affect," trans. Michael Hardt, *boundary 2* 26.2 (1999): 77–88; Michael Hardt, "Affective Labor," *boundary 2* 26.2 (1999): 89–100. For more on Marxian aspects of Foucault's thought see Michel Foucault, *Remarks on Marx: Conversations with Duccio Trombadori*, trans. R. James Goldstein and James Cascaito (New York: Semiotext(e), 1991); Gayatri Chakravorty Spivak, "More on Power/Knowledge," in *Outside in the Teaching Machine* (New York: Routledge, 1993), 25–51; Renate Holub, "In Lieu of a Conclusion: Gramsci, Feminism, Foucault," in *Antonio Gramsci: Beyond Marxism and Postmodernism* (New York: Routledge, 1992), 191–203. As Bruce Robbins notes in his review (*Modernism/Modernity* 2.2 [1995]: 114–15), Paul Bové's *Mastering Discourse: The Politics of Intellectual*

Culture (Durham, NC: Duke University Press, 1992) attempts to think through Foucault's thinking about disciplinary systems and capital by rejecting the elitist theorizations of the Marxist vanguard while promoting Antonio Gramsci's insistence on the need for forms of intellectual and social leadership, a path that resonates with Holub's final reflections. Andrew Parker sketches the tensions between the study of sexuality as it emerged in response to Foucault and the history of Western Marxism in "Unthinking Sex: Marx, Engels, and the Scene of Writing," *Social Text* 29 (1991): 28–45. For a recent survey of the relation between Foucault and Marxism see Mark Olssen, "Foucault and Marxism: Rewriting the Theory of Historical Materialism," *Policy Futures in Education* 2 (2004): 454–82.

13. Eve Kosofsky Sedgwick, *The Epistemology of the Closet* (Berkeley and Los Angeles: University of California Press, 1990), 3.

14. Michael Hardt and Antonio Negri, *Empire* (Cambridge, MA: Harvard University Press, 2000), 22. Further references to this work will be made parenthetically in the text.

15. Eric Otto Clarke, *Virtuous Vice: Homoeroticism and the Public Sphere* (Durham, NC: Duke University Press, 2000), 12.

16. Matthew Tinkcom *Working Like a Homosexual: Camp, Capital, Cinema* (Durham, NC: Duke University Press, 2002), 5.

17. Seamus Deane, *Strange Country: Modernity and the Nation: Irish Writing since 1790* (New York: Oxford University Press, 1997), 146. Further references to this work will be made parenthetically in the text.

18. Antonio Gramsci, *Selections from the Prison Notebooks*, trans. and ed. Quintin Hoare and Geoffrey Nowell Smith (New York: International, 1971), 324. All subsequent references will be made to this edition and will be abbreviated *PN*.

19. For more on the problem of the universal, see Judith Butler, Ernesto Laclau, and Slavoj Žižek, *Contingency, Hegemony, Universality: Contemporary Dialogues on the Left* (London: Verso, 2000). Another critical discussion that has taken up the problem of the universal and the contingent, albeit in a different guise, is the growing debate around cosmopolitanism. See Timothy Brennan, *At Home in the World: Cosmopolitanism Now* (Cambridge, MA: Harvard University Press, 1997); Bruce Robbins, *Feeling Global: Internationalism in Distress* (New York: New York University Press, 1999); Martha Nussbaum, *For Love of Country?* (Boston: Beacon, 2002). For modernism's role in this debate, see Jed Esty, *A Shrinking Island: Modernism and National Culture in England* (Princeton, NJ: Princeton University Press, 2003); Rebecca Walkowitz, *Cosmopolitan Style: Modernism beyond the Nation* (New York: Columbia University Press, 2007); Amanda Anderson, *The Powers of Distance: Cosmopolitanism and the Cultivation of Detachment* (Princeton, NJ: Princeton University Press, 2001). Comparatists have also undertaken this debate, specifically as it hinges on the formation of scholarly disciplines. For more see Gayatri Chakravorty Spivak, *Death of a Discipline* (New York: Columbia University Press, 2005); Emily Apter, "'Je ne crois pas beaucoup à la littérature comparée': Universal Poetics and Postcolonial Comparatism," in *Comparative Literature in an Age of Globalization* (Baltimore: Johns Hopkins University Press, 2006), 54–62.

20. Edward Said, *Representations of the Intellectual: The 1993 Reith Lectures* (New York: Vintage, 1996), xiv.

21. Oscar Wilde, "The Portrait of Mr. W. H.," in *The Soul of Man under Socialism and Selected Critical Prose*, ed. Linda Dowling (New York: Penguin, 2001), 31–101; and "The Soul of Man under Socialism," in *The Soul of Man under Socialism and Selected Critical Prose*, ed. Linda Dowling (New York: Penguin, 2001), 125–60.

CHAPTER 1

1. Oscar Wilde, "The Portrait of Mr. W. H.," in *The Soul of Man under Socialism and Selected Critical Prose*, ed. Linda Dowling (New York: Penguin, 2001), 31–101; and "The Soul of Man under Socialism," in *The Soul of Man under Socialism and Selected Critical Prose*, ed.

Linda Dowling (New York: Penguin, 2001), 125–60. These editions will be cited parenthetically in the text, abbreviated "WH" and "SM," respectively.

2. James Joyce, *Ulysses* (New York: Vintage, 1986), 15. This edition will be cited parenthetically in the text.

3. The literature on Wilde is immense. For an introduction, see Jeff Nunokawa, *Tame Passions of Wilde: The Styles of Manageable Desire* (Princeton, NJ: Princeton University Press,
2003); Alan Sinfield, *The Wilde Century: Effeminacy, Oscar Wilde, and the Queer Moment*
(New York: Columbia University Press, 1994); Sos Eltis, *Revising Wilde: Society and Subversion in the Plays of Oscar Wilde* (New York: Oxford University Press, 1996); Shelton
Waldrep, *The Aesthetics of Self Invention: Oscar Wilde to David Bowie* (Minneapolis: University of Minnesota Press, 2004); Ed Cohen, *Talk on the Wilde Side* (New York: Routledge,
1992); Richard Ellman, *Oscar Wilde* (New York: Random House, 1989). For interesting
articles, see John Paul Riquelme, "'The Negativity of Modernist Authenticity/The Authenticity of Modernist Negativity: 'No Direction Home' in Yeats, Dylan, and Wilde," *Mod-
ernism/Modernity* 14.3 (2007): 535–41; Paul K. Saint Amour, "Oscar Wilde: Literary
Property, Orality, and Crimes of Writing," in *The Copywrights: Intellectual Property and the
Literary Imagination* (Ithaca, NY: Cornell University Press, 2003), 90–120; Paul L. Fortu-
nato, "Wildean Philosophy with a Needle and Thread: Consumer Fashion at the Origins
of Modernist Aesthetics," *College Literature* 34.3 (2007): 37–53. For a recent article on
how Wilde continues to challenge the boundaries of literary scholarship, see Petra Dierkes-Thrun, "'The Brutal Music and the Delicate Text'? The Aesthetic Relationship between
Wilde's and Strauss's *Salome* Reconsidered," *Modern Language Quarterly* 69.3 (2008):
367–98.

4. Colm Tóibín, *Love in a Dark Time: Gay Lives from Wilde to Almodóvar* (London: Picador,
2002), 86.

5. Rebecca Laroche, "The Sonnets on Trial: Reconsidering *The Portrait of Mr. W. H.*," in
Shakespeare's Sonnets: Critical Essays, ed. James Schiffer (New York: Routledge, 1999),
391–410; quote on 391. Further references to this work will be made parenthetically in
the text.

6. See Colin MacCabe, "The Voice of Esau: Stephen in the Library," in *James Joyce and the
Revolution of the Word* (1978; rpt., New York: Palgrave Macmillan, 2003), 181–202. Mac-
Cabe includes an important discussion of the dominant modes of Victorian biographical
criticism that Joyce challenges. Wilde challenges the same conventions in "The Portrait of
Mr. W. H."

7. Wilde emerges as a strikingly different figure as he passes through the divergent fields of
lesbian and gay, Irish, and English studies. While queer scholarship has recognized the
subversive rhetorical qualities of Wilde's wit and writing as a reaction to and engagement
with the often violent dynamics of homosocial/homosexual definition, it has largely
ignored the specifically Irish historical and cultural context. Irish studies, and indeed Irish
culture, has long accepted the fact of Wilde's homosexuality but has largely downplayed its
contribution to his literary work. Within the reappraisal sparked by the postcolonial
debates in Ireland in the 1990s, Wilde's wit and subterfuge has increasingly been seen as
part of a broader shared strategy of indigenous resistance to controls of colonial cultural
coding. Both queer and Irish scholars have had to fight to register the importance of sexuality and nationality for Wilde's work. My study argues for the importance of both. For
more consider the different discussions of Wilde in Sinfield, *The Wilde Century*; Declan
Kiberd, "Oscar Wilde: The Artist as Irishman," in *Inventing Ireland* (Cambridge, MA: Harvard University Press, 1997), 33–50; and Linda Dowling's introduction to *The Soul of Man
under Socialism and Selected Critical Prose.*

8. While the introduction of affect will unfold through the reading of Wilde, I come to the
philosophical problem of affect through the reading of Gilles Deleuze. Affect is a concern

that runs through the entire corpus of his work but to my mind is helpfully introduced by the work on Spinoza; see *Spinoza: Practical Philosophy*, trans. Robert Hurley (San Francisco: City Lights, 2001); *Expressionism in Philosophy*, trans. Martin Joughin (New York: Zone Books, 1992). Also see the excellent course transcripts on Spinoza available online at www.webdeleuze.com.

9. Eve Kosofsky Sedgwick, *Epistemology of the Closet* (Berkeley and Los Angeles: University of California Press, 1990), 3.

10. Wilde offers a sophisticated and seminal meditation on the dynamics of homosocial/homoerotic epistemology, and ultimately it is these dynamics, if we are to follow the pioneering scholarship of queer theory that emerged in the 1990s, that have proven to be key to the "greatest mystery of modern literature." Along with Sedgwick, much of the pathbreaking work in 1990s queer scholarship focused on the politics of queer epistemology and performativity, including the seminal work of Judith Butler in *Gender Trouble: Feminism and the Subversion of Identity* (New York: Routledge, 1990) and *Bodies That Matter: On the Discursive Limits of Sex* (New York: Routledge, 1993). Queer scholarship has more difficulty engaging Marx, historical strains of Marxism, and problems of capitalism and value. Works that undertake this engagement include Eric O. Clarke, *Virtuous Vice: Homoeroticism and the Public Sphere* (Durham, NC: Duke University Press, 2000); Amy Villarejo, *Lesbian Rule: Cultural Criticism and the Value of Desire* (Durham, NC: Duke University Press, 2003); Rosemary Hennessey, *Profit and Pleasure: Sexual Identities in Late Capitalism* (New York: Routledge, 2000); Amy Gluckman and Betsy Reed, eds., *Homo Economics: Capitalism, Community, and Lesbian and Gay Life* (New York: Routledge, 1997); and John D'Emilio, *Sexual Politics, Sexual Communities* (Chicago: University of Chicago Press, 1998). For a seminal exploration of affect and problems of value in a postcolonial context, see Gayatri Chakravorty Spivak, "Scattered Speculations on the Question of Value," in *In Other Worlds: Essays in Cultural Politics* (New York: Routledge, 1988), 154–75. For a consideration of affect and value in the Irish context, see David Lloyd's work on James Connolly: "Rethinking National Marxism: James Connolly and Celtic Communism," *Interventions: A Journal of Postcolonial Theory* 5.3 (2003): 371–81; and the special issue on Connolly, *Interventions: International Journal of Postcolonial Studies* 10.1 (2008). For a look at the emergence of aesthetic and economic value see Mary Poovey, *Genres of the Credit Economy: Mediating Value in Eighteenth- and Nineteenth-Century Britain* (Chicago: University of Chicago Press, 2008).

11. Erskine asks the narrator, "What would you say about a young man who had a strange theory about a certain work of art, believed in his theory, and committed a forgery in order to prove it?" (33).

12. "The equation of the incompatible, as Shakespeare nicely defined money." Karl Marx, *Grundrisse: Foundations of the Critique of Political Economy*, Trans. Martin Nicolaus (New York: Penguin, 1993), 163. This edition will be cited parenthetically in the text and abbreviated G.

13. Karl Marx, *Capital: Volume 1*, trans. Ben Fowkes (New York: Penguin, 1992), 128. This edition will be cited parenthetically in the text and abbreviated C.

14. According to the *OED*, the word "theory" comes from the Greek *theoria* and indicates "a looking at, viewing, contemplation, speculation . . . also a sight, a spectacle."

15. Postcolonial theorists have addressed the importance of the diversity of aesthetic forms in terms of the struggle against colonialism. One of the most influential recent models for understanding forms of colonial and postcolonial culture has been Homi Bhabha's work on hybridity. As Edward Said has noted, there are also important aspects of Frantz Fanon's analysis of postcolonial culture that are not as frequently taken up—particularly as Fanon emphasizes the limitations of nationalist cultural forms. For more, see Homi Bhabha, *The Location of Culture* (New York: Routledge, 2004); Edward Said, "The Politics

of Knowledge," in *Reflections on Exile and Other Essays* (Cambridge, MA: Harvard University Press, 2002), 372–85; Frantz Fanon, *The Wretched of the Earth*, trans. Constance Farrington (New York: Grove, 2005).

16. For a discussion of queer initiation in American culture see Michael Moon, *A Small Boy and Others: Imitation and Initiation in American Culture from Henry James to Andy Warhol* (Durham, NC: Duke University Press, 1998).

17. The French is from the early French translation of the story, *Le Portrait de monsieur W. H.* (1906), by Albert Savine, available on Project Gutenberg: www.gutenberg.org/etext/15372 (accessed January 10, 2012).

18. The relationships among discourses of affect, emotion, sentimentality, and melodrama are complex and often contradictory. They emerge in a variety of different historical and interpretative contexts. The point here is not to reify a transcendent model of affect over and against an equally hypostatized model of sentiment, but to think through the particular distinctions that Wilde crafts and to elaborate what these distinctions enable in this study.

19. "It is clear then that no Authoritarian Socialism will do" ("SM" 131).

20. The relations between a masculine—and thoroughly homophobic—intellectual friendship set against an abject femininity comes to an orgy of violent contradiction, projection, and repression in the final passage of *Women in Love*, in which Birkin reflects on the dead body of Gerald, under the gaze of Ursula: "He forgot her, and turned to look at Gerald. With head oddly lifted, like a man who draws his head back from an insult, half haughtily, he watched the cold, mute, material face. It had a bluish cast. It sent a shaft like ice through the heart of the living man. Cold, mute, material! Birkin remembered how once Gerald had clutched his hand, with a warm, momentous grip of final love. For one second—then let go again, let go for ever. If he had kept true to that clasp, death would not have mattered. . . . But now he was dead, like clay, like bluish, corruptible ice. Birkin looked at the pale fingers, the inert mass. He remembered a dead stallion he had seen: a dead mass of maleness, repugnant. He remembered also the beautiful face of one whom he had loved. . . . Ursula stood aside watching the living man stare at the frozen face. . . . 'Haven't you seen enough?' she said." D. H. Lawrence, *Women in Love* (New York: Penguin, 1995), 480.

21. Wilde's passage points to the diffused influence of Spinoza. Consider the following passage from the *Ethics*: "We see, then, that the mind can undergo great changes, and pass now to a greater, now to a lesser perfection. These passions, indeed, explain to us the affects of joy and sadness. By *joy*, therefore, I shall understand in what follows that *passion by which the mind passes to a greater perfection*. And by *sadness*, that *passion by which it passes to a lesser perfection*. The *affect of joy which is related to the mind and body at once* I call *pleasure* or *cheerfulness*, and that of *sadness*, *pain* or *melancholy*" (161). Benedict de Spinoza, *A Spinoza Reader: The Ethics and Other Works*, trans. and ed. Edwin Curley (Princeton, NJ: Princeton University Press, 1994). Thanks to Eric Clarke for his observation that Spinoza had a broad, and largely unexplored, cultural influence in the nineteenth century. Lionel Trilling points out that Matthew Arnold read Spinoza: see Trilling, *Matthew Arnold* (New York: Columbia University Press, 1939), 19. George Eliot, whose philosophical interests and reading ran deep, translated the *Ethics*. For work that has been done on Spinoza's influence, see Marjorie Levinson, "A Motion and a Spirit: Romancing Spinoza," *Studies in Romanticism* 46.4 (2007): 367–408; Elizabeth Deeds Ermarth, "Negotiating Middlemarch," in *Middlemarch in the Twenty-First Century*, ed. Karen Chase (Oxford: Oxford University Press, 2006), 107–31. Wilde also echoes the young Marx, especially in his invocation of communism as socialism: see Karl Marx, *Economic and Philosophic Manuscripts of 1844*, trans. Martin Milligan (Amherst, NY: Prometheus Books, 1988), 99–114. Sedgwick has explored the relations between Wilde and Nietzsche as well as their scholarly reception and circulation: see "Wilde, Nietzsche, and the Sentimental Relations of

the Male Body," in *Epistemology of the Closet* (Berkeley and Los Angeles: University of California Press, 1990), 131–82.

22. While working on this chapter, I happened upon what might be thought of as *the smallest mystery of modern literature* in this very line. In the original essay, "The Soul of Man under Socialism," which appeared in the *Fortnightly Review*, volume 49, in February 1891, the line reads: "You *perfection* lies inside of you" (299). However, in the earliest copyrighted edition I was able to locate, the first authorized edition, owned by Arthur L. Humphreys, the line reads as I have quoted it: "Your *affection* lies inside of you" (my emphasis) (London: A. L. Humphreys,1912; I have not been able to view copies of the 1904 and 1905 versions). Robert Baldwin Ross, the executor of Wilde's estate and his lifelong friend, oversaw the production for publication of this edition. For the American authorized edition of Wilde's work, again with editorial help of Ross, published in Boston by John W. Luce & Co. between 1905 and 1909 the line reads with the term "perfection." Given the very early confusion, mistranscription, change, variance, or subterfuge—depending on one's taste for conspiracy theories—contemporary versions of both can be found. It should be noted that the latest authoritative Oxford edition uses the term "perfection" and makes no note of the history of this switch: *The Complete Works of Oscar Wilde*, ed. Josephine M. Guy (Oxford: Oxford University Press, 2007), 241. Ross provides a very interesting preface for the London Humphreys edition from 1912 in which he deploys a variation of the term "affection" and writes: "Unique among Wilde's writings it is no exaggeration to say that 'The Soul of Man' is unique in English literature. At least there is no more comprehensive essay with which I am acquainted. Without being in the least desultory, it touches, though ever so lightly, almost every subject on which educated people think when they think at all. And every subject is illuminated by a phrase which haunts the memory. Indeed, many of these phrases have been boldly appropriated without acknowledgement or 'socialised' by some of our leading platform orators. It may interest some of the author's admirers to note that in this essay he acknowledges, what in his previous writings he pretended to ignore—the potentialities of science. In the old aesthetic days, under the influence of Ruskin and the Pre-Raphaelites, Wilde *affected* to depreciate the debt of humanity to modern science. Art was more or less to solve everything. Here he recognizes that science, not art, is going to cure consumption and solve the problem of misery. Indeed, his appreciation of life and its issues, his perception that art and literature are component parts of life and not the whole of life, account in some measure for the eagerness with which the present and younger generation read Wilde, when the fame of his more esteemed contemporaries is already a little dimmed and their canons of art, literature and life are being readjusted" (my emphasis) (London: A. L. Humphreys, 1912), viii–ix. It may be too fanciful to imagine that Ross, Wilde's queer friend, surreptitiously substituted a notion of *affection* for a notion of *perfection*, in a phrase that already bears the trace of Wilde's rebellion against Matthew Arnold's formulation of perfection through the force of the state. Nonetheless, such a possibility is glimpsed, perhaps, in this passage from the preface in which a certain notion of *affection* is at the crux of Wilde's unique style and politics, set before the world with the *affections* of an intimate friend, and in which the literary value of phrases is made available to "socialization." We know that Wilde himself was not beyond literary appropriation and redistribution, even claiming that he frequently signed his name at the end of books that he enjoyed: see Paul K. Saint-Amour, "Oscar Wilde: Literary Property, Orality, and Crimes of Writing," in *The Copywrights: Intellectual Property and the Literary Imagination* (Ithaca, NY: Cornell University Press, 2003). In the spirit of just such appropriation and redistribution, to resist the constraints of verification, and to invoke the curiosities of this history that sent me for a delightful day into the depths of Harvard's Widener Library, I have left the term "affection" in the main body of this chapter. For a recent transcription of "affection" as opposed to "perfection" see *The Collected Works of Oscar Wilde* (Ware, UK: Wordsworth Editions, 1998), 1047.

23. "Fascism sees its salvation in giving these masses not their right, but instead a chance to express themselves. The masses have a right to change property relations; Fascism seeks to give them an expression while preserving property" (www.Marxists.org; accessed January 10, 2012). The connections between Wilde and Benjamin are suggestive—perhaps stemming from their mutual engagement with French decadence. Benjamin's study of Charles Baudelaire is instructive in this regard. See Walter Benjamin, *Charles Baudelaire: A Lyric Poet in the Era of High Capitalism* (New York: Verso, 1997).

24. Matthew Tinkcom smartly explores the complexities of alternative forms of work and labor in relation to cinema in *Working Like a Homosexual: Camp, Capital, and Cinema* (Durham, NC: Duke University Press, 2002). See in particular the introduction.

25. Like Marx, Wilde does not glamorize labor in and of itself. Instead, Wilde promotes a particular aesthetic, that is a particular social mediation and articulation of labor. Thus, he can valorize the freedom of activity, and at the same time condemn sentimental attachments to the nobility of work: "And as I have mentioned the word labor, I cannot help but saying that a great deal of nonsense is being written and talked nowadays about the dignity of manual labor. There is nothing necessarily dignified about manual labor at all, and most of it is absolutely degrading.... To sweep a slushy crossing for eight hours, on a day when the east wind is blowing, is a disgusting occupation. To sweep it with mental, moral, or physical dignity seems to me to be impossible. To sweep it with joy would be appalling. Man is made for something better than disturbing dirt. All work of that kind should be done by a machine" ("SM" 10).

26. Michael Rubenstein, *Public Works: Infrastructure, Irish Modernism, and the Postcolonial* (Notre Dame, IN: University of Notre Dame Press, 2010), 18–19.

27. For a recent discussion of Marx and Utopia, see Nicholas Brown, *Utopian Generations: The Political Horizon of Twentieth-Century Literature* (Princeton, NJ: Princeton University Press, 2005); John Marx, *The Modernist Novel and the Decline of Empire* (Cambridge: Cambridge University Press, 2005).

28. For an excellent discussion of the complexity of the subjunctive, see Eric O. Clarke, *Virtuous Vice: Homoeroticism and the Public Sphere*, "Part 1: The Subjunctive Public Sphere." For thought-provoking work on the relations between queer theory and temporality, see Elizabeth Freeman, "Time Binds, or Erotohistoriography," *Social Text* 23.3–4 (2005): 57–68. Also see the special issue of *GLQ* (13 [2007]) that Freeman edited, titled "Queer Temporalities."

29. In relation to questions of history and literary history, Wilde's story can be conceptualized in very different ways depending on its critical juxtaposition with different companion texts. For example, when thought of in relation to Stephen Booth's edition of Shakespeare's *Sonnets*, Wilde's text can be thought of as one of the many competing theories about the sonnets. For more see *Shakespeare's Sonnets*, ed. Stephen Booth (New Haven, CT: Yale University Press, 1977), particularly appendix 1. A more provocative companion text might be Geoffrey Keating's (Seathrún Céitinn's) seminal seventeenth-century *The History of Ireland*. Written after the *flight of the earls*, the famous final sundering of the old Gaelic order in the wake of Cromwell's brutal rampage through the country, Keating records the history of the island from an indigenous perspective for future generations. Keating writes the work in Irish and weaves his knowledge of Irish written and oral tradition into a modern Christian worldview. In some instances, Keating sanitizes pagan traditions for a Christian audience, but in other instances he is quite open to the autochthonous tradition. Not only is the decision to write in Irish an early and important instance of Irish language politics, it is also an example of a secular and vernacular struggle against the dominance of Latin, a struggle tracked in Pascale Casanova's innovative *The World Republic of Letters*, trans. M. B. DeBevoise (Cambridge, MA: Harvard University Press, 2007). Keating's work, even as it details a strange mix of myth, legend, and Christian allegory,

inscribes a key moment in the transformation from a medieval Christian tradition to a modern secular understanding of historiography. His work is both *unreliable* as a literal historical record and *revelatory* as it theorizes its own practice, a theorization that is at times strikingly modern. In a similar way, Wilde's text is historically dubious, but from a perspective beyond its own horizon, its complex examination of history and affect opens the door for a postmodern historiography. Special thanks to Sarah Connell, a Northeastern University graduate student in the Spring 2008 graduate seminar Introduction to Irish Literature and Film, for her careful analysis of Keating's negotiation of pagan and Christian elements. For more on Keating, see University College Cork's corpus of electronic texts (CELT): www.ucc.ie/celt (accessed January 10, 2012).

30. Wilde's novel *The Portrait of Dorian Gray* suggests violent cultural connections between queer youth and suicide. For a contemporary discussion of these connections see the website of the Trevor Project, which is dedicated to combating the epidemic of suicide among queer youth in the United States. Some stunning facts about suicide among LGBT and questioning youth: suicide is the third leading cause of death among fifteen- to twenty-four-year-olds, accounting for over 12 percent of deaths in this age group; only accidents and homicide occur more frequently; lesbian, gay, and bisexual youth are up to four times more likely to attempt suicide than their heterosexual peers; and more than one-third of LGB youth report having made a suicide attempt. For more, see the Trevor Project website: www.thetrevorproject.org.

31. Seamus Deane, "Dumbness and Eloquence," in *Ireland and Postcolonial Theory*, ed. Clare Carrol and Patricia King (Notre Dame, IN: University of Notre Dame Press, 2003), 114. Further references to this work will be made parenthetically in the text.

32. The difference between the religious martyr and the political rebel in this respect is crucial. In the above citation, as well as throughout "The Soul of Man under Socialism," Wilde rejects the tenets of religious martyrdom. Even his reading and promotion of Christ rejects the medieval image of Christ the martyr, in favor of his humanist portrayal by the Renaissance. Alternatively, he is quite happy to promote forms of political rebellion.

33. For more on the debates over the relations between postcolonial and Irish studies, see Clare Carroll and Patricia King, eds., *Ireland and Postcolonial Theory* (Notre Dame, IN: University of Notre Dame Press, 2003); Derek Attridge and Marjorie Howes, eds., *Semicolonial Joyce* (Cambridge: Cambridge University Press, 2000); Glenn Hooper and Colin Graham, eds., *Irish and Postcolonial Writing: History, Theory, Practice* (New York: Palgrave Macmillan, 2002); Marjorie Howes, *Yeats's Nations: Gender, Class, and Irishness* (Cambridge: Cambridge University Press, 1999). It is not only Irish studies that has a complicated relationship with postcolonial theory. Various strains of Marxism and Marxian theory also have a complicated relationship with postcolonial theory. For more, see Crystal Bartolovich and Neil Lazarus, eds., *Marxism, Modernity, and Postcolonial Studies* (Cambridge: Cambridge University Press, 2002).

34. Lloyd's discussion is instructive: "While canonical narratives rapidly work to recuperate such an event into the moral history of immigrant success in the promised land of the New World, transforming it into a symbolic moment in a universal history, what lingers is that ineradicable trace, in the land as in local memory, of what has passed away. That trace of passing is what does not pass on, even in its gradual decay." David Lloyd, *Irish Times: Temporalities of Modernity* (Dublin: Field Day, 2008), 11.

35. Gayatri Chakravorty Spivak, "Limits and Openings of Marx in Derrida," in *Outside in the Teaching Machine* (New York: Routledge, 1993), 97–120; Jacques Derrida, *Specters of Marx: The State of the Debt, the Work of Mourning, and the New International*, trans. Peggy Kamuf (New York: Routledge, 1994); Gilles Deleuze and Félix Guattari, *Anti-Oedipus*, trans. Robert Hurley, Mark Seem, and Helen R. Lane (Minneapolis: University of Minnesota Press, 1983).

36. Antonio Negri, "Value and Affect," trans. Michael Hardt, *boundary 2* 26.2 (1999): 77–88. Further references to this work will be made parenthetically in the text.

37. Negri begins his argument by noting that during the period of capitalist modernization, capital's ability to measure labor became increasingly vexed, for two reasons: first, the advancing complexity of forms of labor were less easily rendered as "simple, calculable quantities" (78); second, the increasingly abstract nature of finance capital, and the absorption of finance capital by state regimes, made the mediation of the social sectors of the economic cycle more artificial and manipulable. He maintains that the problem with measurement has been fundamentally transformed in postmodernity with the global expansion of markets and the intensification of capitalization through the "absorption of all of social life within capitalist production" (83). Whereas in the phase of capitalism's modernization, labor stood as an alien use value outside the forces of capital and measure functioned to bring labor within the forces of capital, in the global market, in postmodernity, there no longer exists an *outside* to capital, so "the problem of measure cannot be located" (78).

38. Negri explains: "In effect when we look at things from the point of view of political economy—in other words, 'from above'—the theme of 'value-affect' is so integrated into the macroeconomic process that it is virtually invisible. Economics ignores the problem without any recognition of the difficulties. Among the numerous cases, consider two that are exemplary. The first case concerns the domestic labor of women and/or mothers/wives. Now, in the tradition of political economy, this theme can in no way be posed outside of the consideration of the direct or indirect wage of the worker (male, head of family) or rather, in more recent times, outside of the disciplinary techniques of the demographic control of populations (and of the eventual interests of the State—the collective capitalist—in the economic regulation of this demographic development). Value is thus assumed by stripping it from labor (the labor of women—in this case, mothers and wives), stripping it in other words from affect. A second example resides at the extreme opposite end of the spectrum. This case no longer deals with the traditional paradigms of classical economics but with a really postmodern theme: the so-called economy of attention. By this term, one refers to the interest in assuming in the economic calculation the interactivity of the user of communication services. In this case, too, even in the clear effort to absorb the productivity of subjectivity, economics ignores the substance of the question. As it focuses attention on the calculation of 'audience,' it flattens, controls, and commands the production of subjectivity on a disembodied horizon. Labor (attention) is here subsumed, stripping it from value (of the subject), that is, from affect" (79).

39. Negri explains that the movement between the individual and the universal defines affect as the *power of transformation*: "If the relationship between singularity and commonality (or universality) is not static but dynamic, if in this relationship we witness a continuous movement between the singular that is universalized and what is common that is singularized—well, we could then define affect as a power of transformation, a force of self-valorization, which insists on itself in relation to what is common and which therefore brings what is common to an expansion that does not run into limits but only obstacles" (85).

40. What is at stake here is being able to think about collectivities that extend beyond, or differently, than the classic liberal formations of "the people." There are a number of important works in this regard. Bruce Robbins has written a number of articles that intersect this problem, especially through the work of Kant and Gramsci: see "Cosmopolitanism: New and Newer," *boundary 2* 34.3 (2007): 47–60; "The Sweatshop Sublime," *PMLA* 117.1 (2002): 84–97; "Soul Making: Gayatri Spivak on Upward Mobility," *Cultural Studies* 17.1 (2003): 16–26. Recent work that has thought about this problem in relation to the discourses of human rights and forms of biopower/life include Jacques Rancière, "Who Is the Subject of the Rights of Man?" *South Atlantic Quarterly* 103.2/3 (2004): 297–310; Giorgio

Agamben, *Homo Sacer: Sovereign Power and Bare Life* (Stanford, CA: Stanford University Press, 1995); Gayatri Chakravorty Spivak, "Use and Abuse of Human Rights," *boundary 2* 32.1 (2005): 131–89; Antonio Negri and Michael Hardt, *Empire* (Cambridge, MA: Harvard University Press, 2001); Jodi Dean and Paul Passavant, eds., *Empire's New Clothes: Reading Hardt and Negri* (New York: Routledge, 2003). The Irish colonial situation is a productive site to think through the questions of political collectivity, given that the Irish were forced under specific historic conditions to reconceive a whole series of collective social formations. These reimagined collectivities in some aspects called on the memory of indigenous forms that cast relations differently before the English intrusion, in such formations as the clan and indigenous modes of Celtic communism. The Irish also have had to invent new articulations, affects that clearly imagine models of agency within both the limits and the possibilities of diaspora and emigration. See David Lloyd, *Ireland after History* (Notre Dame, IN: University of Notre Dame Press, 2000), as well as his influential *Anomalous States: Irish Writing and the Post-colonial Moment* (Durham, NC: Duke University Press, 1993); Declan Kiberd, *Inventing Ireland: The Literature of the Modern Nation* (Cambridge, MA: Harvard UP), and his more recent *The Irish Writer and the World* (Cambridge: Cambridge University Press, 2005); Marcus Rediker, *Villains of All Nations* (Boston: Beacon, 2005). Much of this work focuses on Irish men, but of course Irish women have also made important contributions to imagining affective modes of collectivity both against and beyond the colonialist state, both against and beyond the determinations of imperial capitalism. For an introduction to Irish feminist takes on problems of collectivity and articulation, see Angela Bourke, *Field Day Anthology of Irish Writing: Volumes 4 and 5: Irish Women's Writing and Traditions* (Cork: Cork University Press, 2002); Carol Coulter, *The Hidden Tradition: Feminism, Women, and the State in Ireland* (Cork: Cork University Press, 1993); Elizabeth Butler Cullingford, *Ireland's Others: Ethnicity and Gender in Irish Literature and Popular Culture* (Notre Dame, IN: University of Notre Dame Press, 2002); Anthony Bradley and Maryann Gialanella Valiulis, eds., *Gender and Sexuality in Modern Ireland* (Amherst: University of Massachusetts Press, 1997). Much feminist work also intersects in interesting ways recent work on sexuality. The Irish and the queer as critical categories function particularly well as critical complements: the queer forcing into view what has been left out of purified versions of Irishness, and the Irish colonial context providing historical context for developments of sexual identity, culture, and politics.

41. Jane Kneller, "The Aesthetic Dimensions of Kantian Autonomy," in *Feminist Interpretations of Immanuel Kant*, ed. Robin May Schott (University Park: Pennsylvania State University Press, 1997), 173–89; quote on 181.

42. Paul Bové, *Poetry against Torture: Criticism, History, and the Human* (Hong Kong: Hong Kong University Press, 2009), 114–15.

43. Sedgwick, "Paranoid Reading and Reparative Reading, or, You're So Paranoid You Probably Think This Essay Is about You," in *Touching Feeling: Affect, Pedagogy, Performativity* (Durham, NC: Duke University Press, 2003), 123–51; quote on 134.

44. Joseph Valente, in *The Myth of Manliness in Irish National Culture, 1880–1922* (Urbana: University of Illinois Press, 2011), argues for the importance of psychosocial receptivity within the political struggles over imperialist gender ideology. The Irish are caught in a double bind that, in brief, marks Irish colonial subjects. hailed by the ideal of British manhood, as too feminized for self-rule if they passively accept British political dominance and too animalistic for self-government if they violently challenge this dominance. The key to frustrating the strictures of this double bind lies in what Valente refers to as a kind of "receptivity": "Just as the imperialist operation of the manly ideal lay not in the properties mandated but in the logic of their arrangement, so the means of frustrating the imperialist instrumentality of the manly ideal lay not in the degree of the Irish acceptance or rejection thereof but rather in the particular manner of its internalization and

reappropriation, a *receptivity* to the pressure of its immediate social currency that winds up unwittingly altering the larger economy of its potential" (25; my emphasis). *The Myth of Manliness* appeared too late to receive sustained attention in this work, but it is very suggestive to me that Valente here hones in on "receptivity" given that the queer politics of receptivity are a recurrent and important feature in the queer genealogy I trace.

45. Oscar Wilde, "The Critic as Artist," in *The Soul of Man under Socialism and Selected Critical Prose*, ed. Linda Dowling (New York: Penguin, 2001), 213–79; quote on 237.

46. Two important recent works that address problems of literary value are Franco Moretti, *Graphs, Maps, Trees: Abstract Models for a Literary History* (London: Verso, 2007); Pascale Casanova, *The World Republic of Letters*, trans. M. B. Debevoise (Cambridge, MA: Harvard University Press, 2007). Casanova engages Irish literature as her primary case study in the analysis of the development of an autonomous literary cultural politics.

CHAPTER 2

1. Mary Burke, *"Tinkers": Synge and the Cultural History of the Irish Traveller* (New York: Oxford University Press, 2009).

2. John Millington Synge, *J. M. Synge Collected Works: Volume II, Prose*, ed. Alan Price (London: Oxford University Press, 1966), 387. All subsequent quotations from Synge's prose works will be from this edition and cited parenthetically.

3. Daniel Corkery, *Synge and Anglo-Irish Literature: A Study* (New York: Russell & Russell, 1931, 1965). All subsequent references to Corkery are from this volume and cited parenthetically.

4. Kathryn Conrad, *Locked in the Family Cell: Gender, Sexuality and Political Agency in Irish National Discourse* (Madison: University of Wisconsin Press, 2004); Margot Backus, *The Gothic Family Romance: Heterosexuality, Child Sacrifice, and the Anglo-Irish Colonial Order* (Durham, NC: Duke University Press, 1999). Further references to these works will be made parenthetically in the text.

5. For more on homosexual panic see Eve Kosofsky Sedgwick, *The Epistemology of the Closet* (Berkeley: University of California Press, 1990), 19–21.

6. J. M. Synge, *The Playboy of the Western World and Two Other Irish Plays* (New York: Penguin, 1987), 78. The next two quotations from this work will be from this edition and cited parenthetically in the text.

7. For the strangeness of Synge's character see David H. Greene, "J. M. Synge: A Reappraisal," in *Critical Essays on John Millington Synge*, ed. Daniel E. Casey (New York: Hall and Macmillan, 1994), 15–27.

8. For more on the critical reception of Synge see Daniel J. Casey, ed., *Critical Essays on John Millington Synge* (New York: G. K. Hall, 1994); Declan Kiberd, *Synge and the Irish Language* (Totowa, NJ: Rowman and Littlefield, 1979); Daniel Corkery, *Synge and Anglo-Irish Literature: A Study* (1931; rpt., New York: Russell & Russell, 1965); Maurice Harmon, *J. M. Synge: Centenary Papers* (Dublin: Dolmen, 1972); S. B. Bushrui, ed., *A Centenary Tribute to J. M. Synge 1871–1909: Sunshine and the Moon's Delight* (New York: Barnes and Noble, 1972); Seamus Deane, *Celtic Revivals: Essays in Modern Irish Literature, 1880–1980* (Boston: Faber and Faber, 1985); David H. Greene and Edward M. Stephens, *J. M. Synge: A Biography* (New York: Macmillan, 1959).

9. Gary Schmidgall, *The Stranger Wilde: Interpreting Oscar* (New York: Penguin, 1994), 301.

10. Synge refers explicitly to Spinoza in his notebooks, and I believe that his introduction to *The Playboy of the Western World* is also indebted to his reading of Spinoza. The final section of this chapter examines the introduction to *The Playboy*.

11. Gilles Deleuze, *Spinoza: Practical Philosophy* (San Francisco: City Lights, 1988), 48–49.

12. Vicky Mahaffey, *States of Desire: Wilde, Yeats, Joyce, and the Irish Experiment* (New York: Oxford University Press, 1998), 5.

13. For more see the introduction.

14. Benedict de Spinoza, *The Ethics and Other Works*, ed. and trans. Edwin Curley (Princeton, NJ: Princeton University Press, 1994), 152–53.

15. Christopher Isherwood, *Christopher and His Kind* (New York: Farrar, Straus and Giroux, 1976), 74.

16. Adrian Frazier considers a similar passage in the writings of George Moore in which the excessive qualities of musical experience are articulated through a homoerotic encounter. Frazier cautions against reading such passages as simple declarations of homosexual identity, noting that particularly in a Parisian cultural context, these queer musical moments were a common trope that signified in multiple directions. Frazier does not dismiss the importance of homosexuality; rather, he smartly suggests that in the hysteria following the Wilde trial, "when everyone else was running from any association with homosexuality, it would have been like Moore to embrace it." *George Moore: 1852–1933* (New Haven, CT: Yale University Press, 2000), 261.

17. John Millington Synge, *J. M. Synge, Collected Works: Volume 2, Plays*, ed. Anne Saddlemeyer (London: Oxford University Press, 1968), 63. Subsequent references to the prefaces will be from this edition.

18. Charles Baudelaire, "A une passante," from *Les Fleurs du mal.* The translation of the poem reads: "Around me roared the nearly deafening street. / Tall, slim, in mourning, in majestic grief, / A woman passed me, with a splendid hand / Lifting and swinging her festoon and hem; / Nimble and stately, statuesque of leg. / I, shaking like an addict, from her eye, / Black sky, spawner of hurricanes, drank in / Sweetness that fascinates, pleasure that kills. / One lightening flash ... then night! Sweet fugitive / Whose glance has made me suddenly reborn, / Will we not meet again this side of death? / Far from this place! too late! *never perhaps!* / Neither one knowing where the other goes, / O you I might have loved, as well you know!" The French and English versions appear on opposing pages in the bilingual edition. Charles Baudelaire, *The Flowers of Evil* (New York: Oxford University Press, 1993), 188–89.

19. Synge reiterates this comparison explicitly: "The women of this island are before conventionality, and share some of the liberal features that are thought peculiar to the women of Paris and New York" (*The Aran Islands*, 87).

20. Michel Foucault, "What Is Enlightenment?," in *Ethics: Subjectivity and Truth*, ed. Paul Rabinow (New York: New Press, 2006), 309–10.

21. John Millington Synge, *The Playboy of the Western World and Other Plays*, ed. Ann Saddlemeyer (New York: Oxford University Press, 1995), xvii. Subsequent references to *The Playboy* will be to this edition.

22. Jacques Derrida explains a similar effect of the feminine: "There is no such thing as the essence of woman because woman averts, she is averted of herself. Out of the depths, endless and unfathomable, she engulfs and distorts all vestige of essentiality, of identity, of property. And the philosophical discourse, blinded, founders on these shoals and is hurled down these depthless depths to its ruin. There is no such thing as the truth of woman, but it is because of that abyssal divergence of the truth, because that untruth is "truth." Woman is but one name for that untruth of truth." *Spurs: Nietzsche's Styles*, trans. Barbara Harlow (Chicago: University of Chicago Press, 1978), 51.

CHAPTER 3

1. See Lucy McDiarmid, *The Irish Art of Controversy* (Ithaca, NY: Cornell University Press, 2005), 170.

2. For a discussion of Casement's Irish background see Jeffrey Dudgeon, *Roger Casement: The Black Diaries* (Belfast: Belfast Press, 2002).

3. Both the Congo and the Putumayo were sites of the brutal exploitation of indigenous populations for the harvest of wild rubber, which had become an important commodity

by the end of the nineteenth century. For more on this see Barbara Emerson Weidenfeld, *Leopold II of the Belgians: King of Colonialism* (London: Weidenfeld and Nicolson, 1979), 232–36.

4. Roger Casement, *The Amazon Journal of Roger Casement*, ed. Angus Mitchell (London: Lilliput; Dublin: Anaconda, 1997), and Roger Casement, *Roger Casement's Diaries: 1910: The Black and the White*, ed. Roger Sawyer (London: Pimlico, 1997). Subsequent quotations from the diaries are from the Sawyer edition.

5. In March 2002 the first fully independent forensic examination of the diaries concluded that they are authentic. Specifically, the notion that a forger interpolated the homoerotic entries was dismissed. For more see Paul Tilzey, "Roger Casement: The Secrets of the Black Diaries," at www.bbc.co.uk/history/society_culture/protest_reform/casement_05. shtml (accessed January 10, 2012).

6. For recent work on Casement see Lucy McDiarmid, *The Irish Art of Controversy* (Ithaca, NY: Cornell University Press, 2005); Séamas Ó Síocháin, *Roger Casement: Imperialist, Rebel, Revolutionary* (Dublin: Lilliput, 2008); Jeffrey Dudgeon, *Roger Casement: The Black Diaries: With a Study of His Background, Sexuality, and Irish Political Life* (Belfast: Belfast Press, 2002); William J. McCormack, *Roger Casement in Death: Or the Haunting of the Irish Free State* (Dublin: University College Dublin Press, 2003).

7. For an introduction to Casement see Lucy McDiarmid, "The Posthumous Life of Roger Casement," in *Gender and Sexuality in Modern Ireland*, ed. Anthony Bradley and Maryann Gialanella Valiulis (Amherst: University of Massachusetts Press, 1997); Roger Sawyer, *Casement, the Flawed Hero* (Boston: Routledge, 1984).

8. Eoin Ó Máille, M. Uí Callanán, and M. Payne, *The Vindication of Roger Casement: Computer Analysis and Comparisons of the Dublin 1910 Diary, the "Nation" Letter 1913, the London 1903 and 1910 Diaries* (Dublin: Roger Casement Foundation, 2000, photocopy), c.

9. Ibid., d.

10. For more see Daniel Nettle and Suzanne Romaine, *Vanishing Voices: The Extinction of the World's Languages* (New York: Oxford University Press, 2000), 1–25.

11. See Philip Alston and Henry J. Steiner, *International Human Rights in Context: Law, Politics, Morals*, 2nd ed. (New York: Oxford University Press, 2000).

12. J. A. Betley and R. J. Gavin, eds. and trans., *The Scramble for Africa: Documents on the Berlin West African Conference and Related Subjects 1884/1885* (Ibadan, Nigeria: Ibadan University Press, 1973), 129. Further references to this work will be made parenthetically in the text.

13. Peter Singleton-Gates and Maurice Girodias, eds., *The Black Diaries: An Account of Roger Casement's Life and Times with a Collection of His Diaries and Political Writings* (New York: Grove, 1959), 90–91. Further references to this work will be made parenthetically in the text.

14. Alston and Steiner, *International Human Rights in Context*, 141.

15. Casement was well known for his generous support of the language movement. See McDiarmid's *The Irish Art of Controversy*, 172.

16. For questions of value in relationship to lifestyle, see Eric O. Clarke, *Virtuous Vice: Homoeroticism in the Public Sphere* (Durham, NC: Duke University Press, 2000), 1–67.

17. Séamas Ó Síocháin, "Evolution and Degeneration in the Thought of Roger Casement," *Irish Journal of Anthropology* 2 (1997): 45–62.

18. Conrad quoted in Michael Taussig, *Shamanism, Colonialism, and the Wild Man: A Study in Terror and Healing* (Chicago: University of Chicago Press, 1987), 17.

19. Quoted in Colm Tóibín, "Sex, Lies and the Black Diaries," *Irish Times*, March 2, 2002, www.irishtimes.com/newspaper/weekend/2002/0302/1014332615285.html.

20. Colm Tóibín, *Love in a Dark Time: Gay Lives from Wilde to Almodóvar* (London: Picador, 2002), 109.

CHAPTER 4

1. James Joyce, *Ulysses*, ed. Hans Walter Gabler (New York: Modern Library, 1992). All *Ulysses* quotations will be from this edition and cited parenthetically.

2. James Joyce, "Drama and Life," ed. Ellsworth Mason and Richard Ellmann, *The Critical Writings of James Joyce* (Ithaca, NY: Cornell University Press, 1989), 39. Subsequent references to the critical writing will be to this volume.

3. For an extended and excellent analysis of Joyce's multivalent engagement with the law see Joseph Valente, *James Joyce and the Problem of Justice: Negotiating Sexual and Colonial Difference* (Cambridge: Cambridge University Press, 1995).

4. E. M. Forster in fact refers to *Ulysses* as a form of inverted Victorianism attempting to cover the world with mud, whereas the Victorians attempted to propagate sweetness and light. It seems appropriate in the lines of this analogy that whereas Arnold connected culture with the force of the state, Joyce in his inversion chooses the more popular bar. See E. M. Forster, *Aspects of the Novel* (New York: Harcourt, 1985), 121–23.

5. Colin MacCabe, *James Joyce and the Revolution of the Word* (London: Harper and Row, 1979), 97.

6. For more on the complexity of Casement's national status see Roger Sawyer, *Casement, the Flawed Hero* (Boston: Routledge, 1984).

7. The entire quote in which this label appears is worth examining: "He's a perverted jew, says Martin, from a place in Hungary and it was he drew up all the plans according to the Hungarian system. We know that is the castle" (292). "Perverted jew" in this context refers on the first level to the fact that Bloom has turned from his religion. "Pervert" stands in relation to the term "convert." However, in this citation "pervert" can also be linked to problems of sexual perversion, as the passage further links Casement and Bloom. The "plans" referred to in the quotation are the plans for *Sinn Fein* (from the Irish for "we ourselves") which Bloom fictionally provided Griffith. That they would come from Hungary is an important historical referent, as Casement's father famously transported an appeal for aid from Hungarian nationalist rebels to the British, and this act secured British involvement in the Hungarian struggle. Casement and Bloom are thus both national figures with ties to Hungarian liberation, and each is associated with the importation of aspects of the Hungarian struggle to Ireland.

8. For more on metaphor and metonymy see Roman Jakobson, *Fundamentals of Language* (The Hague: Mouton de Gruyter, 2002), 90–96.

9. I take the terms "splitting" and "doubling up" from the description of the effects of laughter in the pub:

   ... and the wife hotfoot after him, unfortunate wretched woman, trotting like a poodle. I thought Alf would split.
   —Look at him, says he. Breen. He's traipsing all around town with a postcard someone sent him with U. p: up on it to take a li ...
   And he doubled up. (245)

10. This dissolution is confirmed by Joyce's artistic plans for the chapter. Joyce had wanted to turn the chapter into an opera with the avant-garde composer George Antheil, the famous composer of the *Ballet mécanique*. Though not much remains of the collaboration between the two friends, testimonial evidence points to the importance of the dissolution of character I am suggesting: "[*Ulysses*] has music and it has words, but there the resemblance to other operas ceases. It is, for instance, to be performed, as much as it can be performed, without human players at all, or at least visible ones. (...) No singers appear on the stage. They are concealed below where they vocalize into receivers connected with loudspeakers scattered through the auditorium. This device enables the voices to be heard above the din of pianos and xylophones and also saves the audience the unpleasantness of having to gaze upon singers who do not in the least resemble the characters whose roles they are

assuming." From Mauro Piccinini, *Joyce and Antheil*, at www.paristransatlantic.com/antheil/mainpage/joyce.html (accessed January 10, 2012).

11. This means that in many ways the figure of Casement is refracted throughout the chapter. For example, when the citizen replies, "No . . . It's not signed Shanganagh. It's only initialed: P," it is plausible to suggest that Casement is already introduced. Casement penned articles on Irish politics under the name Shan Van Vocht—the "Old Woman of Ireland." Furthermore, the scandal surrounding the homoerotic Black Diaries revolved around the interpretation of frequently dubious markings and initials, and the basic question of whether the diaries contained Casement's handwriting. The chapter features among its many threads the libel suit associated with the postcard. Central to the suit are questions that echo Casement's situation, including handwriting exams, the mysterious nature of the message, and questions of the public versus private nature of the document (see 260–63). None of these details directly refer to Casement's trial, but they suggest the dissemination of Casement's image throughout the montage.

12. In this context, "dirty joke" is a compelling critical term for Joyce's vulgar humor. "Dirty" resonates with Forester's use of the term in his contradistinction between Joyce's project and Arnold's "sweetness and light." "Dirty" also points to the anality of Joyce's use of language. Finally, to use "dirty joke" in this analysis effects the critical elaboration of common speech (at least in the American vernacular)—a sort of Joycean project in its own right.

13. My suggestion that Joyce leverages a queer inscription of Casement in the chapter contradicts the most substantial reading of Casement's role in the chapter, which appears in Enda Duffy's *Subaltern Ulysses* (Minneapolis: University of Minnesota Press, 1994), 93–129. Duffy claims that Joyce cleanses his representation of Casement of any homoerotic valence. Duffy relies on the authenticity of Casement's historical sexual orientation as evidenced in the Black Diaries to ground his dismissal of the homoerotic. This chapter has argued to the contrary that Joyce leverages the instability of Casement's identity, as indexed by the queer, to destabilize the citizen's nationalist interpretation of Irish history. Duffy concludes Casement's homoerotic diaries "may or may not have been forged" and that "this locks our reading into a disabling ambivalence" (103). This reading of the critical situation enabled by the diaries relies on the authentication of Casement's identity to ground critical agency—without the ability to verify the authenticity of Casement's sexuality, according to Duffy, Joyce (and consequently the critic) must bracket the question of the homoerotic. Given this purported disabling ambivalence, Duffy dismisses the contents of the homoerotic diaries, and displaces his critical gaze from the inscription of Casement in Joyce's text to the public scandal surrounding Casement's trial. He claims: "The diaries' contents are trite and mundane, but in the process of their making-public on the one hand and their reception (with the forgery allegation) on the other, they graphically expose the split between native and colonist versions of the insurgent subject" (103). The dismissal of the content of the diaries, and the shift in focus from the particular textual inscription of Casement in Joyce's writing to the context of their public circulation, allows Duffy to present Joyce's inscription of Casement as a sanitized "tribute" that through "decency" chooses to leave "unsaid Casement's career in Irish insurgency, his execution, and his diaries" (101). The diaries, and by extension the questions of sexuality that attend them, remain in Duffy's reading the "unspoken texts of 'Cyclops'" (101). I believe that the queer inscription of Casement as bugger is critical to the chapter.

14. Immanuel Kant, "Idea for a Universal History from a Cosmopolitan Point of View," in *Immanuel Kant on History*, ed. Lewis White Beck (Indianapolis: Bobbs-Merrill, 1975), 15. Further quotations in the text will be from this edition.

15. The importance of memory is a key theme to Emmet's speech as is the will to violence: "I wish that my memory and my name may animate those who survive me, while I look

down on the destruction of that perfidious government which upholds its domination by blasphemy of the Most High" (www.robertemmet.org/speech.htm, accessed January 10, 2012).

16. This term is taken from Joseph Valente, "The Double-Bind of Irish Manhood," in *Semicolonial Joyce*, ed. Derek Attridge and Marjorie Howes (New York: Cambridge University Press, 2000), 106.

17. In that the "Cyclops" chapter both holds up for parody the citizen and British colonialist practices and discourses, I agree with Emer Nolan's assessment of the political charge of language in the section. Nolan in some sense attempts to rehabilitate the citizen, but in a perhaps more important way, she points to Joyce's insistence on engaging the political complexities and difficulties of a multivocal historical situation and not simply endorsing the perspective of a particular character: "Their very words bear the mark of their colonial experiences, and expose the grounding of the modernist textual experiments in a specific and brutally material history. We can see that Bloom does not bring 'multivocality' to the scene, but that this is already there, produced by the colonial situation itself." Emer Nolan, *James Joyce and Nationalism* (New York: Routledge, 1995), 119.

18. This reformation has an important historical precedent in the operations of the Irish Renaissance. As the native patrimony was translated into English, the explicit sexuality of the original Irish had to be purged for Victorian middle-class (particularly evangelical) models of chastity. For a contemporary commentary on the sexual richness of the Irish-language cultural tradition, and the complicated translation of this tradition into English, see Nuala Ní Dhomhnaill, "Why I Choose to Write in Irish, the Corpse That Sits Up and Talks Back," in *The Longman Anthology of British Literature: Volume 2*, ed. David Damrosch (New York: Longman, 2003), 2899–2912.

19. Ernst Bloch, Georg Lukács, Bertolt Brecht, Walter Benjamin, and Theodor Adorno, *Aesthetics and Politics: The Key Texts of the Classic Debate within German Marxism*, ed. Fredric Jameson (London: Verso, 2002), 64.

20. Jean-François Lyotard, *The Differend: Phrases in Dispute*, trans. Georges Van Den Abbeele (Minneapolis: University of Minnesota Press, 1989), 9.

21. Joseph Valente, *James Joyce and the Problem of Justice: Negotiating Sexual and Colonial Difference* (Cambridge: Cambridge University Press, 1995), 8–9.

22. Oscar Wilde, *The Picture of Dorian Gray* (New York: Penguin, 2000), 50.

23. Jonathan Arac, *Impure Worlds: The Institution of Literature in the Age of the Novel* (Bronx, NY: Fordham University Press, 2010), viii.

CHAPTER 5

1. Patrick McCabe, *The Butcher Boy* (London: Picador, 1992); *Breakfast on Pluto* (New York: HarperPerennial, 1999). Further references will be to these editions. I would like to thank Joe Valente for his plenary talk at the Queering Ireland conference, which took place at St. Mary's University, Halifax, in September 2009. The talk, which addressed Jamie O'Neill and Patrick McCabe, and the ensuing discussion over pints were key to shaping my thinking in this chapter.

2. "Social fantastic" is a term that McCabe promotes to describe his aesthetic in an interview with Christopher FiztSimon. "St. Macartan, Minnie the Minx and Mondo Movies: Elliptical Peregrinations through the Subconscious of a Monaghan Writer Traumatised by Cows and the Brilliance of James Joyce," *Irish University Review: A Journal of Irish Studies* 28.1 (1998): 175–89; quote on 176.

3. Karl Marx, *Economic and Philosophical Manuscripts of 1844* (New York: Prometheus, 1988), 105. Henry Sussman explores the intersection between the aesthetic and the social in *The Butcher Boy* in particular in "On the Butcher Block: A Panorama of Social Marking," *New Centennial Review* 4.1 (2004): 143–68.

4. Take, for example, Francie Brady's description in *The Butcher Boy* of a fountain built for Queen Victoria: "There was one thing I knew about that fountain. They had put it there for Queen Victoria the same time as they built the Jubilee Road in honor of her visit to the town that year. Except for one thing—she never came. . . . I dropped a spit onto a fag box and thought of all the school kids and old folks *Hooray for Queen Victoria!* Except for one thing—where the fuck was she?" (103). James M. Smith explains that *The Butcher Boy* indicts "a protracted process of decolonization dominating Irish society well into the 1980s. [It] emerged in a decade that witnessed a distinct shift in Ireland's willingness to confront its past" (114). "Remembering Ireland's Architecture of Containment: 'Telling' Stories in *The Butcher Boy* and *States of Fear*," *Éire-Ireland: A Journal of Irish Studies* 36.3–4 (2001): 111–30. Tim Gauthier examines *The Butcher Boy* within neocolonial dynamics: "Identity, Self-Loathing and the Neo-Colonial Condition in Patrick McCabe's *The Butcher Boy*," *Critique* 44.2 (2003): 196–211. Martin McLoone explores the historical resonances in "The Abused Child of History: Neil Jordan's *The Butcher Boy*," *Cineaste* 23.4 (1998): 32–36.

5. Ireland was one of the first countries in Europe to have access to radio; television came later. While the BBC broadcast in Northern Ireland in the late 1950s, it was not until the early 1960s that RTÉ began broadcasting in the Republic. For more on this history see Lance Pettitt, *Screening Ireland: Film and Television Representation* (Manchester, UK: Manchester University Press, 2000).

6. Richard Dienst, *Still Life in Real Time: Theory after Television* (Durham, NC: Duke University Press, 1994), 4.

7. The film and novel versions of *Breakfast on Pluto* diverge more significantly than those of *The Butcher Boy*. The chapter addresses these divergences, one of which is the naming of the main character: Pussy in the novel and Kitten in the film. To distinguish between the two, when referring to the novel I will use "Pussy," and when referring to the film I will use "Kitten." When referring to both, I will use "Patrick."

8. Henry McDonald, "'Endemic' Rape and Abuse of Irish Children in Catholic Care, Inquiry Finds," *Guardian*, May 20, 2009.

9. John Banville, "A Century of Looking the Other Way," *New York Times*, May 22, 2009.

10. James M. Smith *Ireland's Magdalen Laundries and the Nation's Architecture of Containment* (South Bend, IN: University of Notre Dame Press, 2007), 24.

11. One of the expressive strengths of queer colloquial language is the easy shifting between gendered pronouns. This is a strength that *Breakfast on Pluto* takes advantage of and that I maintain in this chapter's prose.

12. Key events that take place only in the film version include Kitten's encounter with her mother and her younger half-brother (who is also named Patrick) and the reconciliation with her father, Fr. Bernard.

13. In an intensely disturbing scene in the film, the British policeman, who, just scenes earlier, is shown smashing Kitten's skull into a wall, intervenes to get Kitten off the street. He drives her to a regulated peep show "unionized" by sex workers. While trying to convince Kitten on the ride over he shouts, "Patrick! You'll get killed out there!" This does not seem to cross his mind while beating Kitten when she is in custody.

14. Peter Mahon concludes that *Breakfast on Pluto* offers an important psychoanalytic theorization of political violence: "By affirmatively 'working through' maternity, violence, and incest beyond the name of the father, Pussy also opens up the possibility of a reconfigured Irish nationalism that is no longer shamed by the name of the father in an effort to assure itself a line of pure descent that would originate in the land. In other words, *Breakfast on Pluto*'s affirmative, worked-through, and reconfigured Irish nationalism is not—indeed could not be—closed to non-Irishness precisely because it affirms an incestuous and promiscuous site of maternal bonding where the name of the father is no longer heard as

either the first or last word." "Lacanian 'Pussy': Towards a Psychoanalytic Reading of Patrick McCabe's *Breakfast on Pluto*," *Irish University Review: A Journal of Irish Studies* 37.2
(2007): 441–72.

15. Marcia Landy, "The International Cast of Irish Cinema: The Case of Michael Collins,"
    boundary 2 27.2 (2000): 21–44; quote on 44.
16. Matthew Tinkcom, *Working Like a Homosexual* (Durham, NC: Duke University Press,
    2002), 4.
17. "Where do they be taking you says the old fellow with the eyebrow up. You needn't think
    you're not seen. Then he looks down to the other end of the ward and the other fellows
    nodding away. I told him to travel through the wastes of space and time like in Dan Dare
    that's where they're taking me and he looks at me" (148). Laura G. Eldred explores the
    diversity of cinematic genre in the film in "Francie Pig vs. Fat Green Blob from Outer
    Space: Horror Films and *The Butcher Boy*," *New Hibernia Review* 10.3 (2006): 53–67.
18. For a discussion of narrative disjunction in the film see Carole Zucker, "The Poetics of
    Point of View: Neil Jordan's *The Butcher Boy*," *Literature Film Quarterly* 31.3 (2003): 203–8.
19. Spatial disjunction permeates *The Butcher Boy*. Places are not what they seem. Characters
    are disoriented, unable to coordinate location with meaning and affect, history and time.
    Home, for instance, not only has multiple references—the Brady home versus the Nugent
    home, the home for orphans in Belfast at which Francie's father and Uncle Alo grew up—
    but has sharply contradictory associations. These contradictions are perhaps most clearly
    brought into focus when Francie violently transforms the Nugent home into a "school for
    pigs" and defecates on the living room floor. The town itself is a forgotten and peripheral
    site, a small town in rural Ireland, and yet seemingly the center of world affairs. This polar-
    ized sense of location is captured hilariously in the movie as the busybody women of the
    local shop measure the scope of global geopolitics through the scale of village life and
    opine that "it will be a bitter, bitter day for the small village if the world comes to an end."
    The Pig-Toll Tax scenes, in which Francie demands that Mrs. Nugent and Philip pay a pig-
    toll tax before they are allowed to pass on the sidewalk, show the deep psychic and polit-
    ical antagonisms over the meanings of space and movement. The brilliance of Francie's
    satirical assault is that it combines incongruent spatial measurements. The first is the his-
    torical place of the pig in Irish society. English colonialist rhetoric made much of the
    fact of the Irish peasant practice of housing humans and livestock in a single (compart-
    mentalized) structure. The association of the Irish with pigs in English propaganda is
    long-standing and has at its roots this particular "border" issue. The discourse further de-
    velops into the tendency to represent the Irish themselves as pigs. The second spatial dis-
    course that Francie's joke invokes is the rationalization and capitalization of the island, a
    process first undertaken by colonial authorities as they attempted to subjugate the indige-
    nous population and a process continued by the government of the Republic. Francie's
    Pig-Toll Tax cleverly invokes both of these discourses. For more on the politics of pigs and
    cleanliness see Joseph Nugent, "The Human Snout: Pigs, Priests, and Peasants in the Par-
    lor," *Senses and Society* 4.3 (2009): 283–302. As Francie sets out to find "beautiful Bun-
    doran by the silvery sea" where his parents spent their honeymoon, he bikes into a liminal
    terrain. He comes across a farmer dropping himself into a well to hide from the nuclear
    threat of Khrushchev's invasion—"Khrushchev youse communist bastards!" When Fran-
    cie finally arrives in Bundoran, he finds that it was not the place he thought at all—nothing
    like the gorgeous romance repeated incessantly by his parents' friends and family. Indeed,
    just as he thinks he has found Bundoran and the origin of his parent's relationship, that
    idealized town disappears with the stark revelations of the innkeeper and Francie throws
    himself into a bottle of whiskey. The film translates this ideological and psychic loss into its
    montage of violent jump cuts set to cacophonous jazz riffs. The movement of images on
    the screen thus translates Francie's emotional trauma into a spatial form.

20. The list of commodities—cattle, bombs, and butter—also has an important circulatory history. Cattle and bombs are still important products of global import and export. Perhaps more surprising is the history of the seemingly most domestic and cozy of Irish images—butter. Apparently, according to Nini Rodgers's *Ireland, Slavery, and Anti-Slavery*, an important boom in the Irish butter industry was owed to the superior butter-making science of the Irish, which allowed them to make butter that could survive longer in the warmer climate of the Caribbean. The industry thus owed its flourishing to buttering the toast of the European slave plantations of the century. Certainly, this history should not preclude its contemporary enjoyment. For more see Nini Rodgers *Ireland, Slavery, and Anti-Slavery* (London: Palgrave Macmillan, 2009).

21. Quoted in Colin Lacey, "Patrick McCabe: A Comedy of Horrors," *Publishers Weekly*, November 1998, 50–51.

22. Ann Cvetkovich discusses trauma in both temporal and spatial terms in the introduction to *An Archive of Feeling: Trauma, Sexuality, and Lesbian Public Cultures* (Durham, NC: Duke University Press, 2003).

23. The image also conjures the vexed figure of Mother Ireland. For more on the history and politics of this figure see Elizabeth Cullingford, "Virgins and Mothers: Sinéad O'Connor, Neil Jordan, and *The Butcher Boy*," *Yale Journal of Criticism* 15.1 (2002): 185–210.

24. The idea that the human spectator operates as a particular kind of image on the same plane as cinematic images is the premise of Gilles Deleuze's work on the philosophy of cinema. Richard Dienst explains: "Just as Bergson understands human memory as part of the open universe of images, Deleuze will begin his analysis of cinema from the scandalous premise that 'viewers' themselves must always be considered images on the same place as filmic ones. There is no radical disjunction, but only various types of movement, between the time and space 'onscreen' and the time and space of spectatorship. Thus any contiguity or contact between images—the seen and the seeing—passes through a specific 'kind' or type of manufactured image, a 'cinematographic concept' whose many forms and permutations Deleuze will classify and describe" (148). One way of thinking about Francie's psychotic break is to say that the novel and film track his journey, as an image, to a conjuncture, at which point he is no longer able to function, circulate, expand, or transform— he therefore literally "breaks down," as Francie says of his own mother. For an examination of the philosophical and political work that Deleuze's conception of the cinematic enables see the introduction to Kara Keeling's *The Witch's Flight: The Cinematic, the Black Femme, and the Image of Common Sense* (Durham, NC: Duke University Press, 2007).

25. Richard Dienst explains that both time and space are key conceptual elements of television that require critical elaboration: ". . . the fundamental concept of television is time. It precedes and envelops any semiotic: As the previous chapters have argued, time is the substance of television's visuality, the ground of its ontology, and the currency of its economy. Television has been analyzed as a machine for the prodigious regulated construction and circulation of time. Its limited morphology of representation obeys strictly temporal constraints. There is a structuring movement of flow and segmentation, certainly, but also speeds of transmission and diffusion, intensities of filling and draining that alter images as if from within. An adequate conceptualization of time as an open-ended process of composition and decomposition is a precondition for any homology between televisual images and exchange value, not to mention any discussion of how television's systemic *visuality* accounts for the contingent subjective process of *visibility*. Time must be theorized at the greatest level of generality without taking for granted that it bears sense, narration, or discursivity" (159).

26. The novel marks the boys' relationship as queer early by measuring their affection through the lines of desire in the Brady household. As Francie's mother asks him to make up for his father's failures, Francie and Joe's relationship is cast as a site for the true articulation of

love, loyalty, and desire: "Then she looked into my eyes and said: Francie—you would never let me down would you? She meant you wouldn't let me down like da did I said no I wouldn't let her down in a hundred million years no matter . . . But it didn't matter for me and ma were great pals after that. . . . She gave me my dinner and says Francie if you ever have a sweetheart you'll tell her the truth and never let her down won't you? I says I will ma . . ." (4–5). Clearly, in the novel and the film, Francie has no other sweetheart than Joe. *Breakfast on Pluto* also explores what can be productively thought of as a queer relationship between mother and son.

27. The novel and the film both suggest that the boys access John Wayne largely through television. So even though Wayne is more accurately a cinematic image, he is also part of the work's examination of the powers of television.

28. This description of Billy is offered by Jordan in the DVD commentary.

CHAPTER 6

1. Jamie O'Neill, *At Swim, Two Boys* (New York: Scribner, 2003), 82. This chapter is dedicated to the memory of Siobhán Kilfeather.

2. An interesting grammatical feature of the Irish language marks the form and response to this question. In Irish there is not an independent form of "yes" and "no." Instead, in an affirmative response to an interrogative, the verb is simply reconjugated and repeated, and in a negative response a negative conjugation is offered. Notice in this light that Jim and Doyler never say, "Yes, we are straight."

3. Jonathan Padget, "The Language of Love: Author Jamie O'Neill Discusses His Gay Novel, *At Swim, Two Boys*," *Metro Weekly* (Washington, DC), May 9, 2002, www.metroweekly. com/feature/?ak=267.

4. Henry Abelove, *Deep Gossip* (Minneapolis: University of Minnesota Press, 2003), 88.

5. For a discussion of how experiences of the 1798 rebellion lingered in the gothic imagination see Siobhán Kilfeather's "Terrific Register: The Gothicization of Atrocity in Irish Romanticism," *boundary 2* 31.1 (2004): 49–71.

6. James Joyce, *The Portrait of the Artist as a Young Man* (New York: Penguin, 1993), 269. On the relationship between O'Neill and Joyce, my argument, while sympathetic in some respects, ultimately runs counter to Jodie Medd's analysis in "Patterns of the Possible: National Imaginings and Queer Historical (Meta)Fictions in Jamie O'Neill's *At Swim, Two Boys*," *GLQ: A Journal of Lesbian and Gay Studies* 13.1 (2007): 1–31. Medd claims that "O'Neill's novel incorporates only to invert Joyce's narrative trajectory" (3). She rests her claim of inversion on what she sees as Stephen's rejection of collective forms of identification and O'Neill's embrace of "individual gay subjectivity through collective identification" (3–4). I note that Stephen's project is not Joyce's and argue that "individual gay subjectivity" is too narrow a metric for understanding the breadth of O'Neill's queer socialist project.

7. Both the agents of the cultural market place and academic critics read in O'Neill's novel an investment in the canon of Irish modernism even if they read the effects of that investment differently. There is yet another way of framing that investment, which is from the point of view of the writer and the production of the text. That is to say, O'Neill cites his continual rereading of Joyce's *Ulysses* as the principal guide for the writing of the novel. This is important because O'Neill comes to the tradition of Irish modernism and to the writing of the novel not through the institutionalized setting of the academy—O'Neill did not attend university—but in the open and ambiguous terrain of the marketplace. He literally steals time from his position as night security and invests it in the writing of the novel. The engagement with Joyce in this instance is thus "directive," as it spurs O'Neill both to writing and to research. He claims that he taught himself to do historical research while working on the novel, beginning his work in the texts of the sixteenth century. This

pedagogical function of Joyce's work activates particular features of the form of the novel, which even as it has been institutionalized into the echelons of high culture retains aspects of more popular accessibility. This is also arguably an identifiable aspect of modernism. The echoes of Joyce reverberate throughout O'Neill's work. We will explore specific instances as this chapter unfolds, but in general we can sketch these echoes: structurally, *At Swim, Two Boys* condenses the epic sweep of Irish history and politics into the shifting intimacies, insights, and points of view of a handful of local characters in a relatively short time frame—a year as opposed to a day—and in doing this the novel repeats many key aspects of the structure of *Ulysses*. The particular focus on schoolboys and their painful engagement with the adult world around them reproduces many of the same situations that Stephen Dedalus encounters (in *The Portrait of the Artist as a Young Man* and in *Ulysses*), with many of the same issues at stake—conflicts with family, teachers, and friends, and tensions over art, language, religion, political ideology, nationalism, and sexuality. Furthermore, the novel's sustained and central emphasis on portmanteau words that smuggle in both contemporary and historical contexts and meanings also bears the mark of Joyce's influence.

8. Joseph Valente, "Race/Sex/Shame: The Queer Nationalism of *At Swim Two Boys*," *Éire-Ireland: A Journal of Irish Studies* 40.3–4 (2005): 67; Kimberly McMullen, "New Ireland/Hidden Ireland," *Kenyon Review* 26 (Spring 2004): 134–35.

9. The extraordinary history of the novel's publication points in explicit ways to the contradictory processes of the capitalization of literary value and in particular to the circulation of this value as monetary quantity. By all accounts the publication of *At Swim, Two Boys* was a dazzling success. According to the wild speculations and interviews unleashed by an effusive public relations machine, the novel secured for the then thirty-nine-year-old Irish author a record-setting deal with Simon and Schuster. The signing package—rumored to be upward of $1.5 million—established publication and distribution rights for Europe and North America, and covered a film deal as well. The PR materials that accompanied the release of the novel in both Europe and North America stressed that publication was also a considerable personal success for O'Neill. Previous to the chain of events that led to his "discovery," the writer had been a discarded detail of the British tabloids. In the 1990s he had been the lover of the British talk show host Russell Harty, who had died unexpectedly, leaving O'Neill heartbroken, homeless, and destitute. He toiled for ten long years on his novel while working night security on the ward of a mental hospital for a mere two hundred pounds a week, a sum that cannot have gone very far in London. After striking the deal with Simon and Schuster, O'Neill, in a reversal of the centuries-old flight of the Irish, packed up and returned to Ireland to live on the western coast of Galway with his French dancer-turned-shiatsu-therapist lover, Julien. O'Neill claims that he had always wanted to return to Ireland but that one can only return as "a success." Ireland does not extend what he refers to as "that great weight of tolerance" to her queer children, but she does respect success. As he explains to the Washington, DC, gay rag, *Metro Weekly*, "You can do anything you want there as long as you buy a round. If you can't buy a round, you're hardly a human being. It's no place to be poor."

10. Karl Marx, *The Eighteenth Brumaire of Louis Bonaparte*, available at www.marxists.org/archive/marx/works/1852/18th-brumaire/ (accessed January 10, 2012).

11. On this point, the popular reviews of the novel are clear and correct: the work does self-reflexively circulate forms of authorial value. The reviews that accompanied the launch of the novel emphasize O'Neill's relationship with the canon of Irish modernism; in particular, they point to the influence of Joyce and Wilde on O'Neill's prose. In a blurb reprinted for the opening pages of the American edition of the novel, Felice Picano exclaims: "The secret is out, James Joyce and Oscar Wilde had a child: his name is Jamie O'Neill." The agents of the cultural marketplace are thus in agreement with McMullen in the sense that

they too read the novel as capitalizing on Irish culture, and in particular as capitalizing on the canonical value of Joyce and Wilde. Even if their analyses of the novel on this question coincide, certainly the motivations of these agents and McMullen are different. The publishing and media industries read O'Neill's investment in the modernism of Joyce and Wilde as their own potential profit. McMullen offers an ideological cultural critique suspicious of the political effects of the novel and even proffers her own remedy: "To the extent that it resuscitates romantic Ireland, O'Neill's novel would benefit from a blast of the post-modern equivocation" (135).

12. Ruth Amossy, "The Cliché in the Reading Process," *Sub-Stance* 35 (1982): 34–45; quote on 34. Further references to this work will be made parenthetically in the text.

13. Certainly Amossy is aware of this broader ideological function of cliché. Nonetheless, she focuses on the question of cliché in primarily narratological terms.

14. This phrase plays out, at the level of particular words, a conflation of the domestic and the economic remarked upon by Jim's "fellow" (33) classmates. The class status and wealth of his classmates allows them to abstract ideologically their own domestic spheres of home and family from the taint of the brute necessity that under girds the economic. Thus they grill Jim about his family's material inability to maintain this distinction: "His first day at Presentation, a boy had approached: 'The fellows wanted to know, is it true that you live in a corner-huckster's?' Jim had said no, it was the Adelaide General Stores and some of these fellows sniggered. 'Do you sleep at night in a bed?' Jim slept on a settle-bed made up in the kitchen, so he said yes, but they were up to that dodge. 'In a bed-room?' He shook his head" (33).

15. In a more playful way, this phrase and the related title phrase of this chapter point to trans-valued political terms. In particular, they echo what I have argued (chap. 3) is a particularly Joycean anality and vulgarity. Doyler is even referred to as a "vulgarian" by Polycarp (120). Jim's "arse" is also both the physical and the mental center of his swimming lessons with MacMurrough (370). For more, see the discussion of the "bugger's tool" in chapter 4.

16. The cinematic is an important organizing component of this text; remember that the record-breaking publication deal included the rights for film production.

17. Seamus Deane, "Dumbness and Eloquence: A Note on English as We Write It in Ireland," in *Ireland and Postcolonial Theory*, ed. Claire Carroll and Patricia King (Notre Dame, IN: University of Notre Dame Press, 2003), 118.

18. Immanuel Kant, *Kant's Political Writings*, ed. Hans Reiss (Cambridge: Cambridge University Press, 1991), 54. All subsequent references will be to this edition.

19. A similar process was seen in Synge's *The Playboy of the Western World* and the development of Christy Mahon's eloquence and romantic prowess.

20. A similar line of analysis could be followed in relation to Doyler, in particular in relation to the practical philosophical aspects of his embodied physicality. Consider, for example, how our self-declared "ignorant heathen whoring bastard working Irish man" (89)—a description that achieves its own level of roughneck elegance—is also cast as the model of the "thou-shalt-nots" from the *Christian Politeness* manual that Jim reads in school (80).

21. The same kinds of open debates around cliché occur around the literary. Consider the following passage in which Brother Polycarp leads the boys in a Latin lesson:

> "The horse do not ye credit, O Trojans."
> "Credit? What does credit mean? Can you not speak the King's English, boy?"
>
> That time in Dalkey when the pig was squealing. They had it hoisted from a beam and the buckets were waiting below to collect the blood. When the bells came they laid off the slaughter to say the Angelus. All through the bells the squealing and the thrashing legs and so on, while men prayed. How it riled his father and he said to the men no God would sanction such cruelty to his creatures. The men laughed,

> wiping their blades on the bloody cloths, and his father told him afterwards that we are a race immured to cruelty. He had meant inured.
>
> "Quidquid id est, timeo Danaos et dona ferentis." The brother's eyes roved the room. "Construe . . . Courtney."
>
> That old saw—is it from there it comes? Really they had it wrong. Beware of gifts bearing Greeks, it should be.
>
> Supercilious. But why would he think he was being coarse? Did he truly believe I meant my own . . . ? No one would say such a thing to a brother. It made no sense. Courtney is thrilled by it. He thinks it means something vulgar. Ignorant fool.
> (130)

Again we have the invocation of Joyce, particularly *The Portrait*, in which Stephen debates the meaning of words in the marketplace and in which he contemplates the inability to police the sexual of charge of language. More important, though, we see in the repetition of the Latin translations the simultaneous transmission and formation of both forms of cultural cliché and forms of literary language. In the debates and images surrounding the contemplation of language in the passage we also see the political struggle that simmers behind the scenes.

22. This connection between language and politics is literalized by MacMurrough (and the Rising itself): "Post office! MacMurrough repeated to himself. At last, the Republic of Letters!" (545). A more violent conjugation of this connection is caught in the description of that "bloody machine gun—like a very loud typewriter" (547).

INDEX